AF262899

Creative Ozone

CREATIVE OZONE

The Artists of Westbeth

Miriam Chaiken

EMPIRE STATE EDITIONS

AN IMPRINT OF FORDHAM UNIVERSITY PRESS

NEW YORK   2026

Visit us online at www.fordhampress.com/empire-state-editions.

For EU safety / GPSR concerns: Mare Nostrum Group B.V., Mauritskade 21D, 1091 GC Amsterdam, The Netherlands, gpsr@mare-nostrum.co.uk

Library of Congress Cataloging-in-Publication Data available online at https://catalog.loc.gov.

Printed in the United States of America

28 27 26   5 4 3 2 1

First edition

*I dedicate this with profound thanks and humble gratitude
to the Westbeth residents who took time to talk
with me at length about their life in this remarkable
community, and who are now no longer living.
May your memories be a blessing for us all.*

Bill Anthony

Helène Aylon

Shami Chaikin

Magda Dajani

Joan Kaplan Davidson

David Del Tredici

Neil Derrick

Jack Dowling

Ron Faber

Carol Hebald

Ralph Lee

Ethan Maile

Juanita McNeely

David Seccombe

Shelley Seccombe

Hugh Seidman

Edith Stephan

Jamie Zaretsky

CONTENTS

Creative Ozone

INTRODUCTION

IN 1970, MY father's siblings Shami and Joe moved into adjacent studio apartments in a formerly derelict building in Lower Manhattan, and they stayed for the rest of their lives. Nothing about their move was remarkable, nor were the spaces they occupied, except for the building that they called home—Westbeth. Two decades later, their oldest sister Molly also moved into Westbeth, and all three siblings had studio apartments facing the Hudson River, with million-dollar views of the Statue of Liberty.

My father's siblings were all eligible to live at the rent-stabilized apartments at Westbeth because all three were artists. Molly, or Miriam as she was formally known, was a writer of children's books; Shami was an actor, singer, and dancer; and Joe was an acclaimed actor, director, and playwright. Shami was one of the first residents in the building and lived to see the 50th anniversary of the building's occupation, where she was one of a handful of Westbeth's original occupants who moved into one of the 384 apartments in 1969.

The building is bounded by West and Bethune Streets, which gave rise to its name. Westbeth, the brainchild of philanthropist Jacob Kaplan, his daughter Joan Kaplan Davidson, and architect Richard Meier, was designed as affordable living and workspace for people in the arts. Kaplan was known for his support of the arts, civil rights, and historic preservation projects around New York City, and he took a chance on an untested architect right out of school, a classmate of his son Richard. After scouting possible buildings for renovation, they settled on a maze of unconnected buildings that had formerly been used as the Bell Telephone Laboratories. These buildings were the site of important inventions such as the microphone and color TV, and after being converted to open lofts by Meier, they continued to be the loci of creativity and innovation.

Today, this "Vertical Village" is recognized on the National Register of Historic Places and has been home to thousands of artists in its half-century. Westbeth remains the largest and oldest artists' residence in the world (Alduino 2020).

Since the 1980s, I have been visiting my aunts and uncle at Westbeth, in this highly unusual building. Although parts of the building are 13 stories tall, other wings are 11, 3, or only 2 stories tall. Reaching some apartments requires insider knowledge of the labyrinth of the building, as some floors can only be reached by stopping at a lower floor, crossing the length of the building, and then resuming your journey through another bank of elevators. There was access to rooftops at several locations in the building that served as playgrounds for resident children. The long, dark hallways create echoes of footsteps and conversations despite the curving, undulating ceilings that are supposed to enhance acoustics.

Members of the Westbeth community include both the famous and obscure. Visual artists Helène Aylon, Hans Haacke, Karen Santry, Lorraine O'Grady, and Juanita McNeely created works that inspire and infuriate. Dancers and choreographers such as Vija Vetra, Sally Gross, and Edith Stephan tested the limits of expression through the physical form. Actors and directors from Westbeth created twentieth-century avant-garde theater, such as my uncle Joe Chaikin's Open Theater company and Gloria Miguel's Spiderwoman Theater. Others, such as Pawnee Sills and Moses Gunn, excelled in more traditional theatrical performances alongside giants such as James Earl Jones. Ed Field's poem about his experiences as a young aviator shot down in World War II won him accolades for recounting the worst day in his life. Ralph Lee's life in theater was overshadowed by his legacy for creating Greenwich Village's legendary Halloween Parade and the iconic Landshark character on vintage Saturday Night Live. Madeleine Yayodele Nelson and her Women of the Calabash group brought "world" music to global stages long before it was fashionable. Artistic iconoclasts challenged art conventions and wove political activism with artistic expression.

I began holding conversations with members of the Westbeth community with the goal of writing a book about this remarkable community of eccentric souls. As a cultural anthropologist, I approached Westbeth residents not just as a family member of a resident but as a curious social scientist trying to capture their stories and oral histories. Yet my role in this project is far different than other research I've conducted, as I now count many Westbethers as dear friends, and I look forward to my regular visits more as a trip to see extended family rather than just research.

Having spent nearly thirty years working as a cultural anthropologist in remote villages in sub-Saharan Africa, I had come to think of Westbeth as very analogous to the villages where I have worked. Everyone knows a little about everyone else's business. Everyone shares in each other's successes and catastrophes. Everyone has at least a mild case of PTSD following the successive horrors of the 9/11 attacks a few blocks away and the devastation of Hurricane Sandy. Everyone talks about the good old days when they were young. Everyone complains about the expenses/neighborhood/weather/transportation—just pick one. Everyone pulled together to protect each other and the vulnerable elderly when confronted by the COVID-19 pandemic. Such is life in a village.

Today, there is both a middle-aged and a younger generation of artists in Westbeth, in addition to a few of the venerable original residents. The younger artists admire their elders but also sometimes covet choice units that the elders moved into decades ago. Yet these elders are a few of the many who have put Westbeth on the map.

This book will tell the story of Westbeth, its people, its role in the history of Greenwich Village, and the triumphs and tragedies that have taken place within this one square block of New York City. I write about Westbeth as an anthropologist, weaving together pieces of information shared by the community. Many current and former residents of Westbeth sat for hours with me to tell me the stories of their lives.

To write this ethnographic description of Westbeth, I have interviewed artists as old as 98 and many of the now middle-aged generation who spent their childhood in Westbeth. I have combed through print and digital resources documenting Westbeth and listened to recorded oral histories collected from some who played a pivotal role in its creation. I have collaborated with others who share a fascination with this community of artists, including photographer Frankie Alduino, who recently published a book of stunning photos of the Westbeth elders. I am very grateful to all who shared their stories—stories enough to fill an entire shelf of books.

My spinning of the tales of Westbeth is built on my decades of field research on four continents, where I learned about how communities worked and how the ordinary person was actually extraordinary. The book owes an acknowledgment to Margot Lee Shetterly, whose book *Hidden Figures* was an inspiration. She told us about the lives of African American women mathematicians whose work was instrumental in the success of early NASA missions. Like her protagonists, the people of Westbeth have fascinating lives and have made a mark in the arts and the city of New York, yet remain largely unknown. A chance meeting with Margot made me think about the people at Westbeth in a new light.

The following pages include portraits of many individuals, but the overall goal is to create a window into the community as a whole. As an eager listener, my role as the anthropologist is to create an ethnography, a description of the community that is greater than the sum of the individuals. Traditionally, anthropologists use pseudonyms when writing about people, but in Westbeth, everyone hopes to be recognized for their accomplishments and the significance of their work, so I have used their true names. This story is told through the voices and lived experiences of the people of Westbeth.

The community collectively serves as a model for other cities hoping to foster a vigorous arts presence by supporting affordable housing and workspace. The story of Westbeth is of resilience and, recently, of renewal. This summary of its fifty-plus years is a lesson about purposeful communities and what works.

We begin this story with a dive into the history of the building and its earlier incarnation for nearly a century as the locus of innovation when it was the Bell Telephone Research Lab. Chapter 2 tells of the transformation into Westbeth as the concept of a purposeful community of working artists takes shape as the first generation of residents arrive in 1969–70. The origins of Westbeth coincide with a period of intense political and social justice activism in the US, and the third chapter illustrates how the social conscience of the original residents became a through line in the community in both individual and collective action. Left-leaning perspectives are evident in their artistic works and in their half-century of activism promoting social justice and equality. Amidst this politically engaged context, a younger generation grew up in the building in a climate of permissiveness and freedom. Chapter 4 focuses on the self-described feral children and how growing up in this unusual context shaped their own futures, as many have gone on to become artists themselves. While the magical upbringing fostered creativity among many in the second generation, the community had more than its share of troubled residents whose tragic lives also influenced and sometimes traumatized those who grew up at Westbeth. Chapter 5 focuses on the "weird neighbors" and the stories of eccentric hoarders and recluses, and those whose lives tragically ended in suicide, giving the building the macabre nickname of Westdeath.

Examining Westbeth as a microcosm of important trends in the broader context of New York City, Chapter 6 focuses on the transformation of the gritty, industrial neighborhood into one of the most expensive zip codes in the world. The gentrification has made the area cleaner and safer, but at the cost of some of the character of the place and the characters who frequented the area. Chapter 7 looks at the disasters that have affected the community, beginning with the events of 9/11 at the World Trade Center, only a few blocks away. Like 9/11, the whole city was also traumatized by the 2020 COVID-19 pandemic, but the impact of both of these pale in comparison to the emotional and infrastructural devastation wrought by Superstorm Sandy in 2012.

The final chapter looks at Westbeth today as a multigenerational community with social innovations to ensure the safety of the most vulnerable and to optimize opportunities for the most productive—much in the same way I have seen in remote villages in Asia and sub-Saharan Africa where I have worked. Despite challenges and problems, Westbeth began its next half-century as a dynamic, forward-looking village that can be a model for other purposeful communities around the world.

1

Creative Ozone

FOR A TOURIST visiting New York City, one must-see area is Greenwich Village, where fans of *Sex and the City* seek out the Magnolia cupcake bakery, and shoppers frequent the trendy and expensive boutique stores in the Meatpacking District. In this neighborhood, a Tesla dealership in a glass-fronted showroom is neighbor to some of the most expensive residential real estate in New York City, including a block-long building owned by the De Beers diamond family, shiny glass towers where Martha Stewart and fashion designer Marc Jacobs have owned apartments, and where artist and filmmaker Julian Schnabel built his rose-colored high-rise apartment, Palazzo Chupi. While strolling the recently re-bricked roads near Gansevoort Street, modern art aficionados pop into the new Whitney Museum and go to the Chelsea Market. While in the area, everyone climbs the stairs just outside the Whitney to the High Line, one of the most popular tourist destinations in New York. The High Line is a stretch of elevated railway that runs for nearly a mile and a half uptown and has been converted from its original industrial use to one of the most innovative parks in the world. The High Line contains tens of thousands of plants ranging from full-grown trees to seasonal perennial flowers. Along its course, visitors stop to hear busking musicians, buy ice cream, enjoy the views from the amphitheater, and splash in the water feature.

The first segment of the High Line was only opened in 2009, expanded in subsequent years, and is now one of the top tourist destinations in New York, drawing millions of visitors each year. The railbed where the High

Line is built originally ran through the western edge of Greenwich Village, parallel to the Hudson River, and was used to move millions of tons of industrial products, meat, dairy products, and produce from the factories and meatpacking plants in the neighborhood. Completed in 1934, this elevated train ran right through factories, including the Bell Telephone Research Laboratories and the American Biscuit Company at the level of about the third story, so trains could run and be loaded and offloaded without pausing for street-level traffic (see Fig. 1). By the late 1960s, traffic on the High Line trains began to wane, and the last train ran on these tracks in the 1980s, after which the railbed remained an abandoned industrial eyesore for many years. Many local business owners and politicians called for the total demolition of the High Line bed and trestles, and a segment from Gansevoort Street where the entry to the park now stands, south to the Bell Labs at Bank Street was removed in 1991 (Fig. 2) ("The High Line" 2020).

Looking at this neighborhood today, which exudes affluence and even excess, one may find it hard to imagine what it looked like fifty years ago when the Westbeth Artists Housing was opened in the maze of buildings formerly housing the Bell Labs. This book explores the origins of the Westbeth Artists Housing and the mark this experiment has made on the people who make up this community and on the larger art world. Westbeth is in the heart of the West Village and bounded by four blocks—Bethune on the north, West on the west (hence the name merging the two street names), Bank Street on the south, and Washington on the east. Officially opened in 1970, Westbeth remains the largest and oldest arts community in the world and has been home to thousands of artists, both famous and obscure, in its first fifty years.

The oldest segment of the interlocking buildings that make up Westbeth was built in 1861 when a wood-planing mill was built on the corner of Bank and West Streets to make planed timber for the booming construction that was taking place across Manhattan. Later converted to a box factory, then partially damaged by a fire in 1895, this building was purchased in 1897 by Western Electric, which did research for the Bell System. Over the next several decades, the Bell Labs built additional buildings on the site, including a 13-story headquarters building facing West Street, an 11-story building along Bethune Street, and a building along Washington Street that included a third-story opening for the High Line rail to pass through, permitting shipping of products manufactured at the Bell Labs (Fig. 3). For over sixty years, the Bell Labs remained at this site and generated some of the most important technological innovations of the twentieth century (Sheire 1975).

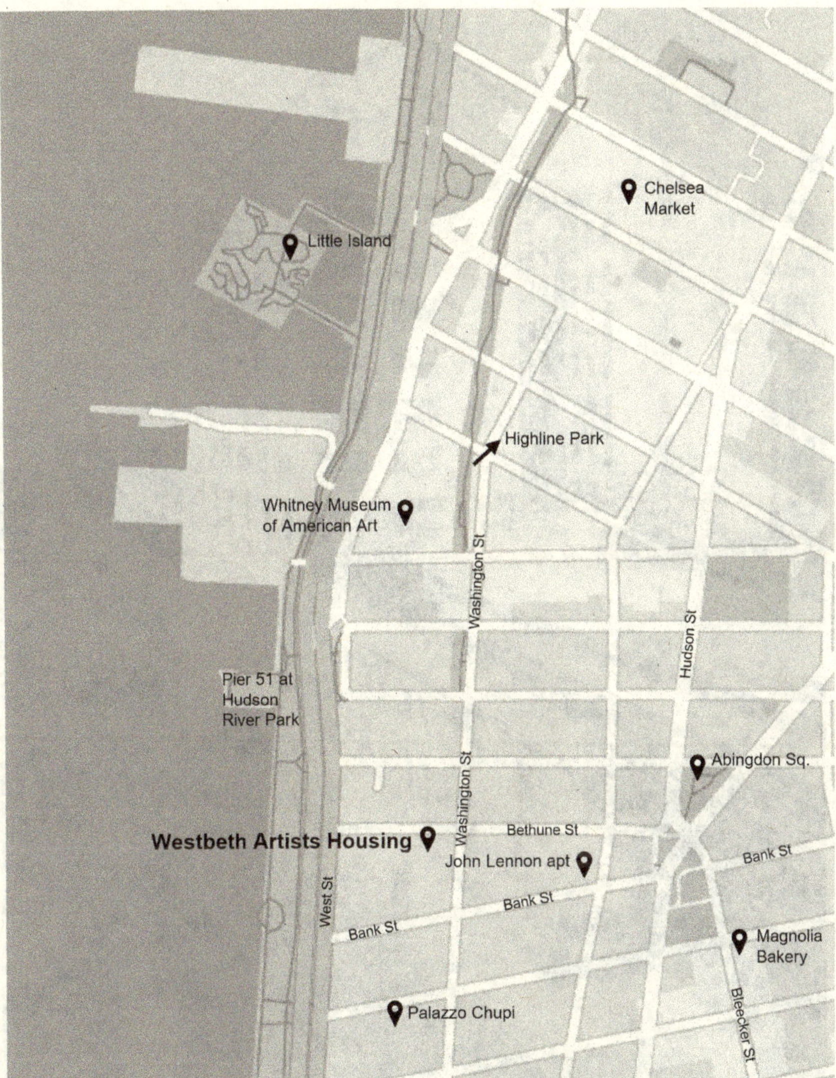

Figure 1. Google Map of Westbeth Neighborhood. Prepared by Mehran Pourakbar.

As we are bombarded by advertisements offering the most reliable, most affordable, or most friendly mobile telephone service or devices that will enrich our lives and include the latest bells and whistles, it is hard to remember when there was only one telephone company—Bell. Divisions of this monopoly manufactured phones and other electronics, provided access to

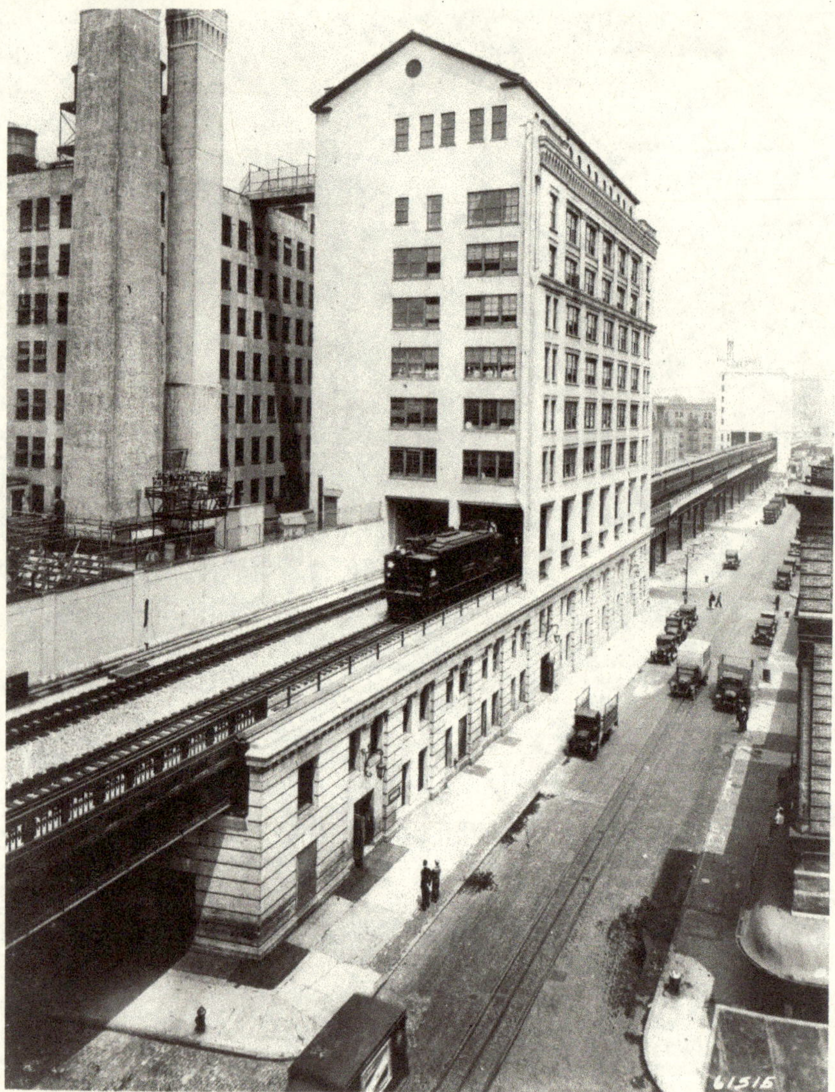

Figure 2. Bell Labs and High Line Train ca. 1930. Image Courtesy of AT&T Archives and History Center.

the cables to permit phone transmission, and engaged in research to further technological innovations. Until Ma Bell was broken up into subsidiaries and "Baby Bells," the Bell Telephone Company was an extraordinarily powerful economic engine with almost monopolistic control over technological innovation.

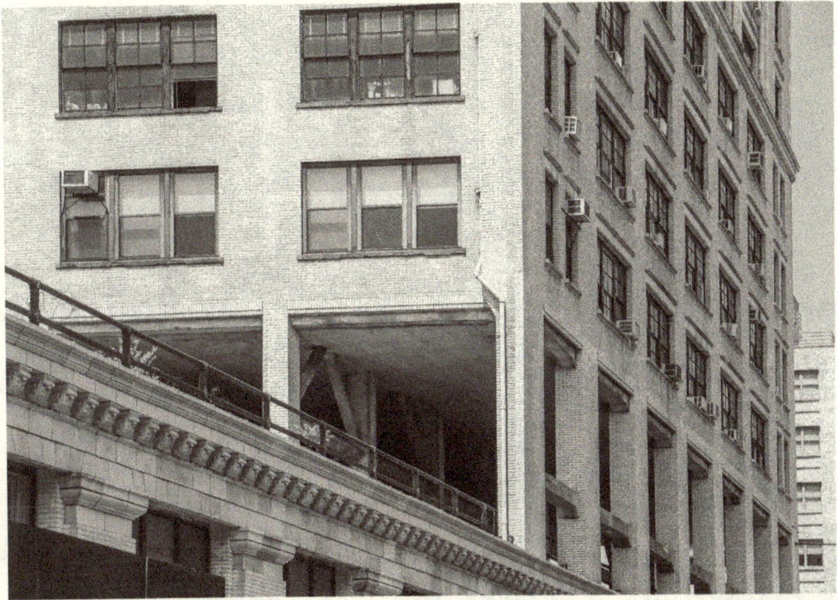

Figure 3. High Line railbed through Westbeth building 2024. Image Courtesy of Tom Conelly.

The Bell Labs

The Bell Labs complex in the West Village was the site for many of the most important technological breakthroughs of the twentieth century, and some of the most powerful scientific intellects worked at the Bell Labs, including Albert Einstein and Alan Turing. The top floor of the building facing the Hudson River included the executive offices, with exquisite, tiled floors and rich wood paneling that remain today. The elevator lobby that led to the executive offices also includes the original mosaic tile work, reminiscent of some of the most beautiful handmade tile decorations found in the oldest New York City subway stations. On the top floor at the opposite end of the complex, the Bell Labs constructed an auditorium where technological product launches would be held, with the press the first to be privy to the latest and greatest gadgets and systems—a style of product launch that Steve Jobs of Apple successfully emulated decades later. A movie theater at street level on Bank Street was where the first commercial film with sound (*The Jazz Singer*) was shown (1927), and in the same year, the Bell Labs invented the TV transmission and the vacuum tube. The Bell Labs were also responsible for the invention of radar (1919), the coaxial cables and color TV transmission (1929), radio astronomy (1933), a prototype digital computer

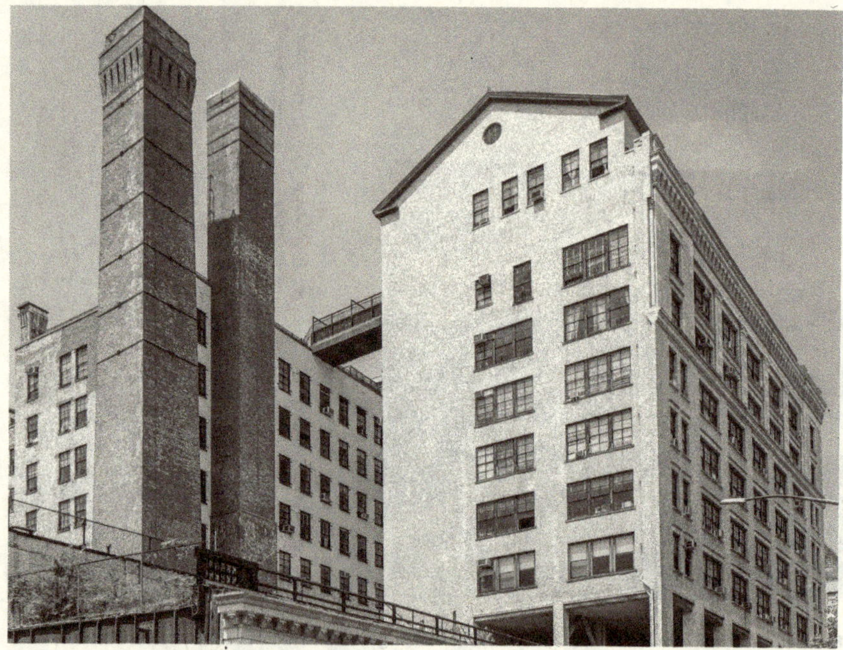

Figure 4. Westbeth from Washington Street. Courtesy of Tom Conelly.

(1938), microwave radio system (1948), transoceanic telephone cable (1956), lasers (1958), and satellite communication (1962) (Sheire 1975). The building's industrial history remains apparent through the utilitarian architecture and dominant smokestacks, which are still visible today (Fig. 4 and Fig. 5).

The square block that was the Bell Labs is responsible for some of the most important and dangerous technological innovations in history. Some foundational physics research done at the Bell Labs was for defense work, including for the development of atomic weapons as part of the Manhattan Project during World War II. The building was the site for many innovations in acoustics and understanding the properties of sound, and the rippled ceilings that remain today were designed to have acoustic properties. The site in the complex where the first microphones were invented is now a rehearsal space for some of the resident musicians. They sense the walls hold sound memories that pass down and inspire the current generation of musicians.

Many people who live in the repurposed Bell Labs—now Westbeth—describe the site as having a humming, sentient, creative force that surrounds all who live there, like a creative ozone that silently seeps in and surrounds

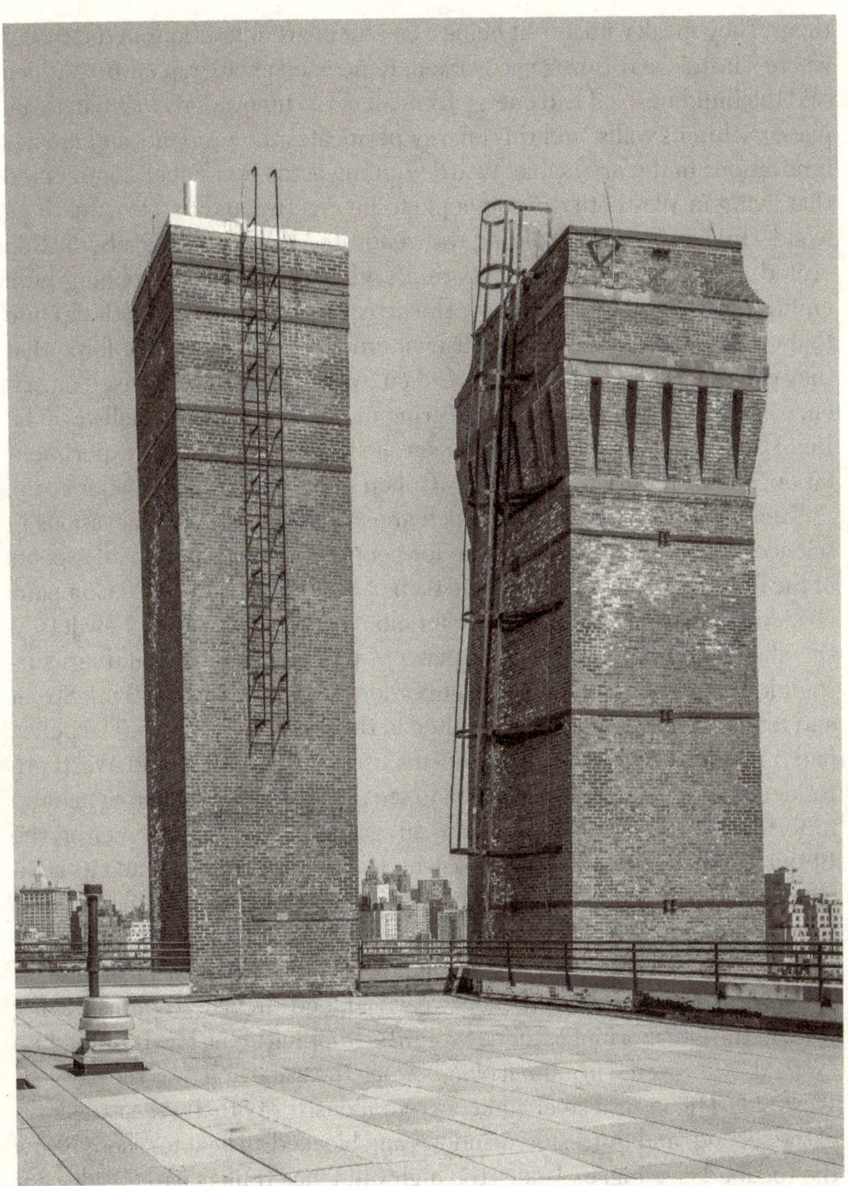

Figure 5. Smokestacks above Westbeth Roof. Image Courtesy of Tom Conelly.

them. They speak with awe at being a creator of art innovations in the spaces where Einstein and Turing had worked. Renowned photographer Bob Gruen said the building itself had energy from all of the innovations that had taken place within its walls, and this energy permeates the residents and creates innovations in the arts. Obie Award-winning actor Ron Faber commented that living in Westbeth drives people to be creative and to "do something wonderful." Before the building was renovated to become Westbeth, Ron visited a friend who lived nearby and said he felt a deep throbbing hum emitted by the building, and now the artists who live in Westbeth tap into that energy and release it in their own creative endeavors, as a force that they can't evade. Filmmaker Jem Cohen, whose films have focused on science, feels inspired knowing that Turing may have walked his hallway. The Bell Labs/Westbeth building has been the locus of innovation, experimentation, and discovery for 120 years (Cohen 2020; Gruen 2018; Faber 2018).

The fact that the Bell Labs, which are so associated with innovations in science, ended up becoming home for people who innovated in all aspects of the fine arts is a most improbable turn of events. When the Bell Company abandoned the West Village lab site for more modern facilities in New Jersey, the abandoned buildings were a maze of partially derelict buildings surrounded by a gritty, industrial neighborhood. A jail was across Bank Street and regularly had escapes that resulted in the sounding of sirens. The police had a paddock nearby for their horses used in patrolling, and Westbeth residents recall taking their children to see the horses and collecting manure to fertilize house plants and windowsill gardens. Across the street on the Bethune side of the building was a grim factory, Superior Ink, and its adjacent parking lot, where ink for the city's newspapers was manufactured. A few blocks on the other side of the site were the major printing presses where the city dailies were printed. Heading uptown was the Meatpacking District, and it was common to see butchers wearing blood-drenched aprons leaving work in the late morning after dawn shifts, stopping at the local coffee shop for food, still covered in animal blood. Along the waterfront was the elevated West Side Highway, a steel and concrete monstrosity that was at the level of the second- and third-story windows and blocked all light for those below the roadbed (see Fig. 6). Under the highway, truck trailers parked adjacent to the mostly abandoned piers that had formerly been busy sites for ships carrying freight to and from Lower Manhattan. As larger ships with containerized shipping became more common in the 1960s, the port shifted to the New Jersey side of the Hudson, where dredged shipping channels permitted the huge vessels to navigate, rendering the relatively small piers on the New York City side obsolete. The buildings on the piers were largely

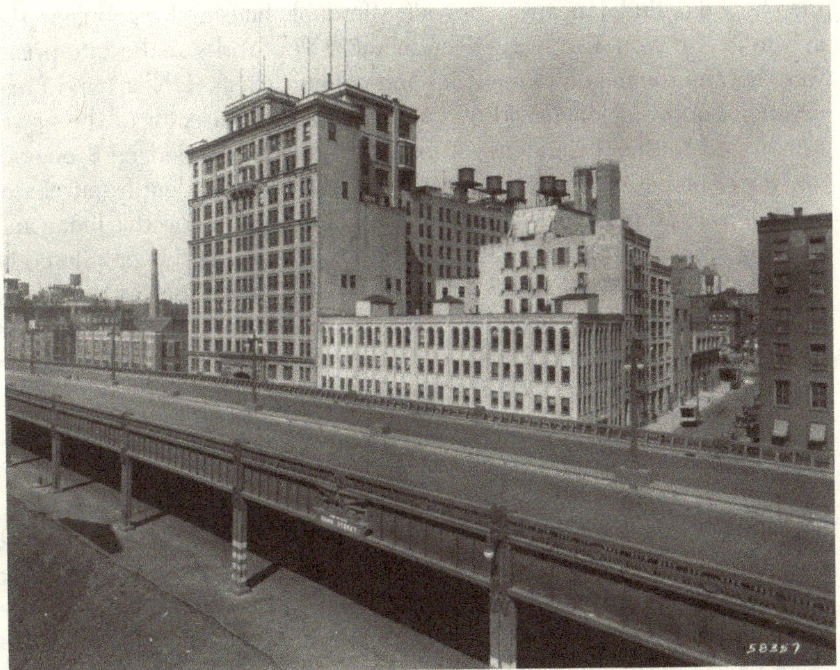

Figure 6. Bell Labs with Elevated West Side Highway ca. 1940. Image Courtesy of AT&T Archives and History Center.

abandoned and collapsing, as were the piers themselves, but the cost of their demolition was more than any of the companies wanted to shoulder, so they were allowed to slowly deteriorate, and pieces fell into the Hudson. In this context of urban decay, the trucks and empty warehouses along the river became notorious as places for gay men to rendezvous for anonymous sexual encounters, and for gay and transgender sex workers to solicit clients. Alongside these sexual activities, the neighborhood gained a reputation for drug dealing, which brought about all the problems associated with widespread drug use, including violence and fights (Holst 2020; Prete and Sonnenberg 1995; Strausbaugh 2013; Waldman 2002).

Given this context, it is hard to imagine anyone looking at the derelict lab complex and deciding that it looked like a perfect site to move in families and create living and working space for four hundred artists. But that is precisely what happened, thanks to the vision of philanthropist and historic preservation advocate Jacob Kaplan and Roger Stevens, a successful theatrical producer President Kennedy appointed to establish a national arts' cultural center (now the Kennedy Center). As supporters of the arts, both men hoped to find a means to provide affordable housing for people in the arts to live in New York City. Even in 1967, New York's real estate prices were beyond the means of many up-and-coming artists (Dolkart and Preservation 2009; Kaplan Davidson 2019). As the first director of the newly established National Endowment for the Arts, Stevens pledged $100,000, and the Kaplan Fund provided a match as seed money to identify, purchase, and renovate property in Manhattan that would be an innovative living and working space for artists. Smaller projects of this sort had been piloted in several European cities, and several cultural institutions such as Yaddo and the McDowell Colony permitted short-term residencies to support artists in doing their work, but the concept of a full-time living and working space was unprecedented in the US (Dahl 2014).

Westbeth Imagined

Kaplan and Stevens were exploring vacant real estate in Manhattan, assuming renovation would be less costly than a new build, when they discovered the empty Bell Labs complex. They set out to negotiate the purchase of the property, which they secured for $2.5 million, and to find financing for the renovation of the buildings. Securing adequate funding for the full renovation would prove daunting, as traditional mortgage guarantees, such as those available through the Federal Housing Authority (FHA), were intended to support purchases of single-family homes, not industrial properties. The amount of FHA funding available as a guarantee for any given property was calculated by the number of bedrooms and, thus, the probable number of occupants. The Bell Labs buildings ranged in size from 2 to 13 stories, and spaces as small as equipment lockers and as vast as production facilities, so determining the equivalence in the number of bedrooms was daunting. Ultimately, the solution was found through the creative designs of the architect selected to spearhead the Westbeth renovation.

Jacob Kaplan's son had just completed architecture school when the project was beginning, and he recommended a classmate whom he saw as a very creative designer to take on this massive project. The classmate, now famed architect Richard Meier, had a meager track record of output at this point, designing only one residential property for his mother, so entrusting him with the Westbeth design was a leap of faith. Kaplan's confidence in Meier's talent proved well founded, as he went on to design many famous buildings around the world, and was the youngest person to win the Pritzker Prize, the equivalent of the Nobel Prize, for architecture (Kaplan Davidson 2019).

Kaplan hired Dixon Bain, who had a background in finance, to manage the fundraising and logistics for the project and tasked his daughter Joan Kaplan Davidson to oversee the project and represent the Kaplan Fund, where she served as vice president. Bain and Kaplan Davidson would oversee the construction of Westbeth and develop a plan for selecting future residents. Meanwhile, Meier hired another young architect, Tod Williams, who had been researching utopian architecture and communities, as his assistant. Williams soon became the first resident of Westbeth, as he occupied space in the building throughout the construction and for several years after the first residents moved in (Kaplan Davidson 2019).

The project began by measuring every square inch of space to within 1/8th of an inch for the three quarters of a million square feet of the Bell Labs (Williams 2007). The complex of buildings ranged from two to thirteen stories, ceiling heights ranged from 13 to 18 feet, and many of the exterior walls were 48-inch-thick brick construction. The first task was determining how interior space would be divided to make apartment units and spaces set aside for artists' studios, practice, performance, exhibition, and for commercial leases. Meier's final design resulted in 384 residential units, ranging from single-room studio apartments under 400 square feet to two-story, 1300-square-foot three-bedroom units. The word *bedroom* should realistically be in quotation marks because neither in the architects' renderings nor in the final construction were interior walls erected to delineate bedrooms. Meier's fictional bedrooms had to meet FHA standards to secure a mortgage guarantee and the zoning and code departments in New York City. So, he came up with a creative solution by using a formula for the number of windows in a unit to equate to the number of bedrooms. The building had hundreds of original windows, which had been untouched during the renovation. Meier drew solid lines in his plans to delineate fixed walls between different units, but within units, he drew dotted lines from each window to the opposite interior wall to approximate a bedroom count in order to satisfy FHA. After much wrangling and negotiation, FHA and the city of New York were mollified, thus creating the first adaptive reuse loft conversion in New York City and opening the door for many subsequent projects that repurposed industrial properties (Williams 2007; Dahl 2014; Bain 2007; Dolkart and Preservation 2009).

With the financial guarantees from FHA to cover the mortgage in the event of default, the Kaplan Fund and the newly created Westbeth Corporation could borrow $12 million for the purchase and renovation of the Westbeth complex. The FHA security permitted the Westbeth Corporation to secure a thirty-year mortgage from Bankers Trust to realize the Westbeth project.

Several buildings in the interior courtyard were considered too damaged to renovate and were razed, which also allowed light to stream into apartments. The plans envisioned workspaces, living spaces, some that permitted both work and living, and ground floor properties reserved for commercial development. The planners assumed that commercial galleries, performing arts ensembles, and recreational facilities such as restaurants would clamor to rent space within Westbeth. What the planners failed to acknowledge was that, at the point when Westbeth was first suitable for habitation, the rest of the surrounding neighborhood was derelict and dangerous. In addition, the new residents of the building fit the "starving artists" stereotype, and none had the financial means to afford restaurant meals or rental of venues. Many of the commercial spaces envisioned failed to generate income for the complex in any meaningful way for many years.

Ultimately, the creative adaptive reuse of the industrial skeleton, using design elements such as color, and facing the challenge of FHA and zoning conventions won praise and awards for the Westbeth project and its architect (Dolkart and Preservation 2009).

Westbeth Design Innovations

Meier was keenly aware of the need to economize on the per unit cost for each apartment's renovation and also aware of the unusual backgrounds that the future residents would bring. Ideally, the ways that space within a given unit should be configured or subdivided would vary considerably if the resident was a dancer compared with a writer or composer. Visual artists are often limited in what they produce by the size of the space in which they work. Future Westbeth artists with children would have different needs than a single artist. Ultimately, it was decided that each unit would have a small, enclosed white tiled bathroom, a small kitchen with standard cabinets and appliances, parquet floors, and no interior walls. Each unit had two "closets"—large cupboards on casters that could be used to make room dividers and, if pushed together, provided enough space to sleep on top, given the high ceilings. Each resident would be free to configure interior space as best suited to them, carving out workspace and living space from the empty shell.

Two architectural innovations are unique to Westbeth. First are the half-moon balconies that function as additional egress for fire protection (Fig. 7 and Fig. 8). Meier did not want to block light into apartments that look out

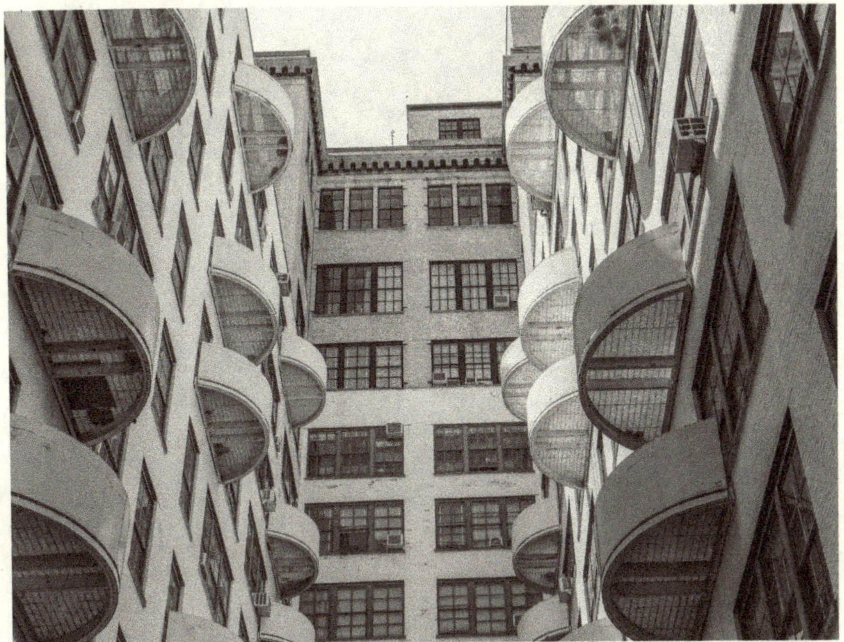

Figure 7. Westbeth courtyard and halfmoon balconies. Image Courtesy of Tom Conelly.

to an interior courtyard (rather than units with an exterior wall looking at the main streets), and he did not like the ugly black metal scaffolding that characterized most traditional fire escapes. He designed a half-moon-shaped balcony that bridged windows in two adjacent units, which provided a means to exit in the event of a fire and climb in the window of the neighboring apartment. He assumed, as it turns out rightly, that if there were a fire in one unit, the solid brick walls would contain the fire to that unit and not spread to the adjacent apartment. There have been several fires in the building, but for many residents, the half-moon balconies have been primarily used for potted gardens and by children who have locked themselves out of their home and accessed the balcony of their neighbor to shimmy into their apartment. Nadia Dajani spent her childhood at Westbeth and recalls the half-moon balconies. "We were always getting locked out of the apartment, so we would bang on the neighbor's door and breeze right past them through their house, open their kitchen window, and crawl out and around, open our kitchen window, and we'd be home" (Dajani 2020).

Residents Bob Gruen and Juanita McNeely noted that there had been a fire in an apartment very close to their unit that destroyed the entire contents

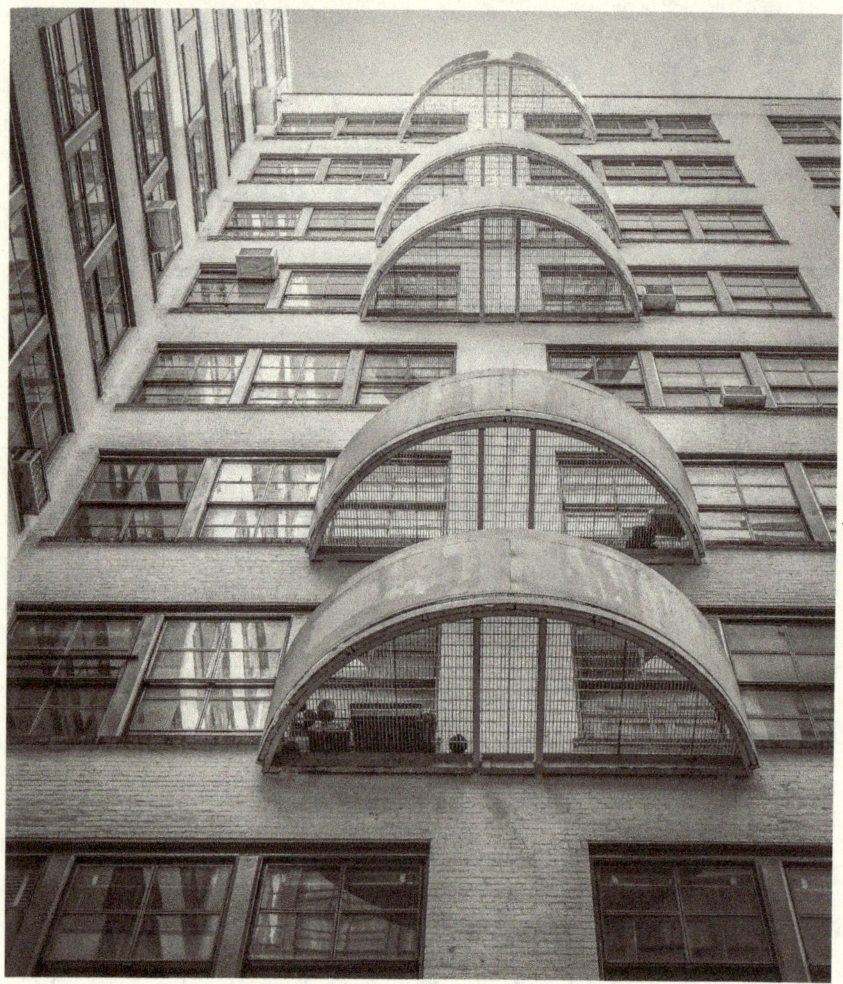

Figure 8. Halfmoon balconies detail. Image Courtesy of Tom Conelly.

of the apartment, but the fire did not spread to their units or any others (Gruen 2018; McNeely 2019; Hurd 2020). In 2022, a terrible fire broke out in Bill and Norma Anthony's apartment on the ninth floor. Tragically, Bill raced into the inferno to try to save his artwork and lost his life in the fire. The entire contents of the apartment were destroyed, but Norma survived and the fire did not spread to adjacent units.

The second innovation was the design of the two-story, two- and three-bedroom units, which residents call the duplexes. In the duplex units, the two floors are not stacked on top of one another as in a conventional house. Each unit had an entry from a hallway on floors 3, 6, or 9, and the entry-level space was fairly small, consisting of the bathroom and enough space for a small studio or a bedroom and some storage. The stairs to the other floor went up or down steeply at a 45-degree angle, and the other floor was essentially on top of or below the adjacent unit and opened to a large, spacious, open area that included the kitchen. Some residents have divided the open floor into conventional living spaces of living, dining, and bedroom spaces, and others, like dancer Sally Gross, kept her space open to serve as her practice and teaching space.

Visitors new to the building are often confused when they can't figure out how to get from one side of the building to the other. Access to the Westbeth complex for nonresidents is through a doorman-monitored lobby, now situated on the corner of Washington and Bethune Streets. A bank of elevators in the lobby reaches all thirteen floors and the basement in the tallest section of the complex. However, because the floors above and below levels 3, 6, and 9 are part of the duplex units, parts of the building are inaccessible from the lobby elevators. The only floors that have hallways that run the length and width of the building are 3, 6, and 9, as, for example, much of levels 2 and 4 are incorporated into duplexes accessed on level 3, as similarly levels 5 and 7 do for sixth-floor duplexes and 8 and 10 for ninth-floor duplexes. Today, duplex apartments all have triangles mounted on the entry door pointing up or down, intended to tell firefighters whether the staircase goes up or down in each unit in the event of a fire.

Meier's period of finalizing the design of Westbeth (1967–69) coincided with a time of great civil unrest and turmoil, but also a time of wild innovation and the Pop Art movement. Painters such as Andy Warhol, Roy Lichtenstein, and Peter Max created vibrant images with intense, bright colors, and they popularized and commercialized their works by reproducing images on everything from posters to T-shirts. These colors influenced Meier as well, and each floor had a different palette of color surrounding the elevator lobby and along the high, undulating hallway ceilings. These were mostly repainted years later with a drab ecru, but samples of the original paint colors show that he used vibrant hues such as Kelly green, hot pink, neon orange, bright blue, and red. The only place where these neon colors remain is on the coffered ceiling squares of the main entrance of Westbeth on the corner of Bethune and Washington, where the orange, red, and hot pink tiles remain (Bain 2007; Williams 2007; Kaplan Davidson 2019; Salpeter 2020).

The layout of the buildings and many of the industrial elements show that Westbeth was not designed to be a residential property. Giant smoke-stacks protrude from the building and climb well above the roof lines, and a huge concrete ramp on the Bank Street side of the complex connects the courtyard to a second-story entrance (see Fig. 9). This has alternately served as a space for artists, including as a lithograph studio with printing equipment, and as home to Temple Beit Simchat Torah, the largest gay and lesbian synagogue in the US. The executive suite on the twelfth floor, where the Bell president kept an office, retains its elegant wood moldings and bay window, and the breach in the building where the High Line railroad tracks passed through is clearly visible on the Washington side of the building. The oldest part of the complex, called the I building (all wings are labeled with letters A through I), is not accessible from within the main Westbeth complex but must be accessed from exterior doors on Bank and West Streets. This building remains the grittiest of Westbeth wings and is used as studio space for visual artists. It lacks many amenities required in new construction, such as elevators for handicapped access and staircases conforming to the current building code. Other modifications at Westbeth were specifically intended

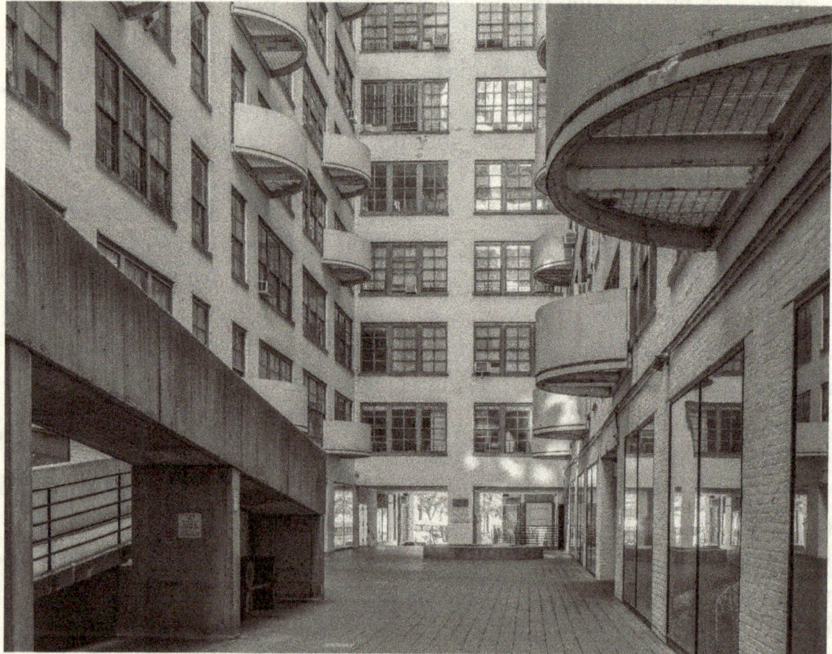

Figure 9. Westbeth courtyard with ramp. Image Courtesy of Tom Conelly.

to make the space more habitable and welcoming, such as the construction of a large water feature in the courtyard. Eventually, the water feature was replaced by huge concrete planters now growing large trees, and round concrete stools for seating, which are heavily utilized in nice weather (Dolkart and Preservation 2009; Kaplan Davidson 2019).

Commercial Tenants

Part of Meier's repurposing of space included room for commercial tenants to generate a revenue stream to help support the building. The first tenant was choreographer Merce Cunningham's dance company and school, which occupied top floor space directly above the entrance. Initially, Cunningham was unsure whether the space was affordable, so a grant from the JM Kaplan Fund permitted the Cunningham company to move into the space and pay their rent for the first three years. The company remained in that space until a couple of years after Cunningham's death, when it was taken over by the Martha Graham Center for Contemporary Dance and the Martha Graham Studio Theater (Dolkart and Preservation 2009).

The theater on Bank Street, where the Bell Labs did product launch events and screened early films, was a commercial theater with a series of tenants for many years. The venue was rented for music and theatrical performances, including concerts by Kiss and Jakob Dylan. Later rented by the LAByrinth Theater Company, a place for actors, writers, and directors to experiment and develop new works, the theater space now houses The New School's Drama Department. Faculty at The New School program include Westbeth residents such as actors Erica Fae and Karen Ludwig ("LAByrinth Theater" 2020; "The New School Drama" 2020; Dolkart and Preservation 2009; Gruen 2018; Ludwig 2018; Greenspan 2019).

From the beginning of Westbeth's occupancy, there have been various spaces used as galleries for the visual artists, and most of the time, there has been a community room equipped for small performances such as concerts, poetry readings, or residents' meetings. Other spaces have been used for various functions, including the Perry Preschool, a vegetarian falafel restaurant, and a commercial photographic gallery.

Westbeth Realized

The first residents began to move into the building in the late autumn of 1969 before the building was completed, and then most of the units were occupied in early 1970. On May 10, 1970, they held the official opening celebration of the building, attended by residents and dignitaries who helped make the building possible, including Mayor John Lindsay. Residents recall everyone signing a large poster advertising Westbeth, which includes all of the first-generation residents' names, and everyone shared food that they had prepared for the event. Susan Berger reported that she prepared Alice B. Toklas's famous recipe for hashish brownies, which Mayor Lindsay happily enjoyed, giving her a knowing big smile (Berger 2020).

Many years after Westbeth Artists Housing opened, the building achieved the distinction of twice being placed on the National Register of Historic Places. The first nomination in 1975 covered the building's history as the Bell Labs, and the second, lengthy nomination in 2009 recognized the building in its current incarnation as the Westbeth Artists' Residence (Dolkart and Preservation 2009; Sheire 1975). The second nomination document included letters of support from 127 residents of Westbeth, including poet Ed Field, choreographers Sally Gross and Edith Stephan, photographers Bob Gruen and Bettye Lane, performing artists including Ron Faber, Arlene Gottfried, Gloria Miguel, David Greenspan, filmmaker Barbara Hammer, and visual artists Barton Lidice Beneš and Lorraine O'Grady.

Making Westbeth Home

As each resident arrived at Westbeth to a blank canvas of space, every artist put their own touch on their space. Some focused on functionality, others on artistry, and most, a blend of the two to create spaces as unique and individual as each resident artist. Almost without exception, every artist interviewed for this project commented on how grateful they were to move into clean, affordable, safe space—as many had been living in rat-infested, squalid spaces, ranging from fifth-floor cold water walkups to illegal squatting in industrial spaces. In the next breath, nearly all commented on how hard it was to live and work in the same space and how no apartment was configured appropriately for their specific artistic activities. Painters wished for better ventilation to vent toxic paint fumes and for a dedicated sink to clean brushes rather than using the bathroom sink for this double duty. Dancers wished for wide-open spaces devoid of furniture to permit them to practice. Musicians (and their neighbors) wished for better soundproofing, especially as performing musicians often had rehearsals at late hours, coinciding with the times they would normally be performing.

Most residents set out to build walls or dividers to compartmentalize their spaces for different usages and, in the case of families, provide more privacy. Today, many units have taken advantage of the very high ceiling heights (13 to 19 feet) and built "treehouses." Visual artists Sandra Caplan and husband Ray Ciarrocchi, Emil Mare, and Christina Maile all built "boxes" that could be closed off and become children's small bedrooms, often no larger than a mattress to permit their kids to have a space to sleep and play. In Christina's apartment, one of her treehouses is above the moveable closets, and her sons Ethan and Julian recall climbing into their nests at night. Another treehouse adjacent to her kitchen now serves as an office, with a window to let light in from the kitchen. She climbs several steps up into the box to work there, and a bureau at the base of the treehouse can be moved aside, revealing precious hidden storage space underneath the loft (Fig. 10, Fig. 11). Emil had learned carpentry skills while in art school and built a sleeping loft for his son, and then renovated when a second child arrived. After the children were long grown and it became difficult for the aging parents to climb a ladder into their sleeping space, the Mares' space was once again reconfigured to have a true bedroom for the couple. Hans and Linda Haacke also built treehouse cubby holes almost suspended from the ceiling as sleeping spaces for their children when they were young. The "treehouses" built in the early years do not conform to any current building codes. In an interview for the Greenwich Village Society for Historic Preservation, resident and architect Tod Williams said that in the early years, residents hauled junk off the street for their makeshift constructions of what he called "psychedelic shanty towns" within residents' units (Williams 2007; Mare 2018; J.a.E.M. Maile 2019; C. Maile 2017; Caplan 2020; Haacke and Haacke 2019).

Others divided their apartments in half vertically, creating large lofts that created a two-story apartment, typically with living and workspace on the lower level and sleeping spaces above. Jack Dowling, Joan Hall, and Karen Santry were fortunate to have apartments on the Washington Street side of the complex, where the ceilings are the highest, and each of them eventually commissioned the construction of a loft with a staircase that covered the middle third of their apartments (see Fig. 12, 13, 14). The ceiling on top of the bathroom near the entry prevented the loft from extending the full length of the apartment toward the interior hallways, and their full-height east-facing windows permit views of the city and the Empire State Building. All wanted to maximize natural light and avoid a cave-like sense by extending a loft floor to break across the windows. These apartments have a kitchen, dining space, book storage, and an office in the below-loft space, a double-height living room with soaring ceilings on the east-facing wall, and an upper-level sleeping and workspace. Lucille Rhodes now lives in an apartment that permits her to break the space into multiple levels.

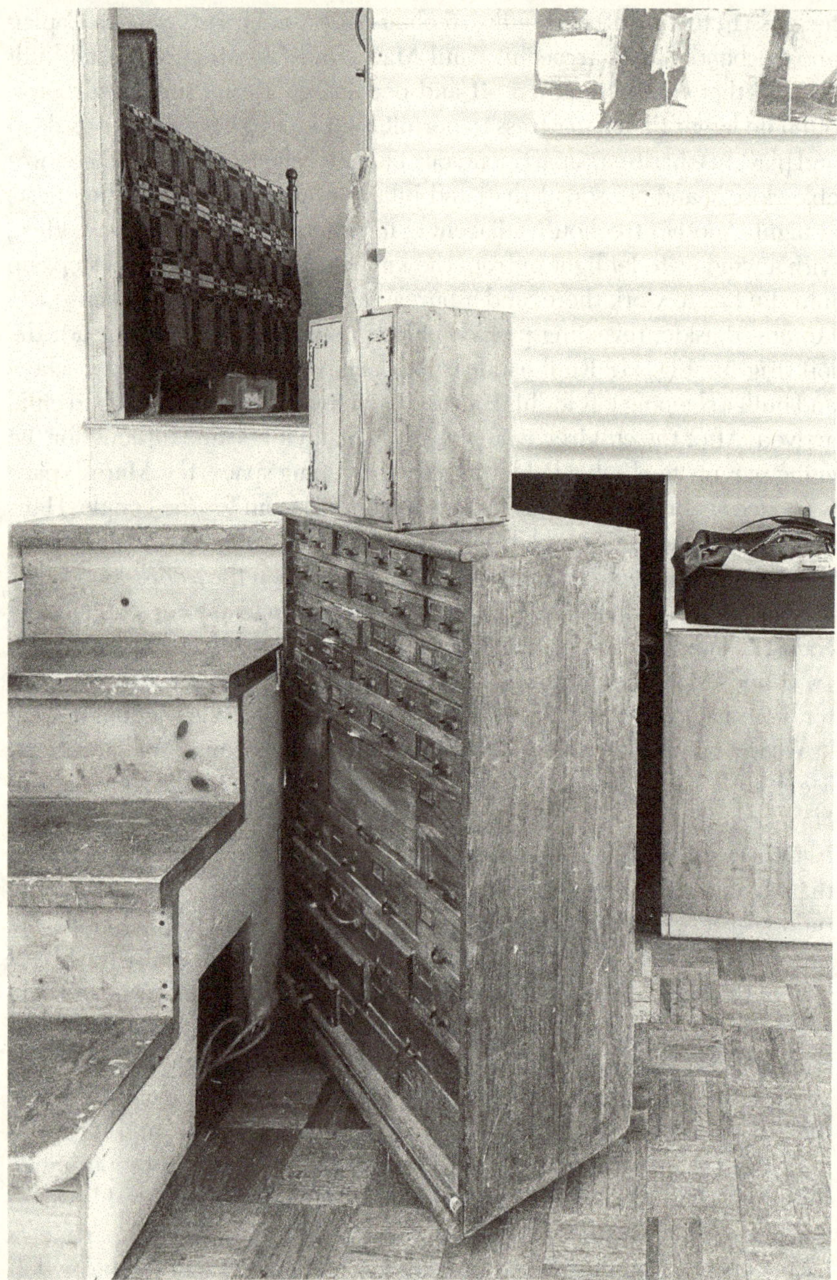

Figure 10. Hidden storage under loft in Christina Maile Apartment. Image Courtesy of Tom Conelly.

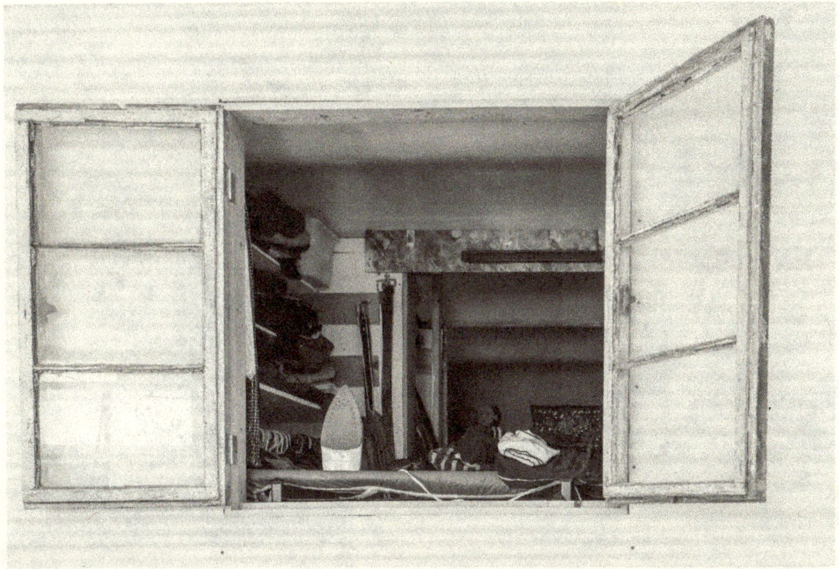

Figure 11. Window in interior loft room in Christina Maile Apartment. Image Courtesy of Tom Conelly.

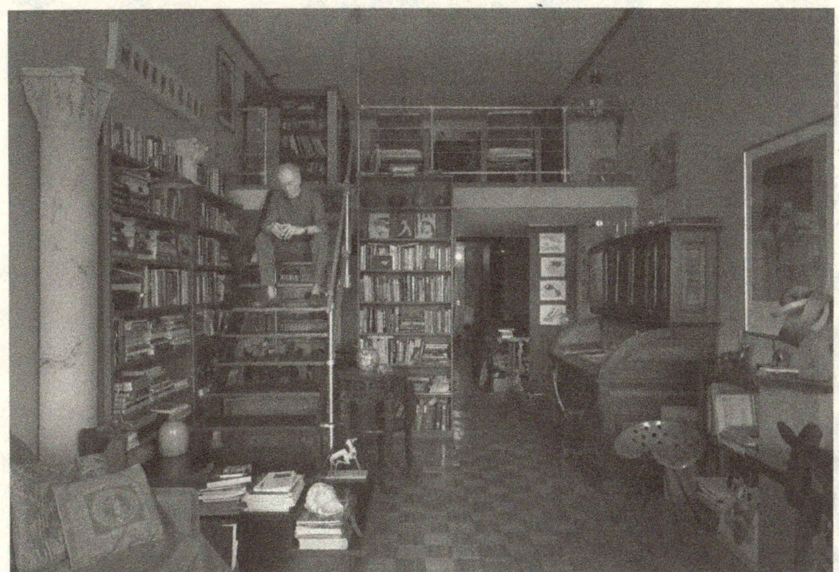

Figure 12. Jack Dowling loft apartment. Image Courtesy of Frankie Alduino.

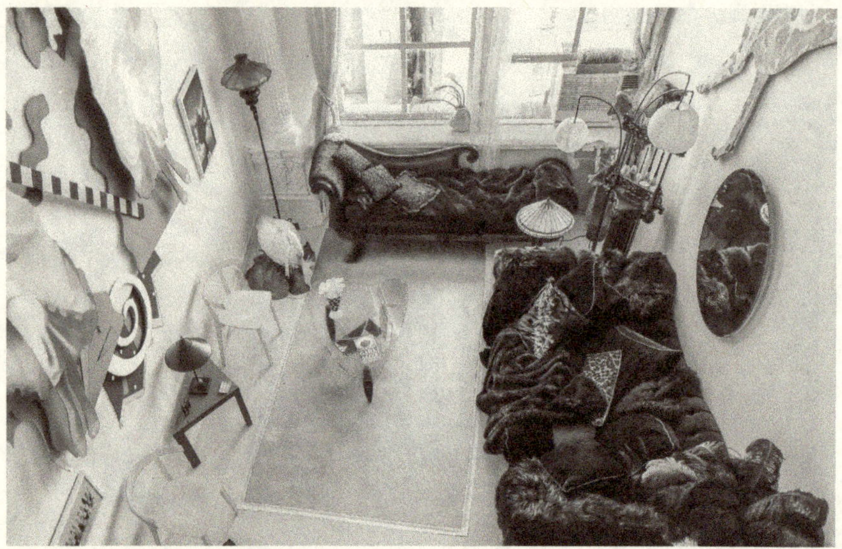

Figure 13. Karen Santry's living room from loft above. Image Courtesy of Tom Conelly.

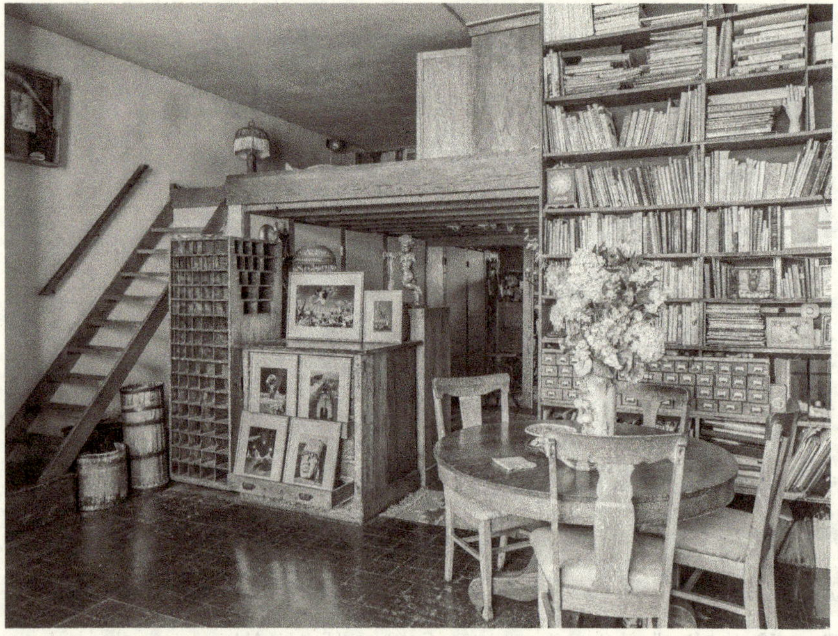

Figure 14. Joan Hall's apartment with stairs to loft. Image Courtesy of Tom Conelly.

Her bright yellow kitchen is near the entry from the hall, and then stairs that are also drawers, similar in design to classic Japanese tansu chests, break her space into multiple levels, each with its own function—a spare sleeping space with a desk, a sofa opposite a wall mounted television at mid-wall level, and finally a sleeping loft on the top level (Dowling 2018, 2020; Rhodes 2019; Santry 2019). These residents are all visual artists, which accounts for their ability to reimagine their blank spaces in three dimensions, and their carefully curated apartments show the exquisite works they have produced and acquired.

The visual artists in the building face special challenges, as they are often doing their work in their apartments, and their work typically requires more space than the needs of a musician or writer. Many have given over most of the apartment space to their working studios, especially painters who need appropriate light to do their work. Patricia Lasch creates three-dimensional constructions of lavishly decorated "cakes" and "garments" that are made out of paint that is poured onto glass from small squeeze bottles and allowed to dry. Her work requires huge sheets of glass as work surfaces, and she creates elaborate "lace" patterns, similar to henna designs on hands or intricately decorated cakes. Her sheets of paint lace are then bent and molded into three-dimensional objects. Her apartment dedicates the majority of her space to her work.

Emil Mare has reconfigured their apartment several times over the decades, depending upon the need for space for children, and then later to reclaim more studio space along the windows as the children grew up and left home. He created a pony wall that provides a visual barrier and frames a living and dining room space, hiding the clutter of his paints and easels on the other side, facing the window for natural light. Photographer Bob Gruen's life's work is massive, as his iconic images of rock and roll nobility are largely in pre-digital formats, and his apartment includes a giant fire-safe vault to protect priceless negatives. Almost the entire apartment is filled with filing cabinets, storage for prints and images, and a workspace for his team, leaving a small space for a sofa and ladder to his sleeping loft above the movable closets. Painter Beverly Brodsky's themes often deal with nature and light, so for her, it was critical that her easels were along the windows of her apartment facing the Hudson. Working in oils doubly complicates her work, as the fumes from the paints and solvents she uses must be vented to ensure her safety. The result is that her apartment is also primarily a studio with just enough space reserved to have a small table and chairs and a place to sleep (Brodsky 2019; Gruen 2018; Lasch 2017).

Rachel Urkowitz grew up in the building and later returned as an adult with a family, taking over her parents' duplex apartment. She needed space for both family and painting, and she built nonstructural interior walls to create separate spaces for her sons to have bedrooms and another divider to wall off her office. She said that structural changes now require approvals and plans drawn up by an architect, but a temporary wall with no electrical outlet is permitted as long as it doesn't impede air or light flow. The Dajani family of four children dealt with the need for privacy in a novel manner. The youngest daughter, Nadia, said her mother bought her a small pup tent, which was set up inside the apartment. Nadia hauled her mattress into the tent, thus creating her own room: "I was able to zip out my sister and brothers and have my own little world. Yes, my mother let me sleep in a tent" (Dajani 2020; Urkowitz 2020).

Secret Spaces

The people who live at Westbeth acknowledge that there are parts of the building that remain a mystery to them, and within the building are hidden spaces that most don't even know exist. In particular, the basement of the building is a scary labyrinth that many have avoided except to use the laundry room or drop off recycling. The basement has been mainly off-limits since the destruction caused by Hurricane Sandy, but adults who grew up in the building remember the basement as the site of epic games of hide and seek and other adventures (Dajani 2020; Dobbs 2020; Hamilton 2020; Lomprey 2020; Oppenheimer 2020; Bottoms-Newby 2020). Before the hurricane, many artists had studios in the basement, and many musical groups practiced and recorded at the music studio in the basement.

The building is so huge that it can be entered from several different points on all sides of the building, and most residents habitually use the entrance most proximate to their unit and often don't set foot in other areas of the building for years on end. The few spaces that everyone passes through, at least occasionally, are the basement laundry room, the ground floor mailbox room, and the main entrance for nonresidents on the corner of Bethune and Washington Streets. Pulitzer Prize–winning composer David Del Tredici rarely sees his fellow Westbeth residents, except when he collects his mail, because he occupies the only apartment that has its own private entrance to the street on the Bank Street side of the building. When I mentioned this to several residents who had been in the building since its opening in 1970, they denied that such a space exists, but indeed, his apartment filled with a grand piano has a door to Bank Street that is hardly visible as it is next to the School of Drama space for The New School.

Sculptor Charlie Seplowin and his family occupy one of two "hidden" apartments that are accessed only by a single flight of back stairs from the tenth floor up to an eleventh-floor landing that is not signed or numbered. When I first visited Charlie, I got lost trying to find his space, and he had to meet me on the tenth floor to guide me up the back stairs to his apartment where they can access the rooftop on the eleventh floor by climbing out the window. His family has taken advantage of the roof access they share with only one neighbor by having a rooftop garden (Fig. 15) (Seplowin 2019). It is fitting that he also has the most secretly accessed studio in the Westbeth complex, which he built after losing his main basement space after the Hurricane. On the Bank Street side of the building, on a low third-floor roof, a shaft protrudes from the roof for two stories, which formerly held a large freight elevator when it was part of Bell Labs. This elevator had been removed decades ago, but the rooftop shaft remained, even though its original glass ceiling had long since collapsed and pigeons roosted in the space. Charlie cleaned out several feet of bird droppings and debris, installed

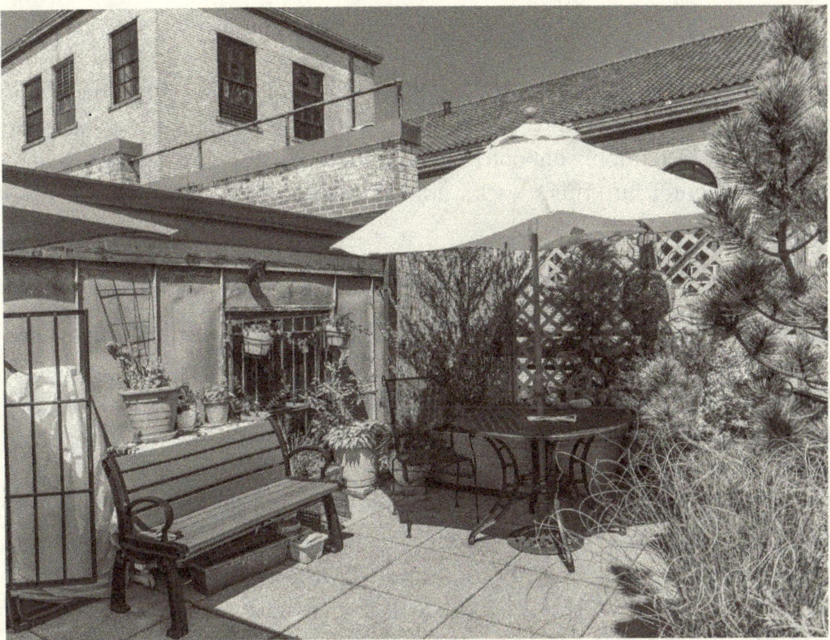

Figure 15. Rooftop garden. Image Courtesy of Tom Conelly.

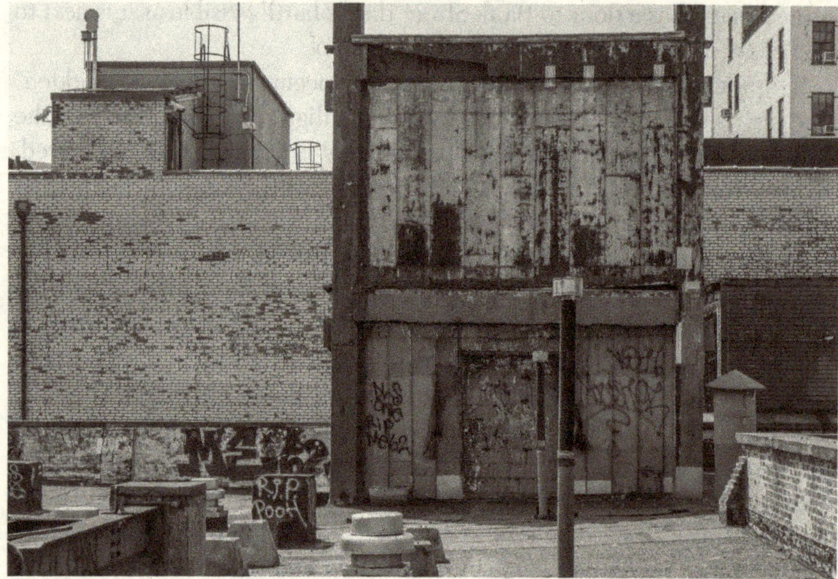

Figure 16. Charlie Seplowin's secret studio in former elevator shaft. Image Courtesy of Tom Conelly.

a new roof on the structure, and created a two-story studio from the abandoned elevator shaft where he now can work. This hidden studio can only be accessed by climbing out onto a roof at the third-story level and traversing the roof to enter into this secret studio (Fig. 16).

Apartment as Art

Many of the apartments in Westbeth are full of amazing art, and many are examples of creatively repurposed space that suits the needs of residents. Some are beautifully remodeled, with elegant custom-built furniture and fittings, while others are worn and overwhelmed by the art produced over decades. Many apartments have ingenious use of space, such as one where the resident built a platform over an open staircase to create a loft for an extra bed, or another that uses floor rugs to define different functions for eating, sleeping, and working for "rooms" without walls. Given the tight quarters in most units, the Westbeth artists have become masters of creative storage solutions, such as using pulleys intended for flying scenery flats into the fly loft above a stage to suspend bicycles from the 15-foot-high ceilings. Another uses the bathtub for storing bins of clothing that are stacked in the hall between showers, and suspended three-tiered mesh baskets intended for storing produce hang over the tub to store cleaning supplies, all hidden by the shower curtain. For many residents, their home is an extension of their art. Joan Hall's lovely apartment displays her creative artwork throughout and feels like a Japanese inn with rich wood finishes. David Gillison's spare white apartment provides the suitable framework to make his huge, dramatic, black and white photographs of people from highland New Guinea have the visual impact they deserve (Fig. 17). Lily Rivlin's apartment shows her life as a scholar which underlies her work as a filmmaker, as every wall is lined with books. Painter Juanita McNeely's apartment has huge canvases propped against the wall, sitting on the floor, so she can continue to work on them while sitting in her wheelchair, and other evocative paintings hang on her walls. But most would agree that no apartment could compare with Barton Lidice Beneš's.

Barton lived in a studio apartment until he died in 2012. He filled it to the rafters with art he made and art he found throughout his career. His apartment held antique taxidermy mounted to the walls, African masks, a large hourglass that contained the ashes of two former lovers, a Chinese

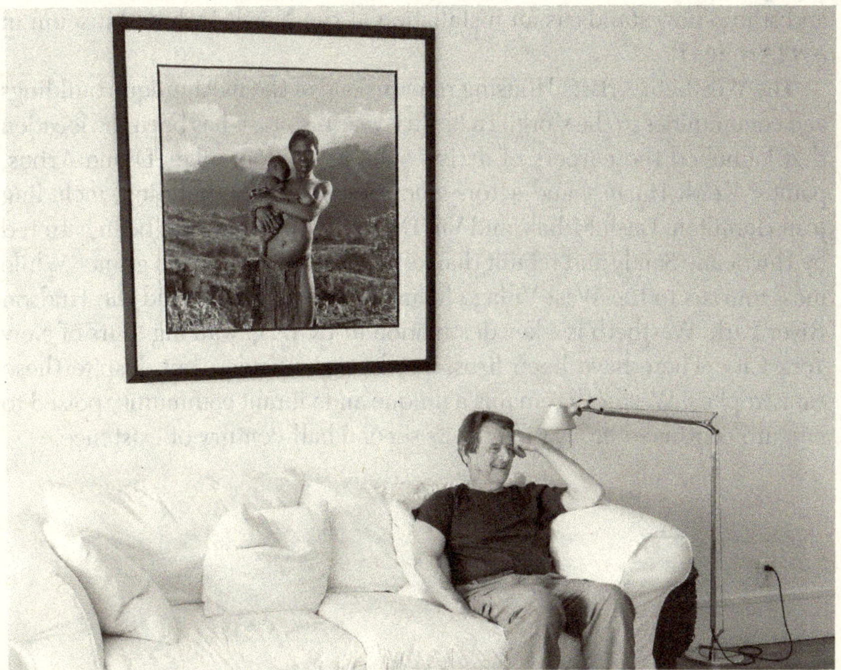

Figure 17. David Gillison. Image Courtesy of Tom Conelly.

opium bed suitable for the emperor, and many of his own artworks. As an artist who wove his own HIV+ status into the themes of his work, he had a decorative cake plate with a dome on the kitchen table that appeared to cover delectable, colorful bonbons. On closer inspection, these confections were constructed from the many pills he had to take each day for his HIV, glued together into colorful bonbons. On another table were ceramic shards from a broken bowl, each with an image of a friend who died of AIDS attached to the fragment. Barton said, "My apartment has become a safe deposit box, a vault of memories. Without the stories, the objects mean nothing, but . . . when the provenance is attached they become interesting, and when they are combined with many more similar objects in a collection, they become art" (Beneš 2002). Barton created a collaborative piece during a residency at the North Dakota Museum of Art and was welcomed by the people of Grand Forks. This came at a time when many people and museums were fearful of displaying art and artists associated with the AIDS epidemic, and he developed an affinity for the people he met during that collaboration. In recognition that his apartment was his greatest work of art, he donated it in its entirety to the museum. Before his death, curators came and photographed and measured the placement of everything, and his apartment and studio now stands as an installation at the North Dakota Museum of Art (Art 2021).

The Westbeth Artists Housing remains one of the most unique buildings and communities in the world. In its fifty-year history, it has been the location that launched the careers of artists such as photographer Diane Arbus, painter Keith Haring, and actors who grew up in the building, including Josh Hamilton, Dash Mihok, and Vin Diesel. The building has been battered by Hurricane Sandy and rebuilt thanks to historic preservation grants. While most tourists to the West Village focus on the High Line and the Hudson River Park, Westbeth is a key destination in LGBTQ walking tours of New York City. There have been fires, floods, and suicides, but despite these catastrophes, Westbeth remains a unique and vibrant community poised to nurture continued innovations in its second half-century of existence.

2

Becoming Westbeth

THE COMBINED VISION of architect Richard Meier and arts advocates Jacob Kaplan and Roger Stevens created the physical campus that would become Westbeth, but the transformation of the raw, industrial spaces into a vibrant community of artists was not a given. The success of Westbeth reflects the successful navigation of legal and zoning regulations, accommodation of architectural legacies, and the creation of a vigorous process for screening potential Westbeth residents.

Meier's Design vs. FHA

Meier's loft conversion design flew in the face of regulations established by the Federal Housing Authority (FHA), specifically for allocating space based on household size. As guarantors on the mortgage for Westbeth, FHA rules for the size of units per family had to be reflected in the allocation of apartments. Given that the building was transformed with the intent to be a combined living and working space for artists and their families, one would expect that a visual artist who painted large canvases or a dancer/choreographer whose performers rehearsed in the apartment would be allocated a larger space than a writer, for whom practicing their craft was not space dependent. However, FHA rules dictated that space must be regulated according to size of family, not genuine space needs. As the lofts had no interior walls, Meier's design used dotted lines on the blueprints from each window across to the interior or hallway wall of each apartment, and these invisible lines were equated with bedrooms. Thus, an artist in a small unit with only two windows was considered occupying a studio, and then more windows equated with one-, two-, and three-bedroom apartments (Bain 2007). Many longtime residents did indeed put up walls to subdivide their loft spaces into actual bedrooms, studios, and living rooms, but at the time the first residents moved into Westbeth, the FHA formula dictated the rules by which apartments were allocated.

FHA rules favored artists with families in terms of accessing space, but even this was not equitable. Regardless of the space needed to practice their craft, single artists typically received studio or one-bedroom apartments, and larger spaces, especially the two-story duplex apartments, were allocated to families. A number of the first generation of artists were single mothers with young children, and they encountered the sexist and antiquated ideas about families that were embedded in the FHA regulations. Patricia Lasch arrived with her small daughter, and because her child was female, she was expected to move into a one-bedroom unit and share a bedroom with her young child, whereas Dolores Walker moved in with a son and was eligible for a larger space so he could have his own room. Hans and Linda Haacke arrived with one small boy, and several years later, a second child was born, also a boy. Their application to move into a larger unit was denied because, according to FHA rules, two children of the same sex would be expected to share a bedroom, even if there was a wide age difference between the children. When Sandra Kingsbury's household added a daughter many years after the birth of her son, she was entitled to a larger space to have separate rooms for her two children (Haacke and Haacke 2019; Kingsbury 2018; Lasch 2017; Walker 2018).

Over the years, most units within Westbeth were reallocated, either to someone from within the community who requested an in-house move or to new tenants who moved in when a unit became vacant. Most people were so desperate to get into Westbeth that they accepted any unit that was offered, even if it was subpar. Bob Gruen was initially located next to the mailboxes, which proved to be a noisy spot for people to congregate all day long, which was at odds with his night owl schedule as a photographer of the rock scene. Photographer David Gillison was first assigned a dark apartment with windows looking directly at a brick wall, and the dreariness and lack of light were depressing after his work in New Guinea, where everything was a vibrant green hue. In both of these cases and many others, requests to relocate within the building were often successful—though sometimes required several years of waiting until they were able to move to a more prime location (Gruen 2018; Gillison 2019).

Getting into Westbeth

As the construction of Westbeth progressed in 1969, Jacob Kaplan charged his daughter Joan Kaplan Davidson with overseeing the selection of artists to become the first generation of residents. Joan shared her father's vision of what Westbeth might become. She said the original plan had been only for painters and sculptors to live at Westbeth, but the broader eligibility resulted from early planning meetings. She convened a committee that included the directors of the Metropolitan Museum of Art, the Museum of Modern Art (MoMA), the Frick Collection, and Lincoln Center for the Performing Arts to make the decisions about criteria for acceptance. They ultimately decided that all disciplines should be included and that the qualifications for placement should reflect both the quality of the work that the artist produced and the seriousness with which they took art as their vocation—meaning they had to be full-time professional artists, not just weekend painters. These leaders wisely determined that they would not be the judge and jury to determine whose work had merit, so they required letters of reference from established professionals in the specific discipline as part of the application. Thus, painters would be evaluated by painters and dancers by dancers, which allowed professionals in that genre to be the arbiter of whether someone was good enough to get into Westbeth. They also felt this would prevent favoring or disfavoring somebody because they were a modernist or a classicist or an avant-garde artist. In one way they were very ahead of the curve, as was an intention to have real diversity within the Westbeth community. They wanted to have families, single people, and people of all different ethnic and national backgrounds (Kaplan Davidson 2019).

Joan Kaplan Davidson and her team assumed that people would move in as the equivalent of a long-term artists' residency. They imagined that young artists would arrive as unknowns at Westbeth and, within five years, would become established and well-known and move on to greener pastures, making way for the next generation of artists. While this was never written into the rules of occupancy, it was an assumption that proved naïve. The screening committee didn't reckon with the ever-increasing cost of Manhattan rental space, combined with a realistic timeline for artists to "make it." For example, several resident visual artists are now regarded as important artists of the twentieth century, but their recognition came when they were octogenarians, not five years after joining the community.

The word of the opportunity for residence at Westbeth spread through the New York art scene, and artists began preparing their applications. Painter Sandra Caplan learned of the opportunity from her friend Elaine

Fried de Kooning, who was married to renowned abstract expressionist Willem de Kooning, while dancer Ze'eva Cohen was encouraged to apply by Joan Kaplan Davidson after she attended one of Ze'eva's performances (Caplan 2020; J. Cohen 2020; Z.e. Cohen 2017).

Applications required both proof that one's income was below the threshold established by FHA and that more than half of the income came from being a working artist. In addition, each applicant had to submit three letters of reference from people with expertise in their area of artistic expression—ideally someone with name recognition. Playwright and actor Dolores Walker had recently performed in an award-winning film and a piece at La MaMa Theater. Later, she learned that her acceptance may have been because La MaMa's director, Ellen Stewart, was on the Westbeth Advisory Committee that screened applicants. Similarly, Ron Faber's off-Broadway performance had won him an Obie Award, and poet Hugh Seidman had just won the Yale Younger Poets Award, and the recognition enhanced their applications' success. Puppeteer Penny Jones submitted letters from the director of a national puppeteer's organization and Bill Baird, and filmmaker Lucille Rhodes was working for writer Norman Mailer at the time, and he provided one of her letters of reference. Perhaps the most creative strategy to gain admission was from Joan Hall, who was at a loss to come up with her third letter of reference, so she painted a large canvas that said "Joan Hall has influenced my work, and you should give her an apartment" and was "signed" by Picasso, which charmed the committee, and she made her way into the community (Fig. 18) (Faber 2018; J. Hall 2018; Seidman 2017; Walker 2018).

For the initial allocation of apartments in 1969–70, an advisory board reviewed the applications to determine candidates' suitability and quality of their craft. This committee included New York City leaders such as urbanist Jane Jacobs and Rev. Howard Moody of the Judson Memorial Church (a frequent venue for experimental theater). Other members were heads of arts institutions, such as the directors of the Whitney Museum, MoMA, La MaMa Theater, and the Julliard School of Music. Established visual artists such as Elaine de Kooning, Sol LeWitt, Robert Rauschenberg, and poet Stanley Kunitz also served on this board (Dolkart and Preservation 2009). Additional members included early Westbeth residents Thalia Selz and Eleanor Munro Frankfurter.

Many early residents recall moving into their apartments in the fall of 1969 before the building retrofit was completed; some were desperate for housing and willing to essentially squat until their unit was finished. Officially, Westbeth opened for residents to move in January 1970. The *New York Times* noted that by the time of their opening ceremony in May 1970,

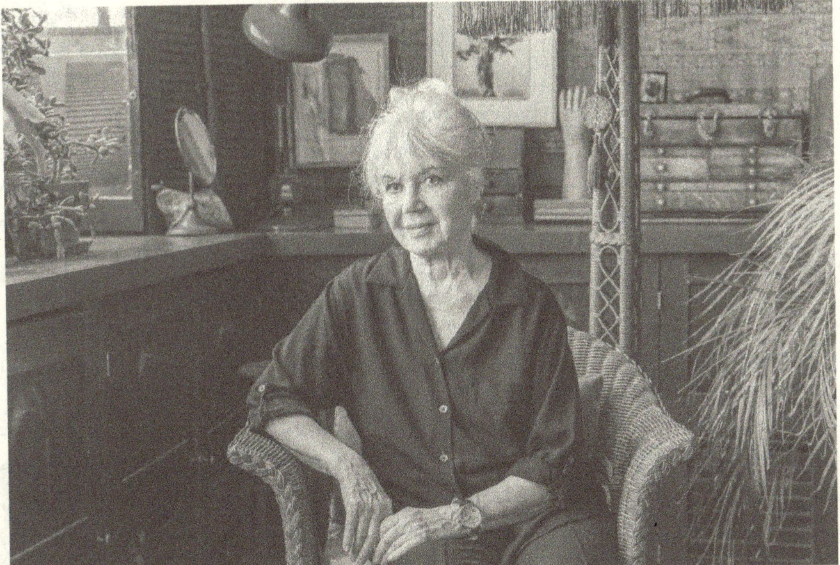

Figure 18. Joan Hall. Image Courtesy of Tom Conelly.

there were over a thousand names on the waiting list, and the building's tenant roster included "150 painters, 49 sculptors, 27 photographers, 19 writers, 26 musicians, 38 actors, 18 dancers, 14 filmmakers, 11 playwrights, seven poets, nine composers, seven print makers, three designers, four graphic artists, five craftsmen, four theater producers, hundreds of children, and a lot of pets" (Dolkart and Preservation 2009).

At the time Westbeth was accepting its first residents, the war in Vietnam was raging, and this political reality colored many aspects of life for the generation of young people. Many residents spoke of their overt actions to protest the war, and many men tried to position themselves so they would be unlikely to be drafted. Doris and Emil Mare said that many of their contemporaries were having children, even though they were financially and emotionally ill-prepared to become parents, just to reduce the likelihood that the man would be drafted (Mare 2018). Others such as actor Jack Davidson had completed his military service and was beginning his career as a performer when he moved into Westbeth. Ken Wade had been drafted but was able to leave the service after becoming a conscientious objector. He left the US for several years to escape the anti-war turmoil, learning to become a painter in Australia and Tasmania. His unlikely sojourn to Australia began when he hitchhiked with a lesbian couple and traveled across the country to the port of Houston, where he sought passage on a ship about to embark for Australia. Ken was a skilled musician who carried two guitars with his sparse luggage and the first mate on the ship asked why he had two guitars. Ken replied that one was for classical music and the other was to accompany his singing. The first mate brought the ship's Captain, and he asked if Ken could play Beethoven on his classical guitar. When Ken answered in the affirmative, the Captain gave him free passage across the globe with the proviso that he be placed in the adjacent cabin and leave the door open whenever he played so the Captain could enjoy the music (Wade 2019).

In the years following the initial occupation of Westbeth, the selection of prospective tenants has been primarily in the hands of the current residents. The admissions committee has participants from the visual, performing, and literary arts, and each applicant is screened by the appropriate committee. Painter Beverly Brodsky recalls being interviewed prior to admission by fellow painter Bill Anthony after a decade on the waiting list, and actor Gloria Miguel put together a portfolio of her performances before being allowed to move in with her son in 1977. Musician Marc Jacoby applied for admission after learning of Westbeth in 1983, when he joined his friend who had been studying art in a class taught by Westbeth resident Arnold Wexler. Marc and his friend attended a party after an art opening in the building, and he was amazed to see famed musicians John Cage, Hiram Bullock, and Gil Evans playing at this event. He submitted his application, which he describes as very rigorous, and notes that people who didn't have their act together would be challenged to provide the documentation needed for admission (Brodsky 2019; Jacoby 2019; Miguel 2017).

The Waiting List

Getting into Westbeth was a goal for many artists who had to endure years and years on a waiting list before receiving word that they were eligible to move in. Eligibility was predicated upon both income eligibility and the significance of one's artistic output. In the early decades, when Westbeth was paying off the HUD mortgage, prospective residents had to have a low income and generate at least half of that from their art. In those early years, monthly rent was based on a sliding scale based on one's annual income.

The waiting list was legendary, and some joked that applicants would die before they succeeded in rising to the top of the list. Indeed, many current residents waited a long time before finally obtaining a unit. Feminist filmmaker Lily Rivlin was visiting her friend Judith Thurman at Westbeth in

1976 when she noticed an offer of a sublet in the building, which she moved into and also applied for a permanent apartment. When she was notified that a unit was available, she told them she was already in the building and was able to retain the sublet unit she was occupying. Painters Karin Batten and Stephen Hall were both single when they applied for admission to Westbeth, but by the time they were successful after twelve and fifteen years, respectively, on the waiting list, their circumstances had changed. Batten had since adopted an infant, who was by this time a 12-year-old boy. Hall had married his wife, Samantha, and they became parents to their daughter, Reef. So, both of these households were able to move into the larger and coveted duplex apartments because they had children (Batten 2018; S. Hall 2019; Rivlin 2018).

For artists living in New York, the Westbeth building took on legendary properties and many imagined spaces and support for their work far more grand and elaborate than the realities in the building. Musician and composer Paul Collins was living in Europe but wanted to return to his native New York City, and he faithfully updated his application for an apartment every year when he visited the US. He recounts bringing his son with him, and each year, the staff commented on how much he'd grown since they'd seen him in the previous year—all the while, Paul hoped that presenting himself as a single dad would make his appeal for an apartment more compelling. He finally got an apartment after a dozen years on the waiting list, and he arrived at Westbeth after flying in from Spain, hauling in all his worldly possessions on a day of driving rain. Paul recalls opening the door of his new apartment to find one large room with a kitchen at the end. After hearing legends of the enormous, well-lit, glorious Westbeth apartments, he expected multiple stories and much more space but ultimately came to love and appreciate the space he had and the freedom that it provided (Collins 2021, 2019).

Several people describe their acceptance to Westbeth as coinciding with a crisis and their acceptance was fortuitous and even lifesaving. Filmmaker Jem Cohen was on the waiting list for twenty years and dutifully renewed his application annually. Though he became convinced he would never get an apartment, he moved into Westbeth just as his living arrangements in Brooklyn became untenable. Puppeteer Penny Jones was finally successful at acquiring an apartment just as her marriage ended and she had nowhere to go. Arriving with her son and a huge amount of furniture, she was later told the Westbeth staff initially wondered if she was running a secondhand furniture business out of her apartment. She used the cabinets and bureaus to create "walls" and divide up her apartment into a room for her son, as well as for storage space for her puppets and rehearsal spaces for her performances. Gayle Kirschenbaum visited fellow filmmaker Lily Rivlin and decided to put her name on the waiting list in hopes of finally being able to leave Los Angeles and return to her native New York. After ten years, she was elated when she found she'd been accepted, even though her first apartment was directly under the abandoned railroad tracks in the building. The ceiling leaked so much that she had to construct a makeshift funnel out of plastic sheeting to channel the water out the window that was coming through the ceiling. Gayle said that her Westbeth apartment "was my ticket back, my way to get out of jobs I hated. It is like winning the lottery" (J. Cohen 2020; Jones 2019; Kirschenbaum 2020).

Building Community and Fighting Factions

Through its fifty-year history, Westbeth has seen multiple generations of artists come and go. Some stayed in Westbeth for just a few years before moving on, and others remained until the end of their days. In the spring of 2020, the building was scheduled to celebrate its fiftieth year of operations when the COVID-19 pandemic emerged, resulting in canceling or postponing all events, but at this point, approximately 10 percent of the buildings' original residents had been there since its inception. Given the diverse backgrounds, artistic foci, ages, and experiences of the Westbeth artists, it is not surprising to know there have been both divisive pressures and opportunities for cohesion and cooperation.

Several power struggles, hot button issues, or confrontations have erupted in Westbeth's history. Early on, Joan Kaplan Davidson and the advisory committee tried to force the tenants to take on the management of Westbeth, which the tenants viewed as eroding their freedom and time to be artists, and they felt the building should be provided with professional managers. Lucille Rhodes recounts a meeting with the tenants' management committee and Kaplan Davidson, where all the members of the committee were aligned along one side of a long table, which she described as looking like the painting of DaVinci's *Last Supper*. In the middle of the table, where Jesus would be seated in the painting, sat actor Moses Gunn, well known for his stentorian bass voice and leadership in civil rights movements, including forming the Negro Ensemble Company. At a tense moment, Gunn rose leaned forward and said, "Don't you mother us! We did not come here to be administrators, we came to be artists." Early tenant meetings were often volatile and arguments broke out over issues large and small, but like the confrontation with Kaplan Davidson, most eventually blew over (Rhodes 2019).

Some years later, a small group of disgruntled residents led by Joel Brody proposed a rent strike when the management proposed a modest rent increase. Although the increase was needed to continue payments on the mortgage and was decided by the building management, some tenants believed the Kaplan family was behind the proposed increase. Conspiracy theories arose, suggesting the Kaplans were aligned with the CIA and the building was being controlled by the CIA. The tenants ousted the then-leaders of the tenant board and hired the lawyer who had successfully represented the heirs of painter Mark Rothko, who sought to regain control of Rothko's paintings from the Marlborough Gallery.

Musician Chuck Israels recalled the divisions over the rent strike as largely fomented by a few who "had an exaggerated sense of entitlement," and he joined others trying to calm the strident tones. He had long known Joan Kaplan Davidson, as his father was the attorney for some of Jacob Kaplan's businesses, and the rent strike made him doubly grateful that he had declined her offer to serve as a resident manager of Westbeth. Although his family was struggling financially at the time, he acknowledged that serving in this role would inevitably put him in conflict with friends and neighbors. Though ultimately unsuccessful, and back rents were eventually paid, the rent strike damaged the collaborative relationships between some tenants and resulted in some long-standing distrust between management and some residents (Solocheck 1976; Gillison 2019; Kaplan Davidson 2019; Israels 2023; Walker 2018).

Some of this distrust remains today, as a few point fingers at other residents who seem to have tenuous claims of being legitimate artists yet remain in the building. Others cite questionable and possibly illegal deals negotiated by building managers in the past. Following the divisive rent strike, Peter Shalleck became building manager in 1975 and was charged with finding revenue streams to help with the debt service. He successfully signed a long lease to the Congregation Beit Simchat Torah, New York's largest gay and lesbian synagogue, which was welcomed by the community. Less popular were his decisions to admit some new residents who did not seem to be artists (and some residents suspect that he accepted bribes for admission) and his leasing of the thirteenth floor to the Ramscale Corporation. Ramscale took over space that had no heating or plumbing and finished the space into a reception venue. Ramscale now occupies the top floor with views facing the Hudson River and the Statue of Liberty, and it has turned into a swanky event space that attracts elite events. Residents express distrust over how Ramscale secured this space and what benefits accrue to the Westbeth community, and it annoys residents when one bank of elevators is commandeered for catering carts and shuttling the wealthy elite to rooftop parties (Solocheck 1976; Chaikin 2017–2020; Del Tredici 2017; Gillison 2019; Ramscale 2021).

Some issues that erupted over the years stemmed from the absence of rules and the laissez-faire attitudes of governance in the early years of the building. Many residents, including Ze'eva Cohen, complained of vermin in the building. After conferring with neighbors, she "borrowed" her mother-in-law's Brooklyn cat, hoping this would remedy the problem, but she found the cat was afraid of the giant rodents and proved an ineffective mouser. Other residents resorted to insecticides and mousetraps; one decided that burning candles would deter cockroaches, and he left town with hundreds of candles burning in his empty apartment. Many residents had pets, and those with dogs commented that they got to know the other dog owners as they went out for walks, but the permissiveness about pets resulted in one ninth-floor resident keeping a horse in his apartment for six months, which had to ride the elevator to go out for walks (Williams 2007; Z.e. Cohen 2017).

One of the continuing sources of friction was the leadership of the Westbeth Art Gallery. Various gallery directors have opted to be more inclusive and show work from many Westbeth residents, while others have sought to elevate the standards and be more exclusive in the selection of gallery shows. When residents were rejected from exhibits in the gallery, hard feelings inevitably ensued. Photographer David Plakke recalls that shortly after he moved in, he began receiving anonymous notes under his door trying to get him to align with one or the other of the factions trying to control the gallery (Plakke 2018). One gallery director was removed due to suspected financial improprieties, but the gallery stabilized and returned to being an important venue at Westbeth when Jack Dowling became director and served for many years.

Over the years, the tenant meetings became less volatile, but many residents recall spirited discussion and arguments about all manner of governance issues in the early years. Bob Gruen noted that everyone had their own visions of what the building should become, and that compromise did not come easily to artists. As he noted, "It takes a certain amount of narcissism. You have to have self-confidence to be an artist" (Gruen 2018).

Other residents describe almost a euphoria upon joining the community and have built enduring collaborations and friendships with other residents. In the initial years, some of the first friendships were forged through children, as adults in the community met each other as their children became playmates (Williams 2007). Tod Williams was part of Richard Meier's team overseeing the building construction, and he lived in the building before it was completed and for several years following the opening. He noted that the presence of children was a civilizing factor for many of the adults, and a symbol of hope, vitality, and a future for the community in its early years. Linda Haacke said that while many of the adults struggled with financial and emotional stress, the building provided children with a free and supportive environment. It was common for children to go downstairs in their pajamas on a Saturday to play with friends or have sleepovers and return home with friends at lunchtime to eat together. In the summertime, a sprinkler in the building courtyard was a magnet for kids, and children would play together from morning until night. Painter Stephen Hall's daughter, Reef, became friends with many older residents, and he said that her daily proximity to people's aging and decline has helped her be aware of the inevitable life cycle in ways that most American children in nuclear families remain insulated from as they grow up, but her interactions with elders were very rich relationships. The building has always provided enrichment events for its resident children, from Saturday puppet shows to film screenings of kid-friendly movies, and for a while, there was playground equipment in the courtyard (S. Hall 2019; Haacke and Haacke 2019; Mare 2018).

Actor and writer David Greenspan and his partner, painter Bill Kennon, say that one of the best things about living in Westbeth is that you don't have to explain or justify yourself to your neighbors—they all understand what it takes to be an artist and don't expect you to eventually get a "respectable day job." Bob Gruen shared this sentiment when he noted, "Moving into Westbeth was important to me for two reasons. For the first time in my life, I had my own apartment with my name on the lease, and secondly, everyone who lives in Westbeth has been recognized as an artist by the US government. I was officially an artist now" (Gruen 2020). Juanita McNeely initially worried that a building full of artists might equate with hundreds of people with giant egos, each trying to outdo the other. However, she soon realized the building was large enough to pick and choose your friends and ignore those who rubbed you the wrong way (Greenspan 2019; Kennon 2019; McNeely 2019).

Singer Eve Zanni describes Westbeth as the spouse she never had, a source of emotional and financial security that permits her to live her life as she wishes. Eve formed the Bliss Choir that meets every Friday to sing for the joy of singing, and she describes the participants as all good friends for whom participating nurtures the soul in the way that food nurtures the body. Lucille Rhodes described a Westbeth experience that she cites as typical. After being away for many weeks, she went to pick up her mail from her box in the lobby. Expecting to pop in and out in a minute, instead, she was waylaid and greeted by others who were happy to see her after a prolonged absence, and she ended up spending more than an hour chatting and catching up when she intended just to pick up her mail (Rhodes 2019; Zanni 2019).

Residents note how, as people aged and became increasingly frail, other residents and building staff were attentive and helpful. Pawnee Sills cited an example of this caring community from when my aunt Shami was in a severe accident and was in nearby St. Vincent's Hospital for many months. Dozens of residents supported her recovery and her extended family. Everyone approached her sister and closest friends, inquiring daily about her progress. Eventually, written updates were posted in the mailbox room to inform everyone of her status. Like many elderly people, Shami fell from time to time, and even though the building staff were not supposed to render aid but rather call an ambulance, there were many occasions where the maintenance staff scooped her off the floor when she was unable to get up on her own. Joyce Aaron noted that the front desk staff is very protective of the older adults in the building, and when Neil Derrick suddenly became blind after surgery on his optic nerve, many residents, including my uncle Joe and aunt Shami, would take him for walks in the neighborhood so he would not be so isolated and to give his partner Edward Field a break from caregiving (Aaron 2017; Sills 2017).

In recent years, there has been a movement to recognize the contributions of the elders of the building with the Westbeth Icons Project. The brainchild of George Cominskie, a team of residents including Ted Timreck and Christina Maile handled technical production aspects while researcher Terry Stoller conducted on-camera interviews with some of the most revered senior residents. Interspersing contemporary conversations with the "icons" with video and still photos of them in their early years, these films document the importance of their contributions. Many of the younger residents have noted that they would never have known that the elders they meet shuffling down the hall or sharing an elevator are Pulitzer Prize–winning composers, or renowned contemporary dance choreographers, or famous actors or poets. Musician Marc Jacoby, who is one of the latter generations of Westbeth residents, noted that there is less cohesion and collective ethos among his generation of residents—in part because they are all still working and need to worry about paying the rent—yet volunteering to help with the sound system for a memorial event for his "elder," such as the celebration of life for Woman of the Calabash principle Madeleine Yayodele Nelson, reflects deep respect for the accomplishments of the older generation (Jacoby 2019; Stoller and Timreck).

Throughout our discussions, many residents cited the leadership and generosity of longtime president of the Westbeth Artists Residents Council (WARC), George Cominskie, as one of the factors most responsible for the cooperative, collective ethos. Some jokingly referred to him as Saint George or the Mayor of Westbeth, as he had a reputation for dealing with some of the most recalcitrant and demanding residents with patience and respect. Lucille Rhodes noted that his generosity earned respect across the community. Bob Gruen suggested he should be president—not just of Westbeth, but the United States. In any community of hundreds of people, perhaps particularly in a community of artists, there are inevitably individuals who are difficult or even mentally unstable, but George has shown equanimity when dealing with the most challenging encounters—even working to ensure there are safety nets around residents who have become vulnerable due to their mental illness or dementia with advanced age. He has also been instrumental in writing grants for programs that enrich the lives of Westbeth residents, such as a grant to improve the infrastructure of the community room, as well as programs to maintain the vitality of the elderly residents, such as singing classes and seated yoga (Gruen 2018; Kingsbury 2018; Rhodes 2019).

The great diversity of Westbeth residents is also one of its strengths. Lucille Rhodes's upbringing instilled in her a sense of tolerance and equity, and she values the ethnic and religious pluralism among Westbeth residents. Actress Pawnee Sills, who had been active in civil rights movements since her youth, said that one of the reasons she felt so accepted and at home at Westbeth was because of the collective emphasis on social justice and equality, which she said fostered mutual respect and friendships. Christina Maile said when the first-generation residents joined the building, they felt very compelled to give back, to be part of a collective community-building process with an ethos of social justice, combatting discrimination, poverty, and violence, and that helped foster cooperation amidst the diversity of residents (Rhodes 2019; Maile 2017; Sills 2017).

Space to Do One's Thing

From the beginning, Westbeth has provided both living space and studio space for its residents, but most agree that the accommodations for visual artists are better than those available to others, especially musicians. The marginal facilities currently available to support the musicians in the building is due in part to damage from a hurricane. Before Hurricane Sandy, many musicians had studios in the basement of Westbeth, and there was even a recording studio. Due to flooding from the hurricane, these spaces were abandoned, and now the music rehearsal room is on the third floor of the building, in the space that was the original sound stage for the Bell Labs, where the first recordings for talking pictures were made. Singer Eve Zanni describes an almost holy significance to the walls—which had been witness to vibrations connecting generations of musicians. Yet, despite the history of the space, its current state is in disrepair. A chronic leak in the skylight in the ceiling necessitated rigging up sheets of plastic that are angled into a funnel to flow down into buckets on the floor. There is no soundproofing, so adjacent apartments hear musicians practicing—often quite loudly if they are with an ensemble—at all hours. The musicians who use the space have gathered old rejected sleeping bags and bed comforters and tacked them to the walls to try to improve the acoustic qualities and muffle the noise. All of the instruments in the room—a drum kit, an upright piano, and an electric keyboard—have been donated by resident musicians. The musicians wish for better space and soundproofing so they can crank up their volume as they would when performing without disturbing the neighbors (Jacoby 2019; Zanni 2019).

The basement of the building covers nearly a whole square New York City block, and this was also divided up and used as studios by painters and sculptors. Even though the lighting and ventilation were substandard and did not meet current building codes, access to space made up for its short-comings. The oldest part of Westbeth is the I building that fronts West Street. It was built in the 1800s and remains largely unrenovated. The building has steep, uneven stairs and dark interior hallways, yet it has been used as a visual artists' space. Some spaces are allocated indefinitely to an artist, while others are awarded for a six-month rotation. One large room holds lithography and printmaking equipment, some of which had been left behind when a famous European lithographer, Sandor Zugor, who had made prints for Toulouse-Lautrec and Marc Chagall, returned to his home country. Christina Maile said that in the early years, the printmakers were all male, guarded their access to the equipment like a secret society, and refused to share keys to the space with others (Fig. 19). Eventually, they all died or left the building. For a decade, the print room remained abandoned until she learned about the space and got keys from the management. Entering the print studio "was like going back in time, with a thick layer of dust every-where, but the tools were left out as if their user had just stepped out and was due back soon." The equipment was rehabilitated and is now used by many visual artists who include printmaking in their repertoire, many of whom are women (Maile 2017).

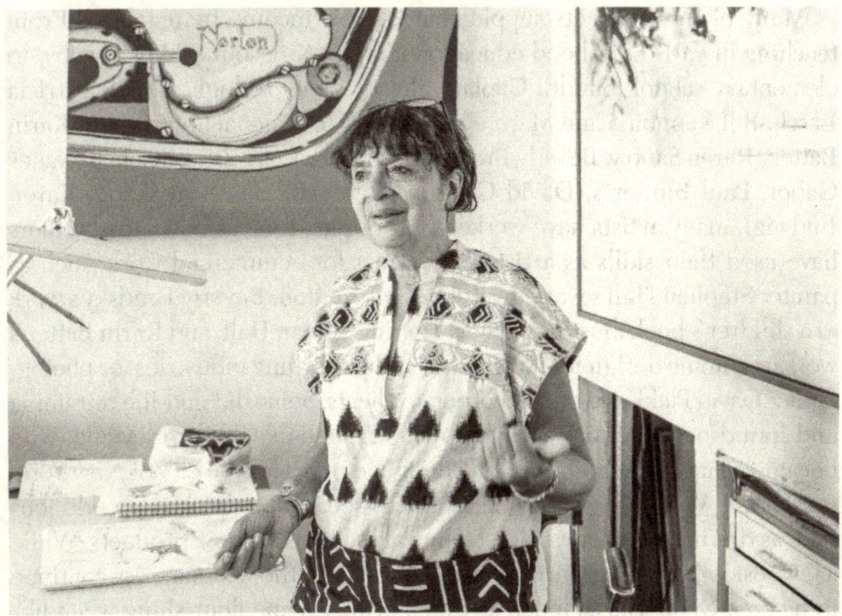

Figure 19. Christina Maile. Image Courtesy of Tom Conelly.

Keeping a Day Job

Artists seeking to live at Westbeth have always had to provide documentation of their financial status as a condition of admission—demonstrating that they obtained the majority of their income from their work as an artist but also that their income was below a threshold to qualify as financially in need. Once admitted to Westbeth, people could become bankrupt, become millionaires, or switch careers entirely and still retain their eligibility for their space. Virtually all of the earliest residents were demonstrably poor when they arrived at Westbeth, and many still qualify for subsidized or Section 8 housing. Longtime WARC president George Cominskie noted that 90 percent of current residents could not afford to live in Manhattan without the rent-stabilized apartment they occupy at Westbeth (Cominskie, Maile, and Lee 2020). The founders of Westbeth had a utopian vision that simply having a roof over their heads would provide a sufficient safety net to permit the artists to flourish and succeed. In reality, most residents had to have a day job or at least a side hustle to make ends meet. This was especially true for artists with children. Many who grew up in the building remember a childhood in poverty.

Many of the residents supplemented their income by teaching. From teaching in early childhood education (Sandra Kingsbury, Marc Jacoby) to elementary school (Sandra Caplan, Sherry Lane) to high school (Patricia Lasch, Bill Kennon, Emil Mare, Pawnee Sills) to regional universities (Karin Batten, Karen Santry, Beverly Brodsky, Ray Ciarrocchi, Ze'eva Cohen, Nancy Gabor, Paul Binnerts, David Gillison, Hans Haacke, Ken Wade, Karen Ludwig), many artists have worked full- or part-time as educators. Others have used their skills as artists to contract for commercial work, such as painter Stephen Hall's work in antiques restoration, Beverly Brodsky's work as a children's book illustrator, Jayne Holsinger, Joan Hall, and Karin Batten's work in graphic design for advertising and publishing industries, or photographer David Plakke's work for corporate clients. Some did mid-life retraining and found new avenues for employment, such as Christina Maile, who became a landscape architect who designed parks for the city of New York, or Dolores Walker, who earned a law degree. Others picked up odd jobs such as driving a taxi or writing technical manuals for new products. While a few residents left their artistic pursuits behind, the vast majority continue to be creative artists as much as time permits, some flourishing when liberated from their "day job" upon retirement.

Synchronicity

Living in proximity to other artists fostered artistic growth for many residents, many exploring different creative avenues because of the rich environment. Joan Hall perhaps embodies this artistic growth best, as in her youth, she was a dancer with a major dance company under the direction of Anna Sokolow while she studied at Julliard, and later she joined the Actors Studio. She soon became a professional mime performer and taught mime theater, but grew interested in visual arts and began assembling collages and art pieces full time. Her mixed media pieces have appeared in major collections, including the Pompidou Center in Paris and the Rufino Tamayo Museum in Mexico City. She also created covers for books, magazines, and music albums. In her senior years, she noted that collages fell out of favor since digital design made it quick and cheap to produce similar works. She added poetry writing to her artistic portfolio and now considers herself primarily a writer. This cross-discipline growth and evolution is common among Westbeth's artists. Allison Armstrong is a well-published writer but switched to painting as her primary medium. She occasionally performs music with her painter friend Ken Wade, as both were trained as musicians. Jack Dowling enjoyed commercial and critical success with his painting when he first came to Westbeth, but after a decade, he switched to writing and was part of several groups that workshopped their written work. Jack noted it was ironic that painting always came easily to him, both the inspiration and the execution, but writing was torturous, yet he came to define himself as a writer (Armstrong 2019; Dowling 2018, 2020; J. Hall 2018; Wade 2019).

In many cases, some artists' productivity soared after moving into Westbeth because their financial status was far more secure than when they were living in expensive New York real estate. Musician Paul Collins said he was writing more music and playing more at 55 living in Westbeth than when he was 25 (Collins 2019).

Bringing Westbeth to the Public

From the early years, the members of the community have been active in creating arts events that attract public attention. Poet Hugh Seidman arrived in 1970 and was happy to meet renowned writer and resident Muriel Rukeyser. Together, they wrote a grant that yielded funding for a long-running public poetry reading event. Actor and playwright Karen Ludwig has long led writing groups where participants meet weekly to write on themes and workshop their drafts. Many residents from the building have participated in these groups, but others have joined the Westbeth Around the Table group, including actors Linda Hunt and Dianne Wiest. In recent years, this group has prepared biannual staged readings of their work, which have been very popular (Ludwig 2018; Seidman 2017).

Since about 2000, Westbeth has tried to create more events open to the general public to raise awareness of the artistic achievements of the residents. The dancers and choreographers began the annual Westfest event, and the public is invited to attend performances staged throughout the building, with multiple dance events happening simultaneously and repeatedly throughout the day. The dance performances are not limited to a traditional stage setting; they dance along hallways, around stairwell banisters, in the courtyard, and in the Westbeth Gallery space. In the same year, residents began opening their apartments to host PEN Literary Fest, where twenty authors from around the world hold salon-style readings of their work, and guests rotate between venues to hear from a number of writers throughout the evening. Twice a year, the visual artists hold open studio visits. In recent years, these events have coincided with resident-led tours through the building, which invite nonresidents to explore the history of the building and its community. These events have been wildly popular and attended by hundreds of visitors (Cominskie, Maile, and Lee 2020).

The Westbeth Gallery has long held exhibits of artists—both from within and outside the community—and the openings of each exhibit are major events in the neighborhood. When the Whitney Museum reopened in its new location a few blocks away, there began a stronger collaboration between the visual artists of Westbeth and the staff of the Whitney. Each year, the Gallery now hosts one exhibit of works by Whitney staff. Many years ago, four separate spaces were used as gallery space. Although the building now uses only one of those spaces for exhibitions, it is a space that has been upgraded with better facilities and lighting, and shows attract attention from across the New York City art scene. Many residents commented that the Gallery had somewhat lackluster shows and reputation for many years until Jack Dowling became director in 1997. At that time, he oversaw the renovations and enlisted a panel to help jury proposals for potential exhibitions. Jack served until 2012, and today, there is an annual call for proposals that results in about fifty proposals that are reviewed by a panel that includes past and current Gallery directors, WARC leadership, and two staff from the Whitney Museum—ensuring an excellent roster of exhibits each year (Cominskie, Maile, and Lee 2020; Batten 2018; Dowling 2018, 2020; Lane 2019; Mare 2018).

Measures of Success

While it is true to say that, except for a few actors who grew up in the building—Vin Diesel, Josh Hamilton, Michelle Hurd, and Dash Mihok—most of the Westbeth artists are not names familiar to households in middle America, many have remained working artists for their whole lives.

Painter Stephen Hall hails from Scotland and retains his trademark brogue. At first glance, he looks like he might be a bartender, which he has been, but his work explores the compelling social issues of the Anthropocene—issues that focus on inhumanity and violence toward our planet and each other. His paintings are at once whimsical and challenging, such as an endangered lemur with guns pointed at his head or an equally endangered orangutan stranded on an ice floe. He has had a number of both solo and group shows and has a small but loyal client base that have collected his work (Fig. 20). Other visual artists have had long-standing representation and regular shows at some of New York's premier galleries and dealers, including the Leslie Tonkonow Gallery (Helène Aylon), June Kelly Gallery (Karin Batten), Peter Hastings Falk (Beverly Brodsky), and Leo Castelli

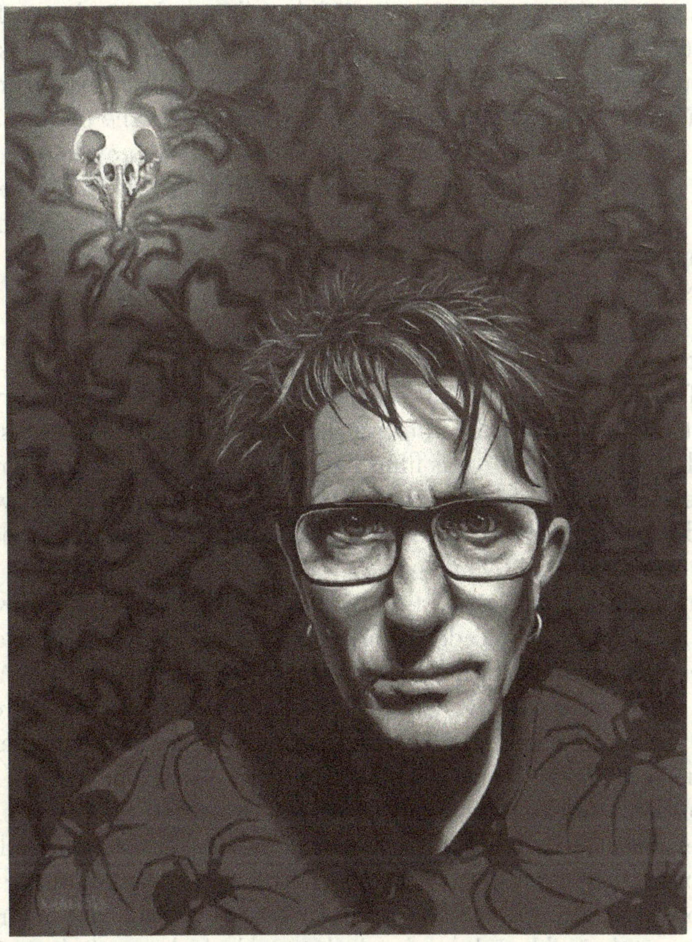

Figure 20. Self-Portrait painting "Dark Study." Image Courtesy of Stephen Hall.

Gallery (Jack Dowling), and their works have appeared in major museums, including internationally. Several painters, including Jayne Holsinger, have won multiple Pollock-Krasner Awards, and Beverly Brodsky received Caldecott Honors for her illustrations for a children's book. Mixed media visual artist Veronica Ryan's work reflecting the African diaspora and her early years in the Caribbean has appeared in the 2022 Whitney Museum Biennial, one of the premier events for contemporary artists.

Painter Karen Santry sometimes does fashion illustration and is currently focusing on larger-than-life action paintings of Kabuki performers, but she got her start painting real performers. While still in graduate school at Penn, her sister insisted she come to a performance in a dicey venue because she thought the performer would make an interesting subject for a painting, and she then met and befriended David Bowie. After the performance, Bowie invited her to join his entourage for a party, where she met Mick Jagger. When Jagger saw her paintings, he encouraged her to be serious about marketing—building on his training from the London School of Economics. She painted portraits of many rock musicians early in their careers before they were world-famous, and Jagger helped her stage a show where every one of her paintings was sold.

Documentary filmmakers have also enjoyed recognition. Lucille Rhodes's film "They Are Their Own Gifts" opened at the New York Film Society and was attended by one of the films' subjects, writer and Westbeth resident Muriel Rukeyser. Lily Rivlin's films have documented important feminist leaders, including Grace Paley, Esther Bronner, and Heather Booth, which earned her recognition as Miller Distinguished Jewish Woman Filmmaker Award (Rhodes 2019; Rivlin 2018).

Many of the performing artists in Westbeth studied with world-renowned teachers and workshop leaders. Karen Ludwig worked with Uta Hagen; Pawnee Sills studied with Lord Richards, Lee Strasberg, and Stella Adler, as did Joyce Aaron, who worked with Stanford Meisner as well. Director Nancy Gabor worked with the three directors who she felt changed American theater, Joe Chaikin, Jerzy Grotowski, and Peter Brook, and learned from each of them. In turn, these performers became teachers, directors, and coaches themselves. Many of Westbeth's performing artists achieved recognition for their work; notably, many actors received Obie Awards for their work off-Broadway. Composer David Del Tredici was enjoying an artists' residency at the Yaddo Colony when he learned he had won a Pulitzer Prize for his composition (Aaron 2017; Del Tredici 2017; Gabor 2018; Ludwig 2018; Sills 2017).

The work of the thousands of artists that have called Westbeth home over its fifty years has put Westbeth on the map and cemented its importance in the arts of its era. While some of the very elderly artists have become frozen in the time of their heyday, others continue to grow and evolve, and a younger generation of artists moves in to continue to ensure that the space is a place of creativity and innovation.

3

▟

You Say You Want a Revolution

WESTBETH'S FIRST RESIDENTS took possession of their raw loft spaces late in 1969, a year remembered for cataclysmic challenges in American society. In the same year that Richard Nixon assumed the presidency, hundreds of thousands of rock music fans gathered at Woodstock to hear Jimi Hendrix shred the national anthem. As Neil Armstrong took his first steps on the moon in July 1969, the Beatles released their final album *Abbey Road*, and in Washington, 250,000 people marched to protest the war in Vietnam. This year saw unparalleled political activism, with Native American activists occupying Alcatraz Island, and the Stonewall riots a few blocks from Westbeth, launching the gay-rights movement. Civil rights campaigns swelled in size in response to the shocking assassinations of Bobby Kennedy and Dr. Martin Luther King Jr. a year before. Demands for more protection for the environment followed the notorious burning of the polluted Cuyahoga River in Cleveland and oil spills off the pristine coast of Santa Barbara, California. All of the activism that characterized the time was manifest in the lives and works of the artists of Westbeth.

I Love Rock and Roll

The soundtrack for this time of upheaval was undoubtedly rock and roll, and one of Westbeth's first residents was witness to every major event. Bob Gruen became known as the quintessential photographer of the rock and roll scene. Bob received a phone call just before Christmas 1969 informing

55

him that an apartment was available in Westbeth. At the time, he was an unknown photographer hanging out at various rock venues and events but living in obscurity. He barely made enough to live on, especially given he was married at the time and had a small child. He said the invitation to move to Westbeth was the best Christmas present he ever received. Many famous and infamous people have stayed at Westbeth at some point, as they visited or sublet from tenants. Gruen said the nickname of the building in the 1980s was "The Hippy Hilton" and noted that even Abbie Hoffman had stayed there when he was on the run (Gruen 2018).

Gruen's break came shortly after moving into Westbeth when he showed some photos he had taken of the Ike and Tina Turner Revue to Ike Turner. Turner liked the photos, and Gruen sealed the deal of becoming the photographer traveling with Ike and Tina Turner by doing prodigious amounts of cocaine with Ike. Gruen went on to work with every rock and roll band of significance, including Elton John, KISS, the Rolling Stones, Joe Strummer and the Clash, Green Day, Patti Smith, and Blondie, and he is especially associated with his work with John Lennon and Yoko Ono. His iconographic photos are instantly recognizable, but the paltry payments he received of $25 to $50 for each published photo meant that he lived paycheck to paycheck and needed the affordable housing that Westbeth provided (Gruen 2020, 2018).

As his career progressed, he became good friends with many of the musicians he photographed and always approached his subjects with respect, rather than stalking them like paparazzi. Joe Strummer of the Clash became one of his great friends. When Strummer was in New York in the 1980s, he would forget what hotel he was staying at, wander over to West Street just below Bob's second-floor apartment, and shout up to him that he needed to crash on Bob's sofa. Bob and Strummer would go out late at night to prowl the music venues, and he always had to be reminded to bring his sunglasses because, by the time they emerged from the bars, it would be bright daylight (Gruen 2018).

While hanging out and waiting with the Clash for a concert later in the day, Bob picked up a bugle that was lying on a table and began to play. Bob then opened all the New York shows by playing a call to arms, to which the audience responded with "Charge!," and then the band would start to play. At a later benefit concert for UNICEF with Paul McCartney and Wings, Chrissie Hynde, the Who, and the Clash, Bob was stopped from entering the party after the concert because the publicist said there were no photographers allowed, but he flashed the bugle still in his hand and Mick Jones said, "He's with the band," and he was allowed to join the party.

Gruen traveled to Japan with Yoko Ono in 1974, and he immediately developed an affinity for the people, the culture, the food, and especially the serenity of Japan. He later returned to Japan for about a year to get sober and centered. Bob notes there were no drugs in Japan at that time, so after a decade of hard living, Japan represented a place to get away and have healthy influences (Gruen 2018).

Unlike other photographers who became paparazzi, stalked famous people, and shot photos intended to infuriate the subject, Bob rejected this objectification. He remarked on another photographer who was punched out by Prince Rainier on the streets of New York City soon after Princess Grace's death, after the photographer stalked him for three days. Bob admired Yoko Ono's philosophy about photographers when she said, "Just stand there and let them take the picture. Then they're done . . . The more you fight against it, the worse the picture is going to look and the more the picture is going to be valuable. So just stand there, smile, they take the picture, and leave you alone" (Gruen 2018).

Bob had a very close relationship with John Lennon and Yoko Ono, beginning from his first months in Westbeth when the famous couple lived quietly around the corner on Bank Street. He worked closely with them jointly and individually and remains close to Ono. Gruen was with them as they recorded the *Double Fantasy* album during an all-night recording session. Lennon had brought along a new jacket that he wanted to wear for a photograph, and although Ono was tired and wanted to go home to their apartment in the Dakota building, she indulged Gruen and Lennon and the couple posed on the street in the early morning light. Bob rushed back to Westbeth to develop the film and print proofs for them to approve in time to make a deadline for a Village Voice publication late that night. As he worked in his apartment, the Westbeth desk staff called Bob and asked him if he was listening to the radio or had the TV on, and then shared the shocking news of Lennon's murder (Gruen 2020). Gruen was devastated and was soon inundated with calls from around the world of people commiserating with him and sharing their grief at Lennon's passing. He was soon called to provide photos of Lennon for memorials, and he said, "I suddenly realized that the whole world was watching, that people everywhere were going to be following the story. Everyone was going to be talking about it . . . and that was my job, to help John look good" (Gruen 2020). By this point, Lennon had become a true New Yorker, and Gruen selected his photo of Lennon wearing a T-shirt printed with the words "New York" on the front, sleeves torn off, arms crossed across his chest, and looking straight at the camera with his sunglass-covered eyes to

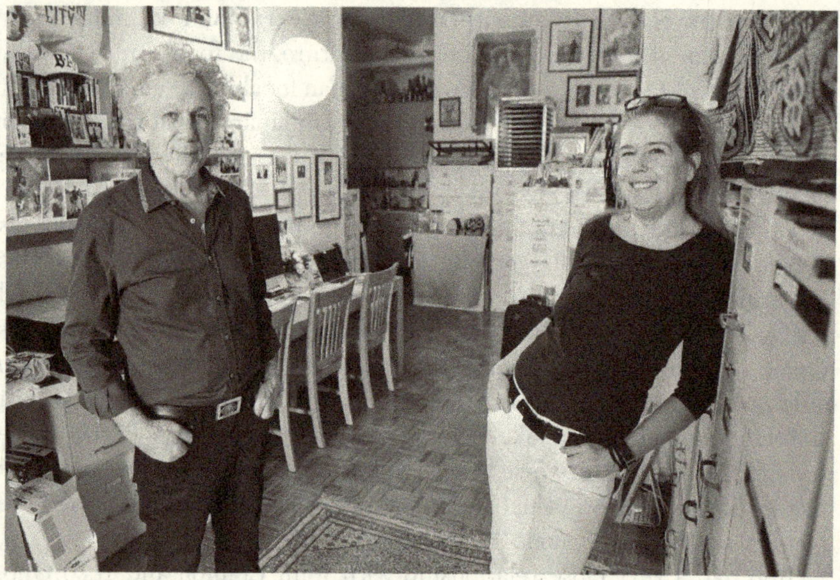

Figure 21. Bob Gruen and Elizabeth Gregory Gruen. Image Courtesy Bob Krasner.

represent the Lennon they all wished to remember and commemorate (Fig. 21).

Taking It to the Streets

From the time of activism when Westbeth was first occupied through to the contemporary women's rights, Black Lives Matter, and pro-science marches, Westbeth residents have engaged in political activism to promote social justice and equity and to protest war, exploitation, and colonialism. For some, their activism was elevated because of the solidarity they developed with other artists in the Westbeth community. A stroll along the hallways shows most doors decorated with some expression of the residents' political views. During the period I was conducting interviews with residents, many of whom were quite elderly, virtually everyone volunteered their feelings of disgust about the policies and actions of President Trump. Karen Ludwig and others marched on Trump Tower in the Women's March the day after his inauguration. Others have protested the perils of capitalist-driven actions, such as when the community turned out in force, led by my aunt Shami Chaikin, to protest the closing of nearby St. Vincent's Hospital, or when Edith Stephan participated in Occupy Wall Street demonstrations when she was in her 90s. Conceptual artist Hans Haacke is famed for his challenge to the museum world, where he saw the contradiction between the influence of museum boards as arbiters of what constitutes art and the fortunes board members built from unethical and exploitative capitalist actions (Merjian 2012; Gopnik 2019). These gray-haired lefties (or, in Edith's case, bright orange hair) have had a lifetime of speaking up for human rights and speaking out against war, intolerance, capitalist exploitation, and oppression.

Some of the earliest activism by Westbeth residents preceded their move to the building. Actor Hugh Hurd joined with fellow African American performers Godfrey Cambridge and Maya Angelou in the late 1950s to mobilize support for Dr. Martin Luther King Jr.'s civil rights activities, and the three went on to form the Committee for the Employment of Negro Performers in 1962. Hurd appeared in performances with multiracial casts long before color-blind casting was commonplace. He joined the 1963 March on Washington with Dr. King, where King gave his famous "I Have a Dream Speech" (Saxon 1995). Neighbor and theatrical producer Irving Vincent counted Hurd as one of his closest friends and describes him as the friendliest person he has known. He dubbed Hurd "the Mayor of Greenwich Village," as he was known by everyone. A short stroll through the neighborhood would take a long time, as Hurd was inevitably stopped for chats by everyone he encountered. Yet despite his friendliness, as a Black man, he was sometimes threatened and challenged in the neighborhood, at which time he relied on his martial arts black belt to fight back. Working for more opportunities in the performing arts aligned with the quest for greater social equity for many Westbeth residents, including collaborator and fellow actor Benny Andrews. Feminist painter Alice Neel did a famous portrait of Hurd, at a time when formal portraits were typically of the establishment elite. Hurd's portrait now hangs in the Crystal Bridges Museum in Arkansas (Vincent 2023).

As a teenager in Nashville, Cordell Reagon joined the Students for Nonviolence Coordinating Committee (SNCC), and used his soulful tenor voice to sing out against racial inequity as part of the Freedom Singers. The Freedom Singers performed across the country, in churches, at political demonstrations, and other events to raise funds for SNCC. The group performed with Harry Belafonte at Carnegie Hall and drew from the rich musical traditions of the African American churches to spread a message of hope and liberation (van Gelder 1996; Goertzen 2016; Project). In New York, Reagon's work with SNCC continued, and he became deeply involved in the anti-Vietnam War protests and environmental activism while continuing to sing and work as a career counselor. Reagon's group, along with other musician activists, used music to convey meaning and build collective action. It is partly because of his work that songs like "This Little Light of Mine," "Ain't Gonna Let Nobody Turn Me 'Round," and, of course, "We Shall Overcome" are synonymous with the civil rights movement. He believed the success of this movement could not have happened without the stirring music that unified people around common ideals (Hoover 1963).

Actor Moses Gunn enjoyed significant critical and commercial success for his roles in films, television, and stage, and political activism was evident in all his performances. Gunn is most famous for his Emmy Award–nominated performance in the groundbreaking TV series *Roots*, which included one episode directed by fellow activist and Westbeth resident Gilbert Moses. Gunn also played a recurring role in the *Shaft* movies. Yet his start was in Jean Genet's controversial play *The Blacks* (1962), which had an all-Black cast and confronted the audience with themes of prejudice, anti-colonialism, and racial stereotypes. This breakout role for Gunn was off-Broadway, but the cast became giants in American theater, including James Earl Jones, Roscoe Browne, Louis Gossett, Jr., and Maya Angelou. Neighbor Irving Vincent became the stage manager for *The Blacks* after the first person hired left the job, and he remained with the ensemble through all the off-Broadway performances and while on tour. Vincent recalls the all-Black cast and crew realized the importance of this piece as the show gained critical attention (Vincent 2023).

Gunn was one of the founding members of the Negro Ensemble Company, an organization dedicated to greater equity and opportunity for African American performers, especially for incorporating the Black experience into mainstream theater. Many of the performers who joined this group in their youth represent the pantheon of great Black actors today, including Denzel Washington, Delroy Lindo, Laurence Fishburne, S. Epatha Merkerson, Sheryl Lee Ralph, Phylicia Rashad, and Esther Rolle. The group also gave performances that gave voice to important African American writers, notably August Wilson.

An extension of some of the civil rights activities came in the form of recognizing the racial disparities in the criminal justice system and the impact mass incarcerations had on communities of color. Several Westbeth residents, notably actor-directors Joseph Chaikin and Nancy Gabor, did programming in prisons to both perform works and to incorporate prisoners into improvised plays. The prisoners created works that told of their experiences with institutionalized racism and created autobiographies that portrayed both their struggles and their triumphs. Gabor says the play that emerged from this collective action, *Choices*, was performed in prisons and other venues, including at alternative theater space Café La MaMa, and was well reviewed. She notes that none of the former convicts who participated in this project ever returned to jail, as the work, and perhaps the catharsis it enabled, helped the men find new direction (Gabor 2018).

Take a Walk on the Wild Side

The nation-wide movements to promote sexual freedom and acceptance of diverse gender identities were embraced by Westbeth residents. A few blocks from the building was the Stonewall Inn, the site of the most important gay rights activism following the Stonewall uprising in 1969. Westbeth photographer Bettye Lane documented the "riots" with sensitive portrayals of the gay activists' confrontations with police. This launched her career documenting protest movements associated with political activism and civil rights (Kiger 2012). The Stonewall Riots came in response to gay bars being routinely raided by the police, who arrested people as they assumed their presence at gay bars equated with illegal drug use and prostitution. Adjacent to Westbeth were the abandoned piers that had served merchant vessels and passenger ships, and the piers were often where gay men sunbathed during the day and met for anonymous hookups at night. Cruising along the piers in search of sexual liaisons was common, as noted by Jean-Claude van Itallie, the playwright collaborator of many Westbeth performers (Strausbaugh 2013).

The Stonewall protests empowered and focused gay activists. Soon after the riots came the first Pride March in June 1970, and gay life became less underground and hidden. Gay entrepreneurs began opening bars, coffeehouses, dance venues, bathhouses, and cabarets catering to gay clientele, including the Mineshaft, the Anvil, and Hellfire bars in the neighborhood (Strausbaugh 2013). Before this time, many gay-oriented establishments were Mafia-controlled, and drug dealing provided additional revenue streams for the Mafia. By the middle of the 1980s, many of these gay businesses closed, as the impact of the HIV/AIDS pandemic was felt. Some closed due to mandates from the city health department (Strausbaugh 2013), others because many gay activists refocused their energies toward caring for vulnerable members of their community and demanding action to address the disease. The nonprofit God's Love We Deliver was established in 1985 to provide care and meals for people affected by HIV/AIDS and now delivers more than four million meals annually to medically vulnerable people in the

New York City region. Others directed their activism toward fighting for resources to prevent and cure HIV, such as the Gay Men's Health Crisis group and Act Up.

During the 1970s and 1980s, many gay artists found Westbeth a safe and supportive place to work—although reports vary on the degree to which the gay members of the community were embraced vs. tolerated. Visual artist Barton Lidice Beneš's work was wholly shaped by the HIV/AIDS pandemic and the social and political responses to this disease. His most noted work included vials, squirt guns, and hypodermic syringes filled with his own HIV+ blood, which some galleries and museums refused to exhibit due to its theoretically dangerous properties. In an exhibit called *Lethal Weapons*, scheduled for exhibition in Sweden, Barton was ordered to heat his pieces in a microwave to destroy any latent pathogens before the exhibition. Despite some pushback against his work, he retained a sense of humor about his very serious subjects and the response to his work. The Swedish exhibit also featured works by fellow Westbeth mixed-media artist Patricia Lasch, who said, "Barton and I, we got ready to go to the opening, and Barton says, 'Will you change clothes with me?' I had this sequin dress with a slit all the way up the side that Freida had given me to wear, so I put on Barton's tux, and he put on my sequined dress. We had a good time" (Lasch 2017).

Many of the gay and lesbian Westbeth residents' work reflected their lived experiences, such as filmmaker Barbara Hammer's works that documented lesbian lives, or painter Jack Dowling's side gig as a partner in Colt Studios that sold gay erotica, primarily black and white photographs (Foley 2020). Poet Edward Field's work is now considered part of the canon of gay and lesbian poetry, but his most famous work is based on his experience of his plane being shot down during World War II and was made into a prize-winning animated short film, *A Minor Accident of War* (Weiss 2019). Reflecting on his nearly fifty years in Westbeth and previous residence in the neighborhood, he noted

> . . . If you wanted to be gay, you had to come to The Village to be gay. If you wanted to be interracial, you had to come to The Village. There was nowhere else you could come to where you could be interracial. So, The Village had a function of a place to let the steam off. (Field and Derrick 2017)

For others, especially those in the performing arts and especially in the early years, their gay identity was often shrouded so that casting directors and others did not exclude them or typecast them. For some, the opportunity to practice their craft was dependent upon being hired by orchestras or theaters, the heads of which might discriminate against an openly gay performer. Pulitzer Prize–winning composer David Del Tredici, actors Shami Chaikin and Joseph Chaikin, and writers David Greenspan and Kate Walter's works reflect diverse influences in addition to their gay identity.

War! What Is It Good For? Absolutely Nothing.

The war in Vietnam was raging at the time the Westbeth building opened, and many of the residents were active in the anti-war movement and continued to protest against violence and war through the decades. During the Vietnam War, my uncle Joseph Chaikin was actively involved in helping draft-aged men evade the draft by teaching workshops on how they could feign mental illness or persuade draft boards they were gay to avoid being drafted. Together with his sister Shami and colleagues from the Living Theater, Judith Malina and Julian Beck, they participated in many anti-war protests and were arrested (Word 2011). As he had a chronic heart defect, his friends tried to persuade Joe not to put himself on the front line and risk arrest, as he might not survive the treatment he'd receive in jail, but he was committed to the cause and did not acquiesce.

Visual artist Patricia Lasch was also involved in anti-war protests and commented that many people in the building were like-minded. She speculated that virtually everyone had an FBI file because of their "suspicious" activities. A single mother living in Westbeth but teaching part-time in Brooklyn, she recounted seeing a man at the school where she was teaching and then seeing the same person outside Westbeth. She suspected she was being followed—as were other activist residents (Lasch 2017).

Westbeth residents continued their anti-war activism through all of the successive conflicts the US has experienced. Painter Jayne Holsinger drew on her Anabaptist upbringing when she noted that in the Mennonite world, there are people termed "true hearts" who are admired because they protect others against all odds, and their pacifist tradition stems from these values (Holsinger 2018).

Sisters Are Doing It for Themselves

Westbeth provided a generation of women the freedom and support to blossom as artists. Some of the younger generation of Westbeth residents, such as musician Marc Jacoby, marvel at the collective impact and wisdom of Westbeth's pioneering feminists—poets Muriel Rukeyser and Ilsa Glazer, visual artists Anita Steckel, Hannah Wilkie, and Juanita McNeely, and performing artists Gloria Miguel and Madeleine Yayodele Nelson. Jacoby commented, "The building is full of powerful women and powerful feminists, and I've learned a lot from them. In fact, everything important I've learned has been from women" (Jacoby 2019).

Many of the women who moved in during the early days were single mothers and struggling artists with very limited financial means, and the low rents and community meant that they finally felt safe and were not dependent on men for a livelihood. Long before women pushed back against exploitative relationships with male superiors with the #MeToo movement, the women of Westbeth experienced overt sexism from men who had power over them. Nancy Gabor turned from acting to directing in large part due to the quid pro quo demands of sex-for-roles that directors expected. Painter Juanita McNeely recounted a professor in her figure drawing class saying to her, "You're too skinny to fuck, so you should just get married and get out of the way" (Gabor 2018; McNeely 2019). Many women artists found solidarity with like-minded women at Westbeth; some intentionally created feminist allies and worked together for consciousness-raising, and others like Juanita McNeely commented that "I was not interested in consciousness-raising; that's the last thing I'm interested in—mine was already raised and wanted to move ahead and make something of myself" (McNeely 2019).

McNeely did develop friendships and collaborations with a group of then unknown artists, including fellow Westbeth residents Anita Steckel and Hannah Wilke, and they were joined by Louise Bourgeois and Alice Neel. These women visited each other's studios to give each other feedback and critique and sometimes show works together. Juanita McNeely continued to paint giant canvases depicting mostly nude women dancing and leaping across the surface, with limbs splayed in ways that defy gravity and anatomy. Her themes of monstrous images of birth, huge vaginas, menstruation, pain, and dislocated limbs was inspired by her own life and her own experiences. While in college, she experienced severe bleeding and was diagnosed with Hodgkin's disease. She was not expected to survive but was successfully treated and continued to produce her art. Subsequent bouts of cancer and a spinal cord injury left her wheelchair-bound for many years, but it did not diminish her productivity; she rotated her canvases that were on the floor propped against the wall so she could reach all corners of the canvases while in her wheelchair (McNeely 2019).

One of her contemporaries was Hannah Wilke, who used her own nude body in photographs and installations to challenge the traditions of femininity and beauty and the objectification of women. Wilke used chewing gum and other detritus to mold small vulvas that she stuck to her body, often while imitating the glamour poses used by models and Hollywood that supposedly reflected the feminine ideal (Museum). She challenged the viewer to be uncomfortable with their gaze and, in her final years, documented her slow demise from lymphoma, photographing herself in hospital beds connected to tubes and machines (Wilke).

Anita Steckel also challenged the historic oppression of women and male control of the art world by her use of erotic imagery, including huge erect phalluses, to intentionally discomfort the viewer. Her explicit art caused a furor during a show in 1973 that resulted in local officials attempting to censor her works. In response, this "led her to form an organization of female artists, known as the Fight Censorship Group, whose membership would include Louise Bourgeois and Hannah Wilke. A mission statement she wrote for the group became a sort of manifesto for many women creating experimental art. "If the erect penis is not wholesome enough to go into museums," it said in part, "it should not be considered wholesome enough to go into women" (Steckel 2021). Famous for her affairs with prominent men such as Marlon Brando and her sideline teaching Latin ballroom dancing as the Mambo Queen, she was a memorable character who didn't achieve fame as a visual artist until well into her 70s (Vitello 2012; Zanni 2019).

Lorraine O'Grady became a conceptual performance artist after she held positions in the federal government and pursued writing at the Iowa Writers' Workshop. She drew on her experiences as the daughter of Jamaican immigrants and her desire to provoke other Black artists to challenge the status quo. Her first attention-getting foray in 1980 was her dramatic entrance to museum openings wearing a gown made of dozens of pairs of long white above-the-elbow formal gloves in her persona as *Mademoiselle Bourgeoise Noire*. Carrying flowers, which she distributed to the visitors, and a whip she cracked to recall the control of enslaved African Americans, she gave spoken-word performances of her poetry that challenged all to reject the hierarchies and privilege associated with the art world. Later, she recruited actors to join her in crashing a parade in Harlem in a performance piece entitled *Art Is* . . . . O'Grady and her fellow performers all dressed in white, carried large ornate gold picture frames and held up the frames around the faces of parade participants, police working the scene, and spectators to "pose" for a photograph as the subject of art. These impromptu pieces of "art" were replicated in styling in a Biden/Harris presidential campaign ad in 2020 (Mitter 2021; Small 2020).

Helène Aylon also explored the impact of hierarchy and misogyny in her work as an ecofeminist artist. Having been raised in an ultra-Orthodox

Jewish family and married at a young age to a rabbi, Aylon created her new identity as an artist, a feminist, and an agnostic after the death of her husband at a young age. She described herself as "post-Orthodox" and recognized in herself and others the lasting impact of their strict upbringing, and notes that they can leave Boro Park (an enclave of conservative Jewish families), but "Boro Park is always in them" (Aylon 2012). Her early works explored deeply Jewish themes, but her move to Westbeth in 1970 exposed her for the first time to an ethnically, racially, and religiously diverse community and had a profound impact on her direction. Strongly influenced by anti-nuke activist Helen Caldicott, she began collecting samples of sand from disaster sites and nuclear sites, and in 1981 held a performance piece in San Francisco that mingled these tainted sands to create an indoor beach. Later, she enjoined Arab and Jewish women in Israel to each collect their bags of sand to comingle as a visceral effort to break down barriers between these two populations.

Aylon said she saw her work as rescuing the earth from patriarchy. After purchasing an old truck and painting a large red cross on the vehicle, she traveled across the country in her "Earth Ambulance," joined by like-minded activists. At nuclear sites and military bases, they would "rescue" pillowcases full of sand to be added to the collection in the back of the ambulance. After traversing the country from Livermore Nuclear Lab and Vandenberg AFB in California to the place where the atomic bomb was developed in Los Alamos, New Mexico, to Colorado uranium mines, her convoy reached New York in time to participate in a rally at the United Nations for nuclear disarmament in June 1982. The culmination of this demonstration was the "liberation" of all of the sand samples across the street from the United Nations, where the sand was poured into plexiglass boxes engraved with the words "They shall beat their swords into plowshares, their spears into pruning hooks, nation shall not lift up sword against nation, neither shall they learn anymore" (Aylon 2012). Aylon tended toward "self-mythologizing" (O'Neill-Butler 2019), but the importance of her collective work for both ecofeminism and Judaica has not been recognized for its true impact (O'Neill-Butler 2019; Greenberger 2020; Gass 2000).

The women visual artists of Westbeth have quietly gained recognition, although in many cases, only after years of working in obscurity. Their works are now held by major museums and collections worldwide, such as the Art Institute of Chicago, the Guggenheim Museum, the Museum of Contemporary Art in Los Angeles, the Elizabeth Sackler Center for Feminist Art at the Brooklyn Museum, and the Philadelphia Museum of Art. They have had their works included in the Whitney Biennial, the Feminist Art Program at Cal Arts, and the Tokyo Museum of Photography, among others. Juanita McNeely and Lorraine O'Grady both had major exhibitions in their 80s. O'Grady's show at the Brooklyn Museum was very positively reviewed, and her rightful place in the world of conceptual artists was cemented (Mitter 2021; Cotter 2021). Veronica Ryan's installation *Quiet as It's Kept* was selected for the 2022 Whitney Museum Biennial, one of the most significant events for contemporary visual artists.

Juanita McNeely had a major show that included several panels that covered two full gallery walls at the James Fuentes Gallery, and the significance of her work is finally being acknowledged (Finnegan 2011). Juanita's major solo show in 2023 at the James Fuentes Gallery in Los Angeles received acclaim in major publications, including *Vogue* magazine and the *LA Times*. The exhibition included huge and challenging paintings of bloodied women inspired by her own illegal abortion that she underwent in the 1960s while battling cancer. Another of her abortion-themed works was acquired in 2023 by the Whitney Museum, the first piece in their vast collection of modern art to depict abortion.

The early generation of women writers who moved into Westbeth formed similar collaborations, including establishing the Westbeth Playwrights Feminist Collective. Initially, many writers living in the building gathered weekly to workshop pieces in progress and to write pieces based on prompts intended to stimulate new directions in their work. When Dolores Walker suggested the theme "rape" as a topic for their writing exercise, she meant it in a metaphoric sense, such as the impact of capitalism on society. But this theme proved too challenging for the men in the group, none of whom showed up for the next writing group session. The women then went on to form the Westbeth Playwrights Feminist Collective. Original members included Westbeth residents Walker, Christina Maile, Gwen Gunn, Susan Yankowitz, Patricia Horan, Sally Ordway, Helene Dworzan, and Helen Duberstein. The first production they staged was *Rape In*, held in space loaned by the New Theater for the City in what is now the Jane Hotel a few blocks away. The play was staged at ten at night and was wildly successful, somewhat to the group's surprise (Maile 2017; Walker 2018; Yankowitz 2019). The group continued to write plays and vignettes, performing around the city and at the Westbeth performance space. A flyer advertising *An Evening of New York Scenes* performed in 1970 for the official opening weekend of Westbeth included works by some of the members of the group, with the collaboration of artists such as Anita Steckel for the staging and Westbeth actors Hugh Hurd, Merlyn Hurd, Pawnee Sills, Peter Salvadore, and Joel Brody (Westbeth 1970). Their plays continued to explore feminist themes and highlight the experiences of women.

Because women were very underrepresented in the backstage trades, the Feminist Collective intentionally hired women to do the lighting design, stage direction, and technical aspects of their productions. Various actors from within Westbeth and beyond participated in their productions, including then-young performers Danny DeVito and Rhea Perlman. Christina Maile recalls playing Scrabble with DeVito and Perlman in her Westbeth apartment, as they all were young, had young children, and had very little money for entertainment (Maile 2017).

Dolores Walker recalls, "From May 1971 to April 1975, we did eight shows, plus touring, plus bimonthly workshops, and we had grants from NEA and NYSCA. It became this huge thing. Our mission was to build a repertory of plays written by women based on self-awareness through individual consciousness-raising. We came to realize that women were often portrayed as victims or comic stereotypes and that even our plays required more men than women, and this raised our own consciousness" (Dace 2001).

The success of the group resulted in the establishment of an advisory board, which brought together prominent feminists both from within Westbeth—poet Muriel Rukeyser and painter Anita Steckel—and from the city at large, including Florynce Kennedy, a women's rights activist and attorney; Carol Greitzer, New York City councilwoman; author Alix Kates Shulman; and founder of *Ms.* magazine, Gloria Steinem.

Their productions brought satire and humor to some challenging topics, and many of their productions were well-reviewed. Some incorporated music, such as *Up! An Uppity Review*, and each production reflected their collective contributions rather than highlighting a single author. Maintaining the ethos of collectivism and collaboration was an important value to the participants rather than elevating one as successful at the expense of others, which was and remains the norm in the cutthroat world of theater and film production.

Of the original members of the playwright group, Susan Yankowitz was the one who persisted in writing for the theater. In reflecting on her work with this group, she said it was very important for each of the writers to present women in a positive light and support the work of their fellow group members to promote solidarity and comradery within the group. The downside of this was a lack of critical rigor, critique, and feedback needed for writers to progress, and she noted that good writers know how to give and receive critique to improve their work (Yankowitz 2019).

For the Times They Are a Changin'

Prior to the opening of Westbeth, the New York theater scene had exploded with avant-garde innovations. Judith Malina and Julian Beck's Living Theater produced new works from emerging European writers, including Samuel Beckett and Eugene Ionesco. Caffe Cino, established in the late 1950s and opened as a coffeehouse, permitted both visual and performance artists to use their space to showcase new works. At a time when gay themes were taboo in theater, Caffe Cino welcomed performances that would be banned elsewhere and effectively gave birth to the off-off-Broadway theater tradition. Café La MaMa followed this model and began producing innovative theater pieces in 1961 under the direction of Ellen Stewart, who later served on the selection committee for applicants to live at Westbeth. In this rich context of experimentation, Joseph Chaikin left the Living Theater company and established the Open Theater in 1963 with collaborators Susan Yankowitz, Nancy Gabor, Lee Worley, Peter Feldman, Megan Terry, Sam Shepard, and his sister Shami Chaikin.

The Open Theater was established as a laboratory to create collaborative works of theater that reflected themes of anti-war, anti-hierarchy, anti-establishment, and experimentation. Joe's sister Shami recalls conversations when Joe envisioned actors working together performing experiments, much in the same way that scientists in a lab may have many failures before achieving a successful outcome in their experiments (Word 2011), which was prescient given both Joe and Shami's later move into the former Bell Lab building.

The Open Theater was composed of diverse performers, and all approached the collaborative process with the same intensity as modeled by Joseph Chaikin. Members of the company used elements of yoga, dance, breathing exercises, psychodrama role playing, and acting to tell stories through performance. The ensemble was highly collaborative, even in its efforts to find venues, as members all chipped in to rent rehearsal and performance space on Spring Street. Participants collectively developed the stories they performed in an organic, improvisational manner, as happened with *The Serpent*, a retelling of the Old Testament book of Genesis. Decades before dance companies such as Pilobolus intertwined bodies on stage, the performers in *The Serpent* explored each other's bodies and engaged in

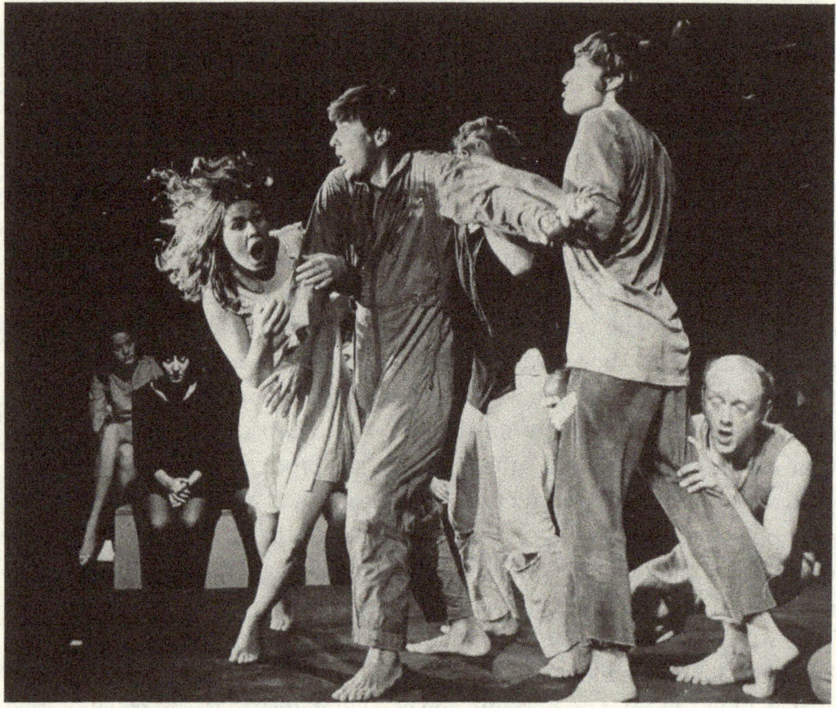

Figure 22. Open Theater Company performing in "The Serpent." Image Courtesy of Kent State University Libraries, Special Collections & Archives.

mock copulation as the narration drones on listing the extensive lineages of descendants outlined in Genesis (Fig. 22).

Company members Ron Faber and Shami Chaikin said that each piece was workshopped through many iterations before finally being written in script form. While Jean-Claude van Itallie is credited as the author of *The Serpent*, the play is a product of the ensemble, not a single author (Word 2011). Several members of the company left, as they felt the "ownership" of their work by a playwright was contradictory to the spirit of collaborative creation that characterized the Open Theater. Playwright and former Westbeth resident Susan Yankowitz recalls that from the outset, the ensemble "had a gravity to it, people took it very seriously. The members of the company approached acting with discipline, integrity, and respect for the community, and the Open Theater emerged as one of the most important theaters in the US" (Yankowitz 2019).

Later works were developed with van Itallie (*America Hurrah* and *Struck Dumb*), Yankowitz (*Terminal* and *Night Sky*), and Megan Terry (*Viet Rock*), and the ensemble toured in Europe with their experimental plays. The company membership waxed and waned, with a few members remaining when the Open Theater morphed into the Winter Project, notably Joe Chaikin's sister and actor, Shami. Joe's vision is compared with theater giants in Europe, but his self-effacing nature deflected praise. His performers noted that at the end of each performance, the stage faded to black, with no curtain call to recognize the actors for their performances. Ron Faber recalls attending a Rabelais play in Paris while the company toured. Many of the Open Theater performers were moved to tears by the hearty applause each performer received at the end of the play in recognition of their work, whereas "for Joe, praise was a distraction from the work," even though the majority of the performers would have liked to hear applause for their performances since they gave their all on the stage (Faber 2018; Gabor 2018).

Joe's intensity and focus on challenging themes was a consequence of his severe heart problems that resulted from having rheumatic fever as a child. He felt his mortality keenly, aware that there might not be much time left, and mortality was a theme woven into many of his works. After suffering a severe stroke while undergoing his third open heart surgery in his early 40s, he was left aphasic and, for the rest of his life, had great difficulty generating speech. His therapy built on his experience as an actor, and friends Sam Shepard and Nancy Gabor noted that he could read words written on a page and even act with the appropriate emotion in the performance, but generating speech remained elusive. Family and friends grew accustomed to Joe's verbal limitations and could discern his meaning when others could not. I recall eating in a Mexican restaurant with him when he wanted their incendiary hot sauce to season his food. He requested "small animal sauce," which mystified the server, but after discussion, it became clear he was requesting their trademark scorpion sauce to spice up his dish.

Although he continued to work in theater directing and performing, his focus shifted to theater for the disabled (Word 2011). Many of Joe's collaborators commented that after his stroke, he was more relaxed, happy, and less demanding, or as Yankowitz noted, he described himself as more open, which he always said in two syllables, oh-pen (Gabor 2018; Faber 2018; Yankowitz 2019).

Joe remained an important figure in American theater despite his aphasia. In the late 1990s, he performed around the world, including an important performance of Samuel Beckett's *Texts for Nothing* in the Netherlands, directed by Paul Binnerts and Nancy Gabor. Gabor color-coded the script with text highlighted in blue representing love, yellow representing fear, and red for anger to help him prepare for the performance, and he was reportedly mesmerizing. His encore was a recitation of the final poem written by Beckett for Joe, which opened with the line "what, what, what is the word" (Gabor 2018).

Many members of the Open Theater lived in Westbeth, and many went on to make important contributions, building on their experiences in the ensemble. Ron Faber continued performing and won an Obie Award (for off-Broadway performances), and Nancy Gabor became a director, coach, and teacher using the techniques developed early in her career in both Europe and the US. Actor Ralph Lee used puppet-making skills that he developed earlier in his career to create new styles of performance, most notably with his creation of the Greenwich Village Halloween Parade. Decades later, this parade is one of the most anticipated events in New York City, but it originated in the early 1970s at Westbeth, with costumed performers stationed along a several-block radius portraying witches and goblins. Unlike other parades in which spectators are stationary as the parade walks by, this parade had the spectators begin in the Westbeth courtyard, where enormous puppet spiders rappelled down the walls from the thirteenth floor, and then the parade attendees followed the route winding through the narrow streets of the West Village, seeing performances at stations along the way. Lee continued this participatory parade style of performance when he established the Mettawee River Theater Company, which has been performing in summers for more than forty-five years. He built puppets for other puppeteers (including Shari Lewis's Lambchop) and life-size puppets that could be worn as costumes for performing, the most famous of which was the "Landshark" for Saturday Night Live (Gabor 2018; Faber 2018; Lee 2018).

Another veteran of the Open Theater, Native American actor Muriel Miguel, left to form a new company, the Spiderwoman Theater, in collaboration with her sisters, Westbeth residents Gloria Miguel and Lisa Miguel Mayo. Considered the first Native American feminist theater company in the US, the Miguel sisters performed across the US and Europe, bringing traditional Indigenous stories and beliefs into theatrical performances (Fig. 23). Taking their name from the Hopi story, the Spiderwoman company sought to weave stories in the same manner that traditional Native women wove cloth (Dace 2001). Although they collaborated with non–Native American writers, the sisters drew on the spiritual traditions they had learned

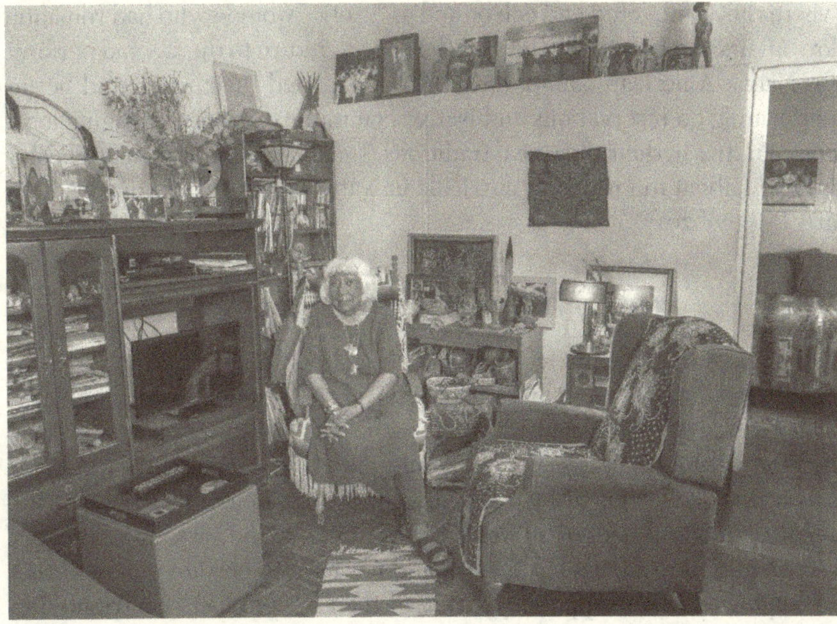

Figure 23. Gloria Miguel, founder, Spiderwoman Theater Company. Image Courtesy of Frankie Alduino.

from their Rappahannock mother and Kuna father, who hailed from the San Blas Islands off of Panama.

The Miguel sisters' father had performed in "Wild West" shows and rodeos held at Madison Square Garden prior to World War II. Although his performances were clearly contrived and reflected the overt cultural appropriation common at the time (e.g., wearing Plains tribes' feathered war bonnets or dressing in buckskin to advertise a new John Wayne movie), his work with these shows brought other Native American performers into their circle. The Miguel Sisters used the stories they had heard from both parents and those of other Native performers who often stayed with the Miguels to create their repertoire of performance pieces and began performing as a company in 1975. Four decades later, they performed at Café La MaMa to commemorate their decades of productivity, and Gloria Miguel continued performing into her 90s. While their performance pieces reflected traditional Indigenous stories, they added strong feminist and anti-colonialist themes to their works. They toured extensively and repeatedly in Europe, where people had a long-standing fascination with American Indian cultures and traditions. Gloria Miguel reflected fondly on their many European tours, where they were feted and celebrated as "exotic" women who had romantic love affairs, but eventually they felt the need to return to the US and perform for Native American communities. They extended their reach and began performing on reservations and Native community centers, engaging local communities in their theatrical traditions. Today, the Spiderwoman Theater is taught about in university curricula in Native American Studies and the arts (Miguel 2017).

You Can't Always Get What You Want

From the earliest years at Westbeth, members of the community have challenged authority and hierarchy. Many of these actions are highly principled and reflect significant risk to the participant—loss of support, sponsors, mentors—while others seem oddly misguided. The epitome of the latter was a rent strike staged by a few disgruntled residents. Periodically, the rents are modestly raised at Westbeth, as would be the case anywhere, but a few entitled residents felt they should not have to pay any rent and that society owed them support by virtue of their art products contributed to the greater good. Various conspiracy theories raged and gained prominence, including a rumor that the head of the residents' board was calling for an increase in rents, and he received threatening letters, often anonymously, accusing him of being in league with evil corporate and governmental interests. The great majority of artists were grateful for their highly subsidized spaces, but a few entitled members felt their "specialness" should be recognized by the city and that they should be allowed to create unfettered by the mundane responsibilities of making a living. Although those who advocated for the rent strike were a small minority, they were disruptive to the cohesion and ethos of the artists' community (J. Cohen 2020; Faber 2018; D. Gillison 2019).

In a similar vein, a small group began promoting a rumor that the creation of Westbeth was not a reflection of the philanthropic largesse of the J. D. Kaplan Fund but rather a CIA plot supported by the corporate world to round up, control, and potentially stifle the creativity of the Westbeth artists. Rumors said that the creation of Westbeth was an effort to keep all the left-wing artists in one place, to observe them and prevent them from engaging in acts of rebellion, and potentially to lock them in if the situation got out of hand. This brief movement and the rent strike disheartened those who had significantly invested in ensuring Westbeth's initial success, especially Joan Kaplan Davidson. Davidson was motivated by a deep appreciation for the arts and a desire to further her father's philanthropic programs, and she responded to the rent strike by stepping back from Westbeth for many years (S. Gillison 2006; D. Gillison 2019; Mare 2018; Walker 2018).

A similar anti-establishment movement involved Westbeth conceptual artist Hans Haacke and others, as they created the Art Workers' Coalition. Inspired by anti-Vietnam War protests in the US and France, artists began to demand the right to retain their intellectual property, even if a work was purchased by a collector or museum. When Greek artist Takis removed his work from the Museum of Modern Art in protest, this spurred discussion in the art community about representation and ownership of an artist's works. A group, including Westbeth residents Hans Haacke and Carl Andre, convened at the nearby Chelsea Hotel to create a manifesto of demands for the museum world. They demanded more inclusion of works by artists of color and free access to museums to counter the elitist reputation of these institutions. Subsequent picketing events resulted in brief closures of New York's major museums, and museum directors refused many of the Art Workers' Coalition's demands, but eventually, many of their concerns were addressed by the museum establishment (Haacke and Haacke 2019).

Anti-war efforts also influenced poets at Westbeth, most notably Muriel Rukeyser and Edward Field (Rhodes and Murphy 1978). Field is a prolific writer but best known for his work that describes his experience during World War II when he and fellow crew members were shot down over the sea. In *A Minor Accident of War*, Field recalls hanging on to a life raft until he was at risk of dying in the cold water when the ball turret gunner switched position with Field and ultimately did not survive in the frigid waters. Recently made into an animated film with Field reading the poem, Field's words clearly recall the horrors of war (Field and Derrick 2017; Weiss 2019; Timreck and Stoller 2018).

Muriel Rukeyser was perhaps the best-known of Westbeth's poets and had a long career writing about social justice issues, including the Scottsboro trial and the Vietnam War. She was unafraid of writing about taboo subjects such as women's sexuality, violence, and bodily functions. In retrospectives that analyze her work, she is often cited as one of the early feminist writers, and her writing is always clearly in the female voice (Terris 1974; Rhodes and Murphy 1978; Allison 2006). Westbeth's writers, including Gil Sorrentino, Joel Oppenheimer, Ilsa Gilbert, Carol Hebald, Hugh Seidman, Kate Walter, and David Greenspan, have remained prolific in part because of the financial stability that life at Westbeth affords.

Perhaps more than sex and politics, the most taboo topic to be an artistic iconoclast remains the realm of religion. Several Jewish residents of Westbeth, including Ze'eva Cohen, Shami Chaikin, and Lily Rivlin, chafed against the traditional patriarchy of their religion, especially the celebration of Passover which includes the retelling of the story of the liberation of Jews from enslavement by the Egyptians entirely from a male view (Fig. 24). In the texts used to guide the Passover ritual, the Haggadah, the traditional writing accounts for only men and their sons, and these women, together with their feminist sisters, rewrote a Haggadah that includes the sisters and daughters and a genderless God. Rivlin and her collaborators, including Gloria Steinem and Bella Abzug, revised the Haggadah annually, always selecting an appropriate theme for the celebration. She noted that in 2018, their theme was "Living under the Pharoah," which was inspired by President Trump's administration (Z.e. Cohen 2017; Rivlin 2018).

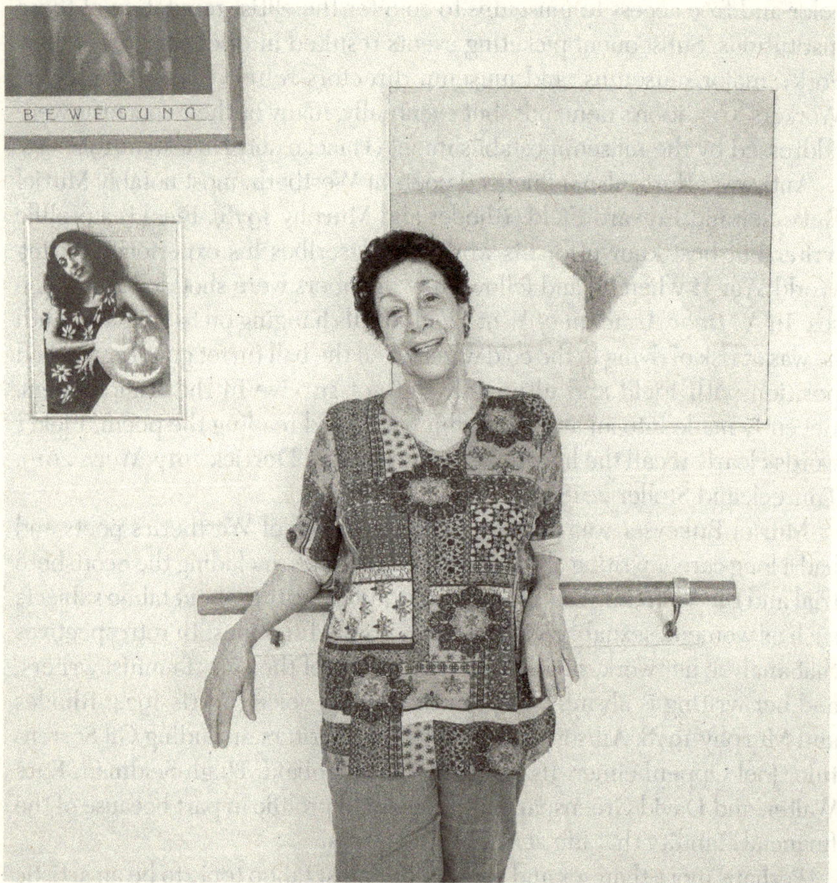

Figure 24. Dancer and choreographer Ze'eva Cohen at the Barre. Image Courtesy of Tom Conelly.

Visual artists and great friends Patricia Lasch and Barton Lidice Beneš used themes deeply rooted in their Catholic upbringing in their iconoclastic works. Barton's multimedia pieces harken to Catholic reliquaries, where items such as slivers of bone or pieces of cloth reported to have come from a saint or holy figure are enshrined or displayed, and the faithful venerate these objects in hopes of divine intervention. Reliquaries reflect James Frazer's concept of contagious magic, where items formerly associated with a person of significance can convey similar power to the holder of this relic. Some of Barton's panels memorialize a single person or event, such as his hourglass that mixed the cremated remains of two beloved friends who died of AIDS, to measure time together through eternity. He is best known for his collage panels that memorialize random contacts with famous people, often with a unifying theme such as a color. His panels include ephemera such as Brad Pitt's used cigarette butt, Marilyn Monroe's lipstick-stained napkin, actor Larry Hagman's gallstone, jellybeans from a jar on President Ronald Reagan's desk, or painter Jean Michel Basquiat's paintbrush. In the middle of his kitchen table, a domed cake plate appeared to be covering colorful sweets but were actually faux petit fours made by gluing his ARV pills used to treat his HIV+ status (Fig. 25). While there is a playfulness in Barton's panels, his work is a direct confrontation to the concepts of holiness

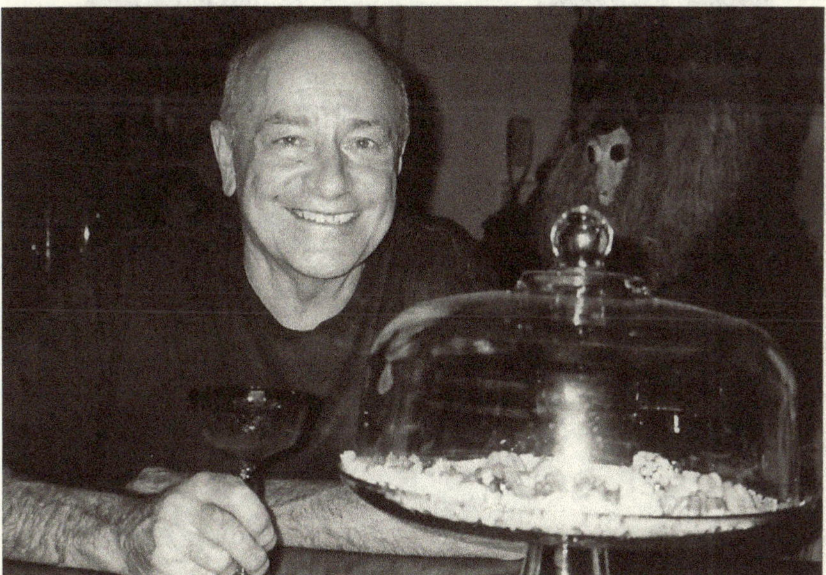

Figure 25. Barton Lidice Beneš and bonbons made of pills. Image Courtesy of Rebecca Chaiken.

and an accusation of idolatry for the generations of Catholics who held the traditional relics as sacred (Beneš 2002). His use of his own HIV+ blood in vials as part of a series on *Lethal Weapons* challenged the bigotry toward people living with HIV/AIDS (Hall 2018; Lasch 2017).

Patricia Lasch's work reflects a complicated relationship with the Catholic Church, and her pieces explore themes of Catholic rites and rituals, the confessional, and the juxtaposition of the permanence of the Catholic hierarchy with the ephemeral qualities of art and life. She began her career as a metal sculptor but later adapted skills she had used decorating cakes in her father's bakery to produce art that reflects the life cycle of Catholic ritual. To create her works, she loads squirt bottles with paint and then "paints" elaborate designs—much like a henna artist paints swirls onto hands—onto sheets of glass to dry into panels of lacelike flexible mesh. Her sheets of paint-lace are then crafted into larger-than-life size ritual garments, such as wedding dresses or baptismal gowns, or other items associated with ritual, such as wedding cakes (Fig. 26, 27). Another series

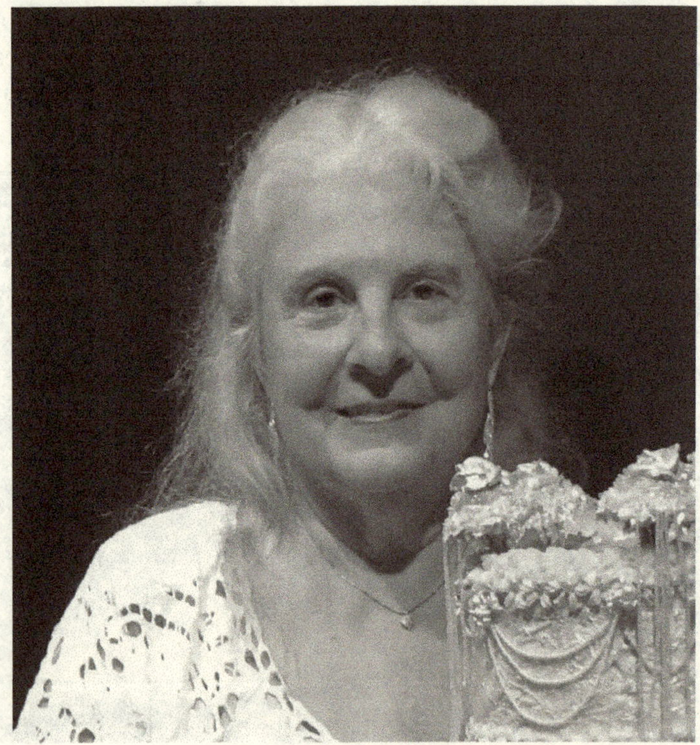

Figure 26. Patricia Lasch and her artwork. Image Courtesy of Patricia Lasch.

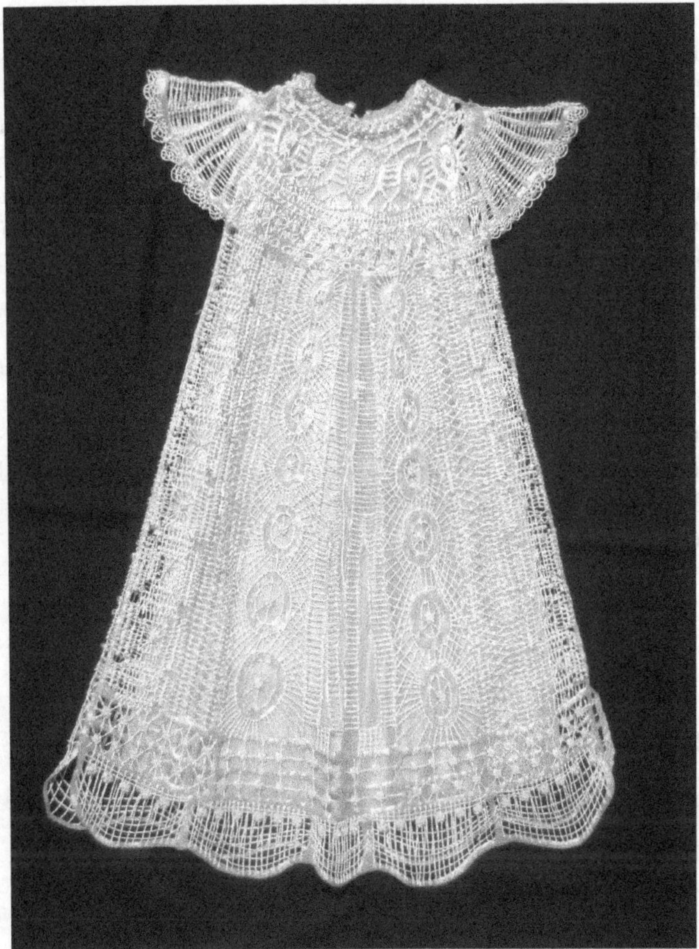

Figure 27. Christening gown made of dried paint, art of Patricia Lasch. Image Courtesy of David Plakke.

uses paint fabric to envelop letters with secrets and confessions. If one opened the envelope made of paint to discover the secret, the work of art would be destroyed. One such letter is a heartfelt thank you note addressed to the family of a man she never met, who lost his life while saving her father when he was a six-year-old child and fell through ice and nearly drowned. Pat's works are simultaneously exquisite and heartbreaking, and force the viewer to see both the bliss and the pain associated with religion (Lasch 2017).

The commitment to left-leaning activism has been integral to Westbeth since its inception at the height of the 1960s social movements. Artists are stereotypically characterized as politically left, and this may be especially true for the early generation, as they included artists such as Peter Ruta and Hugette Martel, who were refugee immigrants (Ruta 2023). Others had personally witnessed the horrors of World War II and were lifelong pacifists and activists as a consequence. The half-century of activism and questioning of authority that was exemplified by the first-generation artists persists vigorously at Westbeth. Anyone who walks the hall will see nearly every door adorned with words and images that express outrage at everything from human rights abuses by the Chinese toward Tibetans to disgust with policies espoused by Republican politicians to opposition to capitalism. Christina Maile summarized it best by noting that, as Westbethians became older, they became less afraid and more willing to be iconoclastic (Maile 2017). Political activism and leftist leanings are in the DNA of the artists of Westbeth.

4

The Family Business

WHEN THE FIRST generation of residents moved into Westbeth, they arrived with their children. Since then, hundreds of children have grown up in the community. Some, like actors Vin Diesel, Josh Hamilton, Michelle and Denise Hurd, and Nadia Dajani; visual artist Gwynne Duncan; and dancers Maya Ciarrocchi and Pele Bauch followed in their parents' footsteps and became artists themselves. All acknowledge they were profoundly affected by the experience of being a child at Westbeth.

While a few of the families may have been financially secure at the time they moved into the building, such as Kirk Lombard's family, whose father Peter was in the cast of the Broadway musical 1776 at the time, most families were living in precarious financial circumstances. Nadia Dajani remembers being in a rat-infested apartment in Harlem with her single mother, Virginia, and three siblings when the opportunity to move to Westbeth arose. Her mother was a freelance writer for a now defunct magazine about architecture, and a man that she worked with felt the Dajanis would benefit from the stability that Westbeth would provide, so he submitted her name as a possible tenant. When contacted with an offer for an apartment, they were told the rent would be $150 per month for a duplex for their family of five. However, because her mother didn't even earn that amount, the admissions committee offered her reduced rent, and the Dajanis moved in with the first cohort of residents (K. Lombard 2020b; M. Dajani 2020a).

Children were very aware of their parents' poverty, partly because there wasn't always food on the table. Jamie Zaretsky recalls his father walking through the neighboring Meatpacking District and coming home with a whole cow head that they would cook. Ethan and Julian Maile recall their mother trying to persuade them that it was just as good to eat their morning cereal with water instead of milk when she didn't have money for groceries, even though she had rented a grand piano for their apartment to nurture their musical talents. Magda Dajani said it was the norm for everyone to be broke every other month, and Susannah Kelly noted that the only upside to being poor at Westbeth was that everyone else in the building was living the same way. Visual artist Patricia Lasch remembers a time when there were posters in the building with information about how to apply for support through Section 8 housing subsidies, which she initially thought was about trying to help low-income families in the building, but later concluded it was more about a strategy to secure fair-market rent subsidies to support the building. Despite the poverty that most families experienced, there was an ethos that it was honorable to have no money and to be only devoted to producing your art—and being focused on financial gain was unseemly (M. Dajani 2020a; N. Dajani 2020b; J.a.E.M. Maile 2019; Kelly 2020; Lasch 2017; Lomprey 2020; Zaretsky 2020).

Most of the families that moved into Westbeth qualified for larger apartments, often the two-story apartments located on floors 3, 6, and 9. Children grew up knowing the kids on their own floor the best and sometimes viewed the other floors as alien territory. Writer Adam Davidson grew up on the third floor and became fast friends with neighbor Ethan Maile, who he viewed more as a brother or cousin than just a playmate. Adam and Ethan rarely associated with kids from the ninth floor because "they were older, and kind of scary. The ninth floor is like another state or something; there were older kids there, like Mark and Paul Vincent[1]—you know, Mark is Vin Diesel" (Davidson 2020). The older kids were both intimidating and "super cool" in Rachel Urkowitz's memory. Older girls were frequently recruited as babysitters for the younger ones, and Caitlin Bottoms-Newby recalls being a fangirl of her babysitters Magda Dajani and Susannah Freed. Magda was the oldest of four children, including younger twin brothers Tarek and Geeby, and she frequently earned a little money from babysitting. She recalls bolstering her babysitting resume as she perfected rolling joints for parents,

---

1 Vin Diesel's legal name is Mark Sinclair, but when he was very young his mother married theatrical producer Irving Vincent. Vincent was a *de facto* father to twins Mark and Paul, and had two additional children with their mother. All of their friends and neighbors referred to Mark and Paul with the surname Vincent as part of this family, and the short version of this name became the actor's pseudonym.

who asked her to take care of this if she had time after putting the kids to bed (Bottoms-Newby 2020; Urkowitz 2020a).

Another way in which Westbeth was unique was the diverse ethnic composition of the population and the inclusion of a large proportion of LGBTQ residents. Michel Dobbs noted that the neighborhoods in proximity to Westbeth tended to be homogeneous—all Italian, or all Irish, or all Puerto Rican—and there were gangs who intimidated the Westbeth kids. Michel describes all the Westbeth kids as outsiders, as all of the children were a highly diverse mixture, and this resulted in them all bonding since they didn't fit into the neighborhood's predominant ethnic milieu. Julian and Ethan Maile reflect this diverse heritage, as one parent was an Anglo WASP, and the other was of mixed Southeast Asian and West Indian heritage. The two brothers look very different, as Julian favors his mother and Ethan, his Anglo father. The Maile brothers said that as children, they didn't recognize the uniqueness of the diverse composition of the Westbeth community, but as adults, they recognized this was an asset. Ethan commented that they "grew up in the future," as it was common for them to interact with ethnically, religiously, and culturally highly varied people. At the same time, they looked back on their childhood and commented that they were all guilty of cultural appropriation long before the term existed, as they would dress up in African clothes with their friend Ayo Nelson, whose mother was one of the founding musicians of the African percussion ensemble *Women of the Calabash* (Dobbs 2020a; J.a.E.M. Maile 2019).

It was also part of the milieu to be surrounded by gay people, and homophobia was a foreign concept in the Westbeth community. The children grew up having many gay neighbors, in some cases single residents who also lived in the building, but also parents of other children. Especially during the early years, many marriages dissolved, and adults found alternative partners, sometimes same-sex partners. The early years of Westbeth coincided with the sexual revolution, and many of the first-generation adults came out of the closet and ended traditional marriages. Ethan and Julian recall a friend whose parents split, and the wife remained in the apartment with her transgender boyfriend. This was just taken in stride as a normal occurrence. When, as a teen, Ethan came out to his mother, coinciding with a time when he struggled in school, his mother's nonchalant response was, "Yes, OK, but this does not get you off the hook for finishing your homework or walking the dog." Children regularly saw the gay and transgender sex workers who worked along the river, and all of these experiences led to very inclusive and accepting attitudes toward others by this generation.

Huck Finn on the Hudson

While most people recall their childhood with great fondness and wonder, all acknowledge that it was a wild place to be a child, and they had very unconventional experiences, several of them describing themselves as feral children. Rachel Urkowitz said the building was like a village, with doors open much of the time and children flowing freely between apartments and families, and other children and the resident adults were like an extended family. Caitlin Bottoms-Newby said living in the building was like kids who grew up in the woods and spent their life exploring their wilderness, except her "woods" were the wilds of Westbeth. Steve Lomprey said, "My sister and I were street urchins; we were always kind of covered in shit and just like an Appalachian version of a New York City street kid in the 1970s," and he described his childhood as "Huck Finn on the Hudson" (Bottoms-Newby 2020; Lomprey 2020; Urkowitz 2020a). Gwynne Duncan described a very communal life and said Westbeth was "kidsville," where children ran wild while their bohemian parents lived their free lives. Michel Dobbs said the Westbeth kids were a sort of gang that looked out for each other and often remained close as adults, as "we knew each other in a way that nobody else could understand" (Dobbs 2020a). For Westbeth kids, the building and the neighborhood were their playground. Summers were full of skateboarding in the courtyard, and the basement was the winter refuge. Two blocks south on Washington Street remained an animal farm, where children would visit to pet the ponies and farm animals (Fig. 28).

Even in recent years, the children of Westbeth remain part of a close-knit community, as Stephen Hall notes that it isn't uncommon for his daughter Reef and her friends to visit back and forth on Saturday mornings still clad in pajamas, and older adults like Hans and Linda Haacke recall their kids floating between apartments in the building all weekend (Haacke and Haacke 2019).

No doubt, the children of Westbeth routinely saw sights that most children did not. Most children routinely saw adults using drugs, especially marijuana, and Jamie Zaretsky said he and his cohort were smoking tobacco and weed at nine or ten years old. Steve Lomprey's apartment faced an interior court-yard with the windows of apartments in the opposite wing directly opposite his, and he recalls seeing completely naked women walking around the opposite apartment wearing nothing but a cowboy hat and boots. On other occasions, he saw artists with their performance pieces, including wearing nothing but layers of cellophane or running around with giant Styrofoam penises. Visiting other apartments within the building provided revelations,

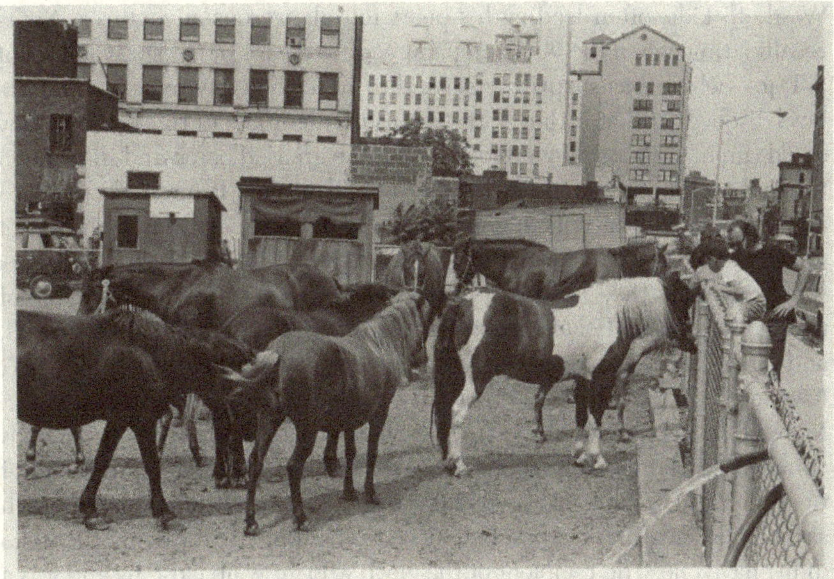

Figure 28. Pony Corral on Washington Street ca. 1972. Image by Leonard Freed Courtesy of Brigitte Freed.

as some were furnished fairly conventionally, while others had the walls laminated with aluminum foil and used UV lights for illumination. Some parents might be home working on paintings or practicing their music, while others sent the children out while practicing their art to avoid the distractions.

Role-playing games were very popular with kids. Some were traditional games, such as Dungeons and Dragons, but kids also made up their own games, acting out popular movies and TV epics. The kids acted out *Mission Impossible,* and the Maile brothers recall their favorite was playing Star Trek with the Vincent twins, Paul and Mark. Like the Maile siblings, their twin friends looked very different from each other, with Paul and Ethan appearing fair and Anglo, and Julian and Mark darker and of indeterminant ethnicity. Although they commented that race as we usually think of it played little part in kids' alliances and playmates, when this group played Star Trek, swarthy Mark (now known as Vin Diesel) was always assigned the role of Lieutenant Uhuru, who was African.

Nadia Dajani was the youngest in her family, and she looked up to her twin brothers. Despite their antics, they always managed to have fun. Her brother Geeby (short for Najeeb) was a charismatic ringleader for the

Westbeth kids, often leading his peers into dangerous adventures. Nadia recalls a time when the boys somehow acquired cans of the spray lubricant WD40—which was surprising since they never had any money—and the boys discovered that if they sprayed this on the floors in the hallway, they could run in their stockinged feet and hit the greased patch and slide down the hall for what seemed like an eternity. She said, "It never occurred to any of us that our parents might be walking down the hallway with bags of groceries and fall. It was so fun for us; we were just holy terrors." Others who grew up in the building commented on Geeby's natural leadership of the packs of kids. Michel Dobbs described it as being under Geeby's spell, and Jamie Zaretsky said that Geeby was royalty. Michel said, "We didn't have to play cops and robbers, because real cops were always chasing us." Many of the people who shared their memories of their Westbeth childhoods commented on how influential Geeby was as a natural leader, protector of the vulnerable, "really smart and really tough," and righter of injustices—such as when he "acquired" a baseball glove from a boy to give to another who didn't have one. The recipient of the glove who grew up close by and was a frequent playmate of the Westbeth kids was Adam Horovitz, who later became famous for his band the Beastie Boys. Geeby grew up to be a roadie for punk bands and later produced hundreds of radio shows. His impact was apparent when he tragically died young of ALS and dozens of former Westbeth friends returned for his memorial (N. Dajani 2020b; Dobbs 2020a, 2020b; Zaretsky 2020).

Sports were extremely important and competitive among the children, especially the boys, and kids like Geeby, with athletic prowess, became influential. Nat Oppenheimer, Kirk Lombard, Josh Hamilton, and Gwynne Duncan recall playing hockey on roller skates in the basement of the building in the winter. In the summer, they skated in the courtyard facing Bank Street or on the abandoned elevated highway along the river. The courtyard was the site for epic skateboard obstacle courses; games of stick ball; a game they invented called "OT," or overhand tennis; and football. Older kids acquired plywood scraps and built skateboarding ramps, and in the summer, kids skateboarded all day. Even though they were not supposed to, they skated and skateboarded down the block-long hallways on the floors with duplex apartments, terrorizing neighbors with both the noise and the threat of collisions (Gilmore 1998; Duncan 2020; Hamilton 2020; K. Lombard 2020b).

Within their apartments, kids would play in the treehouse lofts or cubbyholes their parents had built in lieu of conventional bedrooms, and the steep concrete stairs in the duplex units were used as slides. Children used pillows to slide down the steep staircase at alarming speed. Nat Oppenheimer's father, renowned poet and sports writer Joel Oppenheimer, was famous for many phobias that resulted in his increasing unwillingness to leave his apartment. Between the father's connections with professional baseball players who frequently visited the apartment and were a huge draw for children and the fact that "anarchist poets get along really well with kids," the Oppenheimer apartment drew children in for play and became the epicenter for Saturday-night board game marathons (Bottoms-Newby 2020; C. Maile 2017; J.a.E.M. Maile 2019; Oppenheimer 2020).

The building's basement was both creepy and a magnet for children's play. The basement housed a number of studios for both musicians and visual artists, but it also had giant boilers for the building's heating and other mechanicals that created niches for hiding. Older teens hung out in the basement to listen to the rock bands practicing in their tiny studios, but for the younger kids, the basement was a playground. Rachael Kosch recalls playing "zombies" in the basement, where playmates would hide, and as the searcher came along the labyrinthine corridors, the zombies would jump out to scare them. Games of tag, manhunt, or hide-and-seek in the basement could last for the whole weekend, some recalling that they found such a good hiding place that they remained hidden for six to eight hours, and they would fall asleep while waiting to be found. Kirk Lombard said they would stuff socks with clothing to create soft cudgels and have sock war games in the basement (Kosch 2020; K. Lombard 2020b; Lomprey 2020).

The roofs were also children's play areas, though even more fraught with danger than the basement. There were flat roofs that kids could access at several floors throughout the building, the tallest being the eleventh-floor roof adjacent to the Merce Cunningham Dance Studios. Boys sometimes demonstrated their swagger by standing on the parapets of the building's roof, even eleven stories above the street. Small sheds on the roof that originally held tools or mechanical works for the Bell Labs were converted by kids into makeshift club houses and forts. Younger kids played their games in these sheds until kicked out by older teens who used the shacks for their make-out sessions. Josh Hamilton recalls setting off fireworks from the roof, and one bottle rocket fell into a half-moon balcony on a lower floor roof and exploded, apparently just above the head of a resident. Moments later, the irate tenant burst onto the roof wielding a lead pipe, and instead of thrashing the boys, he dragged them downstairs to their parents to report on their misdeeds. Sebastian Holst remembers throwing rocks at prisoners in the yard of the jail across the street until he was scared straight when seven prisoners escaped and were loose in Westbeth in 1971. Others recall getting pelted with eggs from rooftop bombers (Hamilton 2020; Holst 2020; J.a.E.M. Maile 2019).

The abandoned piers along the Hudson River and the river itself were inevitable draws to the Westbeth children, and both were extremely dangerous places for unsupervised packs of children. Steve Lomprey confessed that he and his friends were responsible for a major fire in 1976 at one of the abandoned piers, that brought firefighters to the piers from across Manhattan. The boys used an abandoned shack on the derelict pier as their makeshift clubhouse, space that had formerly been an office for shipping and still contained abandoned desks and furniture. One of his companions who was a little older took some of the tinder dry paper that had been left for years in an abandoned filing cabinet and lit it on fire and tried to drop it in a wastebasket, but even the dust floating in the air seemed to catch fire, and soon the wooden desk was engulfed in flames. Unable to extinguish the fire, and as befits ten-year-olds, the boys' reaction was to run away, leaving the fire burning, and retreat back to their third-floor apartment to play baseball cards while watching the conflagration from the safety of their windows facing the river. Steve acknowledged they had an unspoken code of secrecy, and he never admitted his role in the fire until he was an adult.

The Hudson was still a conduit for commercial boat traffic, although highly polluted and dangerous. Kirk Lombard regularly fished in the Hudson, and several children got themselves into trouble on the river. Steve Lomprey was part of a gang of boys who were playing in an abandoned warehouse along the river where they used a suspended rope to swing Tarzan-style from end to end of the space. They discovered a derelict wooden rowboat in the warehouse and carried it to the water's edge and tossed it into the river. Somewhat to their surprise, the boat floated. The boys climbed down a makeshift ladder made of slats nailed to the pier's pylons and, armed with scraps of two-by-fours as oars, ventured out into the river. Soon, they were passed by a huge private sailing yacht, and the boat owner looked at these four boys in the rickety boat with appropriate concern—especially as the boat began to take on water, and Steve recalls bailing ferociously with a tiny Styrofoam cup. As the tide was not strong at that time, they were able to row their boat back to the pillar they used to get into the boat, and by the time the last of the four boys climbed out of the boat, it was full of ten inches of tea-colored river water, and it sank immediately (Lomprey 2020).

Nadia Dajani also had a close call on the river. She noticed that, from time to time, a barge full of gravel would be tethered to a nearby pier. In retrospect, she thinks it may have been some of the fill used to build the original World Trade Center towers. One day, the barge was pushed right up against the pier, so she and her friend Beth climbed down the rope onto the barge and spent hours playing throwing rocks at each other and into the water, not noticing the effects of the tide. Suddenly, the gap between the pier and the barge was no longer a few inches, but six feet. The girls began to scream for help and attracted a man on the shore who realized the girls were trapped. He went to fetch Beth's father, and the two men managed to pull the barge close enough to shore to rescue the two girls. Nadia was grounded (N. Dajani 2020b).

Michel Dobbs was part of a gang of boys that included the Dajani twins, and the boys looked for ways to have adventures, including jumping out of second story windows of buildings under construction. Steve Lomprey's cohort used stairwells in the building to demonstrate their athletic prowess, as boys took turns hanging outside the stair railing dangling at the tenth and eleventh floors to see who had the stamina to hang on the longest without falling hundreds of feet (Dobbs 2020a; Lomprey 2020).

Given the daredevil play of Westbeth children, it is somewhat miraculous that few were in serious accidents. Adam Davidson and Josh Hamilton recalled the exception—their friend Matthew Sloat. Josh had Matthew at a sleepover the weekend before, and Matthew goaded him to skip school and explore a nearby construction site, but on the appointed day, Josh said he didn't have the courage to skip school, so Matthew went alone. Tragically, Matthew died at age ten in a construction elevator accident as he sought adventure at the taboo site (Davidson 2020; Hamilton 2020).

Years later, Grace Bergere suffered only broken bones from her brush with death. While playing on the highest roof at Westbeth, she climbed the ladder that scaffolds the chimney protruding through the roof, a leftover from the Bell Labs days. Grace fell down the chimney, more than 180 feet, and the firefighters who were called to the scene were prepared for the worst. When they finally found how to access the base of the chimney, they opened a steel door and saw Grace's small hand reach out. The chimney had many feet of accumulated soot and sediment from when the factory was operational, and this fine powder cushioned her fall just enough that she survived with only broken bones. However, she was black from head to toe, except for the whites of her eyes, due to the ash (Fig. 29) (Hauser 2008).

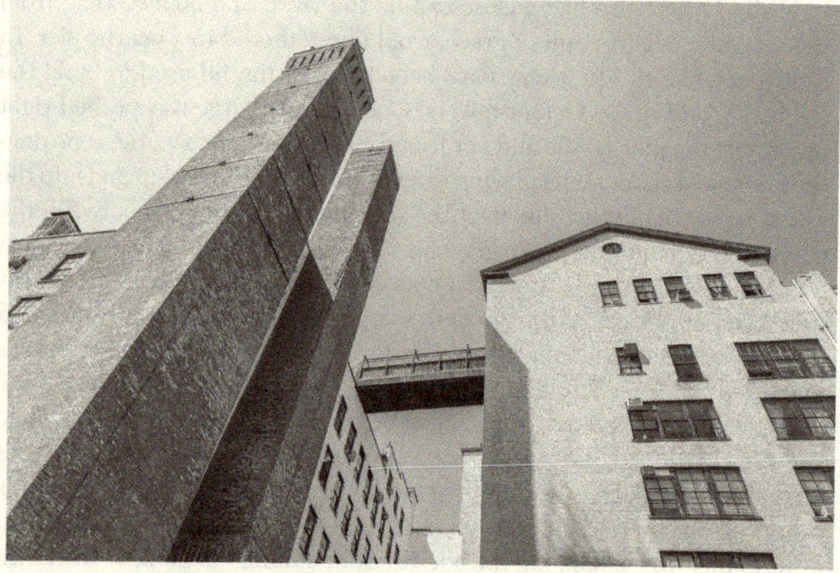

Figure 29. Smokestacks and catwalk. Image Courtesy of Tom Conelly.

Kind of Magical but Also Insane

Nadia Dajani's comment that growing up in Westbeth was "kind of magical but also insane" captures the paradox of the lax child-rearing but enormously supportive community that surrounded the early generation of children. She recalled seeing sex workers and their clients right outside the building and frequent drug use but said, "I was a colossal nerd; I have never in my life done drugs, but a lot of people around me did, and I was certainly exposed to seeing it everywhere. There was sexual freedom, freedom to do drugs, and artists are crazy—imagine a building of over three hundred of them trying to raise children" (N. Dajani 2020b). Interacting with sex workers provided an unusual education for the local kids. Nadia's sister, Magda, referred to the neighborhood as the "transvestite capital of the universe."[2] The sex workers were sometimes taunted from the roof by the kids, and at other times, they would take their breaks in the building's courtyard on the

---

2. Everyone I interviewed who referred to the sex workers who frequented the piers habitually used the term "transvestite," as this is the term they used in the 1970s and 1980s when they were children at Westbeth. Virtually everyone then commented that the term they would use today would be transgendered.

kid's playground. Wearing six-inch heels, they were a fashion inspiration to some of the girls but were also pretty tough, as their clients were truck drivers from New Jersey who would stop below the elevated West Side Highway or park in front of the ink factory on Bethune Street. The Dajani twin boys slept on the lower level of their duplex apartment, only one floor above the street, and Magda recalls hearing her brothers complain "Mom, I can't sleep, the transvestites are fighting again." As he grew older, Josh Hamilton recalled getting an unusual sex education, as he walked his dog late at night or early in the morning (M. Dajani 2020a; Hamilton 2020).

Jenny Lombard, Adam Davidson, and Maya Ciarrocchi describe their parents as more conventional, yet that was within the overall bohemian context of Westbeth. Adam said, "My parents were strict compared to others, but they were Westbeth strict, which is different than any other version of strict. They would say, only smoke pot with your friends and know where it came from, and when I had a high school girlfriend, there was a conversation where my parents said, 'Where would Adam and her be able to have sex.' And yet we took a little bit of pride in how fucked up Westbeth was" (Davidson 2020).

Despite the outward dysfunction, Nadia, like many of her generation, has vivid memories of kids taking care of each other and protecting each other—especially against outsiders, other kids who were not part of the community. Steve Lomprey recalls a time when his six-year-old sister was left home alone, and she climbed onto the window sill and dangled her legs outside the window many stories above the pavement. Teenage neighbor Michelle Hurd, now an actor known for her leading role on *Picard*, was alarmed at the sight of the little child. Michelle quietly crept into the Lomprey's apartment and swooped the little girl off the window to safety (Lomprey 2020).

The Westbeth kids also protected each other from gangs in the neighborhood. Kirk Lombard said Eleventh Street was controlled by a gang of mostly Irish kids, and another was called the Go gang. Lombard's mother saw members of the gang threatening Westbeth kids, and she responded by saying she'd contact their mothers, but when they retorted with "We know who your son is," she realized she may have put Kirk in danger of retaliation. For weeks he tried to slip in and out of school to avoid the gang members, but when he was finally surrounded by the gang and they started to beat him up, he collapsed into tears. Finally, the leader of the gang said, "Oh shit, he's just a little boy," and he picked him up and let him return home without additional torment. Catilin Bottoms-Newby said her dyslexia made her a target for other kids, and she reacted to being in fights on a daily basis by becoming a bully toward others, until she "found boys and marijuana and was off to the races" (Bottoms-Newby 2020).

Many of the children recall their parents' relatively laissez-faire child-rearing practices. Most parents were oblivious to the dangers the kids were experiencing, and they recall their childhoods as a time of great freedom and absence of helicopter parents or warnings of stranger-danger. The exception to this generalization noted by several came in 1979, when a six-year-old schoolboy named Etan Patz disappeared from sight while walking to school alone for the first time. Etan's disappearance caused terror among parents throughout Manhattan, and his disappearance and murder were not solved for many years. Suddenly, parents took to walking their children to school and overseeing their play on the playgrounds (Bottoms-Newby 2020; Lomprey 2020; Zaretsky 2020).

There is a stereotype for kids of Westbeth—either they become great successes, often in the arts like their parents, or they remained "fuck-ups" who grapple with homelessness, mental illness, and addiction. Everyone recalled examples of both, and as Ethan Maile said, he has occupied both ends of the spectrum at various times in his life. The most obvious example of achieving great success is Vin Diesel, who was known as Mark Vincent when he was growing up. His first roles were at the Theater for the New City, housed in what is now the nearby Jane Hotel. While one of his peers said, "I can't believe I have to call him Vin Diesel," Adam Davidson recalls looking up to Vin as a young boy. Adam describes himself as a nerdy kid who liked math, though he is actually a very successful financial writer for major publications. Adam said that even as kids, there were some who were "super cool and popular—not just popular in their high school football team, but popular on an international—like going to Studio 54 scale." Mark was a tough guy working as a bouncer at bars, and even as a teen, he showed his future as an action star. Rachel Urkowitz was a young child when she and several others were trapped with him in an elevator that had stopped on the ground floor, dropped to the basement, and then lurched down into the elevator pit several feet below the basement. Using a lighter to illuminate the dark car, they used the emergency button to call for help, but "Vin sprang into action. He asked someone to hold the lighter, and he fit his fingers into the space between the door and the elevator wall. With some effort, he pried open the elevator door with his bare hands. He directed the other man in the elevator to step up out of the pit onto the floor of the basement and hold the door. Then he lifted me and the other woman out of the elevator and leapt up himself. We dusted ourselves off and walked up the flight of stairs to the lobby" (Davidson 2020; J.a.E.M. Maile 2019; Urkowitz 2020b).

Many who grew up in the community have had a tremendous impact. Josh Hamilton, Dash Mihok, Nadia Dajani, and Michelle Hurd have become well-known actors; Maya Ciarrocchi and Pele Bauch became professional dancers and choreographers; and Adam Horovitz lived across the street but was always part of the Westbeth gang and is now known as one of the Beastie Boys. Christopher Sorrentino became an acclaimed writer like his father, Gil, and Nat Oppenheimer is the engineer who worked with famed architects such as Renzo Piano to create the new Whitney Museum. Adam Davidson is a respected financial journalist, and others have had successful careers in business. There is a perception that "all Westbeth kids are fuck-ups," which is not true. Many of them, some of whom had wildly dysfunctional families, have made a bigger splash than their artist parents and became successful in their fields, even though they are not in the arts (J. Lombard 2020a).

As with any community of size, there are also tragic stories of broken people. Several of the people I interviewed said they had overcome their demons, becoming sober after years of substance abuse or dealing with their mental illness—but they also acknowledged their peers who remain tormented. Jenny Lombard recalled a friend's home as wildly dysfunctional with an alcoholic father. Jenny said that even as a child, she knew things were not right, as the girl's toys were in a box full of centerfolds of naked women, and her brothers were already showing signs of what later was clearly schizophrenia—and as an adult, she speculated about possible sexual abuse in this household. Several middle-aged adults remain living with their now elderly parents because of their problems, and there are stories of young adults terrorizing the hallways, brandishing kitchen knives and screaming about demons, and the notorious Barry, who walks around naked and shouts at people. Some became sucked into the culture of drugs, and some have died of overdoses or become so damaged that they never functioned as normal adults. Kirk Lombard's friend Marcus was his fishing buddy, and although Marcus was African American, he spoke like an Italian fisherman from Brooklyn. Marcus was essentially illiterate and had a very neglectful mother. Even as a young child, when he visited the Lombard's apartment, Marcus would try to steal bottles of liquor. Marcus became an addict and was homeless off and on, and the last Kirk heard, Marcus had developed MS and was living on the streets in a wheelchair. Caitlin Bottoms-Newby said her trauma largely stemmed from her father's departure shortly after moving into the building, and she was fearful of the "long, scary, empty hallways that had the feel of a mental institution" (Urkowitz 2020a; Bottoms-Newby 2020; Davidson 2020; Duncan 2020; K. Lombard 2020b; Zaretsky 2020).

The suicides among adults in the community also caused trauma for the younger generation. Magda Dajani said, "There was one summer where there were at least a few suicides. It was very haunting and affected the entire building; it just set a pall over the building," and many of the younger generation were affected because the suicides were among parents of their peers. Jamie Zaretsky reflected on his childhood in Westbeth and said he wouldn't change it for anything—nor would he ever return. After one visit that was not positive, he sensed a bad energy that he associated with the suicides and his own family's unraveling. Jamie blamed the suicide of his friend Dean's mother on Dean's state now, as he wanders the streets as a lost soul (Prete and Sonnenburg n.d.; M. Dajani 2020a; Duncan 2020; Hamilton 2020; Zaretsky 2020).

In response to the community-wide trauma precipitated by the suicides, Nancy Gabor and my aunt Shami started a gathering for children to talk about their fears, prompted by Nancy's daughter's playmate Dean losing his mother to a suicide. This became an informal therapy group that met for pizza on Friday nights to give the kids a chance to talk about their feelings and feel safe. Gwynne Duncan remembers participating in this group and said it had been important in helping children learn to talk about their feelings and fears, and to process their emotions and deal with their traumas (Duncan 2020; Gabor 2018).

In the early years, the residents also dealt with the inherent dangers in the neighborhood by establishing tenant patrols, where volunteers patrolled the long hallways armed with baseball bats, and women carried whistles to call for help if needed. Maya Ciarrocchi recalled her father participating in these patrols, armed with his father-in-law's pocket knife that had been carved with his initials in Hebrew, which Maya was fairly sure he would never have a clue how to use (Bauch 2020; Ciarrocchi 2020).

Going into the Family Business

Growing up surrounded by artists gave the younger generation an appreciation of how *hard* artists worked and an understanding that creative work didn't materialize out of thin air but required diligence. Nat Oppenheimer said, "The one thing I always tell people that I learned about artists is that they work their freakin' asses off. There's this kind of idea that the artist is sitting there just dreaming, getting stoned, and not being rigorous. Everything I experienced, almost to a person, was the incredible rigor of every day when an artist decides to make a living out of nothing except their creative mind." Erik Moskowitz and Magda Dajani expressed similar sentiments, recalling how, as children, they dabbled in theater and photography, respectively, but at some point, they recognized their lack of dedication to those options focused as artists on the genres they pursued. All of the second generation acknowledged that their exposure to the arts was far more robust than typical. The Dajani sisters recall their mother frequently taking them to museums and giving impromptu talks about New York architecture as they walked through the city. Every summer, long days were spent playing and picnicking in Central Park, waiting until evening to watch Shakespeare in the Park—which Nadia admits she typically slept through after expending all her energy in play (M. Dajani 2020a; N. Dajani 2020b; Moskowitz 2020; Oppenheimer 2020).

Being surrounded by adult artists sometimes resulted in children absorbing artistic influences more by osmosis than by design—in many cases developing artistic talents in completely different genres than their parents' expertise. Caitlin was put into ballet lessons as a preschooler and was eventually selected by the Eliot Feld ballet school for free lessons, which she continued until adolescence. She eventually quit, as she was more inclined to use her dancing skills to roller skate at the Roxy, a famous roller rink in the Chelsea neighborhood where roller disco was the rage. At the same time, she lost interest in classical ballet and replaced that with an interest in boys and disco. Nadia also danced, going twice per week for lessons upstairs in the Merce Cunningham dance studio, where she described herself as the scrappiest little tomboy but loved following along and trying to replicate the professionals' moves. Maya became a professional dancer whose talents were nurtured from a very young age as she attended summer dance camps and the School for American Ballet at Lincoln Center. She later attended a boarding high school that specialized in the performing arts. (Bottoms-Newby 2020; Ciarrocchi 2020; N. Dajani 2020b).

Christina Maile arranged for a resident concert pianist to give piano lessons to her boys and rented a striking white grand piano for their apartment so Julian and Ethan could play. The sons recall that their teacher may have been a gifted musician but was not a good teacher. Nonetheless, the influence was important, as Julian went on to be a professional musician. Josh Hamilton was the son of actors Sandra Kingsbury and Dan Hamilton, and he followed his parents' professional path as he voraciously read books and plays he found abandoned at the building trash chute or at neighbor and actor Joyce Aaron's apartment. He began acting and joined the First Children's Theater at eleven years old and began doing commercials when he was about thirteen. The high school they attended often presaged the career path of the second generation, and the famed LaGuardia High School for the Arts—the basis for the Broadway and television shows *Fame*—was often responsible for shaping students' talents. Nadia wanted to pursue acting, which she now does professionally, but when she tried to get into LaGuardia for acting, she lacked the experience to be competitive. So, she was accepted for vocal music and used that as access to the training she coveted (N. Dajani 2020b; Hamilton 2020; J.a.E.M. Maile 2019).

Susannah Kelly also attended LaGuardia for visual arts, as she demonstrated skill at drawing from early childhood. Her parents encouraged her and supported her choice of LaGuardia and she said, "I was completely supported and encouraged to develop the aesthetics of the artist. It was a double message—on the one hand: We think you're terrific! Go for it! And: Oh, by the way, you'll never make a living. So, it was a mixed message." Yet Susannah did make a living with her art, first as a commercial illustrator, which she hated, and later teaching art for neurodivergent adults and those with developmental disabilities. She describes this experience as her Peace Corps, where she was submerged in a vastly different culture and way of thinking, especially with people with autism. Her ability to design opportunities for her students started her thinking about her own art in very new ways, and she says she learned as much from them as they learned from her (N. Dajani 2020b; Kelly 2020).

Everyone in Michel Dobbs's family was an artist, and early on, he made a conscious decision not to try to compete at the level required to be a professional artist, so he developed his skills at math and, like his friend Nat Oppenheimer, attended the Bronx High School of Science. Michel said that his family supported his different path, and he notes his job involves data analysis. Still, the family quip was that at least one person in the family would know how to balance a checkbook. Nat's father was a poet, and his stepfather, Donald Goddard, was a well-known art history critic who had formerly been married to feminist performance artist Hannah Wilkie. So, at first glance, Nat's career as a structural engineer seemed vastly different than that of his family. But he noted that his father had taken some engineering classes and sketched house plans on graph paper for relaxation. All of these influences and plenty of hard work have made Nat well-known as the engineer on very high-profile bespoke arts projects, such as the design of the new Whitney Museum in New York, and renovations to Frank Lloyd Wright's masterpiece Fallingwater house and the John F. Kennedy Center for the Performing Arts (Dobbs 2020a; Oppenheimer 2020).

While many who grew up at Westbeth became artists themselves, some forged different paths. Kirk Lombard's father was a successful Broadway actor and his grandparents had also been performers, but the family really made a living from a used and refurbished furniture store they ran near Christopher Street. When I asked if he had been encouraged to pursue performing, he responded with a bemused but vehement "fuck no!" (K. Lombard 2020b). Although his primary career is currently as a sea forager who engages in sustainable fishing and teaches about management of marine resources, he is also a professional musician who has built his own instruments for his band. Kirk said it is not surprising that the two arts genres most associated with his generation from Westbeth is heavy metal punk rock and graffiti art—both inclined toward iconoclasm and irreverence for the formal arts, which he attributes to their "effed up" families.

Caitlin, Nadia and her brother Geeby, and Kirk all were swept up in the culture of graffiti tagging and emerging punk music. Geeby developed his own style and became an icon among his fellow teenagers for his ME62 tag. Combined with his athleticism and charismatic nature, he was recalled as the Minister of Chaos among the ragtag latchkey teens of the neighborhood (Ashrawi 2020). Along with fellow Westbeth teens Miles Kelly, Noah Evans, John Gamble, and neighbor Adam Horovitz, the group sneaked into clubs long before they were of age to gawk at Basquiat, Grace Jones, Madonna, and Andy Warhol. They skipped school to go to Yankees games, and all aspired to be part of the bigger scene. They formed bands and developed their music styles and evolved into professionals, most notably Horovitz's band, the Beastie Boys.

You Can Come Home Again

Many of the generation that grew up in Westbeth maintain connections with friends and family in the building, even if they now live elsewhere—and a few left the West Village and never looked back. A sizeable number of now-middle-aged adults living in the building spent their childhood there as children of the early generation of artists. While some remain in their natal apartments with tenuous claims and no role in the art world, many others are now residents and artists in their own right. Visual artist Rachel Urkowitz and writer Jenny Lombard returned to Westbeth as young-ish adults, moving back into their parents' apartments and eventually taking on the space full time. Jenny moved back in 1995 and initially had a series of roommates but later married and had a child who became the third generation in her duplex apartment. Their specific apartment had many major plumbing disasters, so she applied for a transfer within the building, and she was able to move fairly quickly because she was requesting a smaller apartment than her coveted duplex. She now lives with her family on the ninth floor. Rachel also moved back to Westbeth in 1995, and her parents moved out. Over the years as her family grew, she made modifications to the unit to accommodate her children. Today, the apartment is very different than the space she grew up in, and she noted that, unlike the old days when guerilla construction happened as people built out their space, now it is necessary to have plans approved by the building's architect to make any significant renovations. Both now flourish as artists in their own rights (J. Lombard 2020a; Urkowitz 2020a).

A few second-generation residents, like Susannah Kelly, returned to Westbeth to care for aging parents and stayed. She had lived for decades in Hawaii and later, California. Her brother remained in New York and shouldered the care for their parents, but at a point, it became more than he could manage and Susannah moved back into Westbeth. She said it was both odd and familiar to be back in the space where she and her brother grew up, and they both stayed and cared for their mother after their father's death and remained after she passed away. She shared the small entry-level space in the duplex with her mother, and even after her mother died, she found it hard to feel entitled to take up the whole space for herself. She noted that growing up with four people in the apartment where both parents painted large-format paintings in the studio section of the apartment, she grew up feeling only permitted to take up a little corner of space, both in the apartment and in the world (Kelly 2020).

Other second-generation residents applied for admission to Westbeth as artists in their own right, including dancer and visual artist Maya Ciarrocchi and painter Gwynne Duncan. Gwynne waited fourteen years on the wait list before being selected for an apartment, and Maya waited nine years, even though she applied as soon as she graduated from college and began dancing professionally. Maya's acceptance was fortuitous, as she had just experienced the end of a long-term relationship and had moved in temporarily to her parents' apartment while they were away. Initially, she was offered a ground floor apartment, which she didn't accept, and then subsequently moved into a tiny apartment on the third floor. She remained there for several years until her girlfriend moved in with her, and eventually Maya and her now wife were able to move to a larger unit that included what she termed "the magic closet" built by a previous tenant and spacious enough to store clutter out of sight (Ciarrocchi 2020; Duncan 2020).

Although Maya and her wife became active in the life of the community, including serving on the Westbeth Artists Resident's Council, eventually they left Westbeth and moved to space uptown. She admits that most people remain in the building forever and that many thought she was mad for giving up the security of Westbeth, but she said the community "is both a support, but also a smothering blanket" (Ciarrocchi 2020). Nadia Dajani had a similar reaction to remaining part of the community, even though her mother and sister each have units within the building. While she said she wouldn't have traded anything for her experiences growing up there, she says, "Everyone is so all up in your cornflakes" that it could be stifling as an adult (N. Dajani 2020b).

Magda Dajani applied for an apartment at Westbeth as a young single woman, and by the time she was accepted twelve years later, she had married and had two children. The expansion of her household from one to four qualified her for a larger unit. She said the experiences of her children growing up in the neighborhood are very different than what she and her siblings had experienced. Although Magda is grateful for the relative safety for her children brought on by neighborhood gentrification, she, like many, misses some of the grittiness and character of the old neighborhood. Jenny Lombard best summarized this common sentiment when she said, "Westbeth doesn't have the same wacky vibe that it did in the 1970s, but then, neither does New York City" (M. Dajani 2020a; K. Lombard 2020b).

5

Man, You Have Weird Neighbors

IN 1975, JOHN Lennon rang his friend and Westbeth resident Bob Gruen and asked if he could drop in for a coffee after a long night of bar crawling with Harry Nilsson. Bob had recently moved into a unit facing the Hudson River, but one that was hard to find because it necessitated riding the elevators at the entrance to the third floor, traversing the length of the building along the Bethune Street interior hallway, then taking a different bank of elevators to the cul-de-sac hallway where Bob was living. Knowing this labyrinth of Westbeth was not easy to navigate, he advised Lennon to ring from the front desk upon arrival and Bob would fetch him, but instead, Lennon took off on his own in pursuit of the right apartment. Bob waited for nearly an hour when Lennon breezed into the apartment and his first words were, "Man, you have some weird neighbors." Bob recounted Lennon's comments: "Well, I couldn't find your apartment, so I was ringing doorbells trying to find your place." Bob said that upon being greeted by Lennon standing in their doorway on a Sunday afternoon, "everybody opened the door and was like, oh, let me read you my poem! Let me show you this sculpture I made. Oh, I just wrote a song. Oh, let me show you my paintings." This random encounter with Westbeth artists led Lennon to conclude there were some odd ducks among Westbeth's residents, which rings true even today (Gruen 2018).

Artists have a reputation of being free spirits and not bound by many conventions of society—but in Westbeth, some residents pushed this boundary and were not just eccentric but truly odd or sometimes deeply troubled souls. Some artists embraced or flaunted their eccentricity, such as dancer Edith Stephan who proudly dyed her hair carrot orange and wore a swath of sparkly, teal-colored eye shadow at age 98, or actress Pawnee Sills, who always dressed entirely in red, including a red turban, and whose apartment furnishings were all red as well. Poet Edward Field is fond of his reputation as one of the "last Bohemians," and his friend Tobias Schneebaum reveled in his reputation as an alleged cannibal, stemming from anthropological field research with a remote village. Mixed-media artist Barton Lidice Beneš' took pride in his apartment that was full to the brim with curated ephemera—from a life-size stuffed giraffe to a Chinese opium-smoking bed to valuable African masks collected from around the world. His apartment was one giant art installation and is now reinstalled in a museum.

The Hoarders

Many of the visual artists have vast collections of "stuff" saved with the intent to use it in artwork eventually, but in some cases, these collections of items go beyond just clutter and they are truly hoarders. Bob Gruen's neighbor in an adjacent apartment refused to throw out his daily newspaper for decades. At one point, Bob realized that the floor-to-ceiling stack of dry newsprint that his neighbor had stacked along the length of their shared wall presented a huge fire risk and could jeopardize the film prints and negatives that Bob had produced in his career as a photographer. Eventually, the building intervened and forced the neighbor to clear out the accumulated paper, which reduced the fire risk. However, soon Bob realized that the dense wall of paper had an unexpected benefit of sound insulation between their units.

When illustrator Milda Vizbar died, the executor of her estate discovered an apartment full of junk, with narrow paths cleared to permit her to navigate from the door to the bed to the bathroom. As volunteers carefully cleared out her possessions, they discovered financial records leading to hundreds of thousands of dollars, a deed for another apartment in uptown Manhattan (that proved equally full of hoarded stuff), hundred dollar bills squirreled away, and expensive garments still with price tags attached that had never been worn. During her lifetime, no one had a clue that she had amassed substantial wealth or that her apartment was a pack rat's nest.

Christina Maile has filmed many of the Westbeth residents over the years, and she recalls filming famed feminist artist Anita Steckel. She recalls Steckel's apartment was jammed full of her old photos, canvases both finished and in progress, drawings, and "bookcases filled with catalogs and magazine articles about her or her work . . . clothing piled up so densely that she could barely open her apartment door—anyone who entered had to sort of shimmy inside and out. The kitchen was a closet, the stove a shelf, and the sink was full of the kind of odds and ends she thought might come in handy one of these days. Paints, brushes, pencils, papers, were strewn all over, you could read the layers of her apartment like an archaeological dig—uncovering her life strata by strata, canvas by canvas, paper by paper, photo by photo, her body adored, hidden, immortalized like the gold Athena in the Parthenon of her paintings." Like other residents, Steckel's hoarding was partly an effort to hold on to any evidence of past success or glory (C. Maile 2017).

Many of the early residents have passed away and left apartments full of possessions, and even in the cases where they left descendants, there were often mountains of personal detritus that no one wanted and got left behind in the apartment. For many years, volunteers have gathered up the rejected possessions and held a biannual flea market to get rid of the surplus items and raise money for the building beautification fund. My own family's mismatched chairs and china, books, and boots ended up in the flea market after their passing. Residents also shop at the flea market, and the walls of their apartments display original artwork from many of the building's deceased residents whose final works ended up in the flea market. The ability to purchase original artwork at a modest price makes the flea market a draw for hundreds of people from well beyond the neighborhood.

The in-house cleanup team and flea market are a fairly recent innovation as a response to the case of the most notorious hoarder in Westbeth's history, photographer Harry Shunk. Other residents recognized Shunk as the stealthy figure who would haunt the basement trash and recycling area, remove items from the trash, and attempt to hide them as he scurried out of the room, pressing himself against the walls as he moved around the space. His odd behavior earned him the derogatory nickname of "the ferret." Although it seemed like everyone knew of him, few actually knew who he was. Earlier in his life, he was an accomplished photographer who specialized in photographing other artists. After his death, it was discovered that he had thousands of slides and negatives of nearly every significant visual artist of the previous half-century. Shunk had collaborated with dozens of artists but was especially linked with Christo, famous for wrapping huge things, including buildings, in colorful fabric in his art installations. But for most of the time Shunk lived in Westbeth, he was a deeply troubled secretive person who never admitted anyone into his apartment.

Over the years, Shunk accumulated so much junk that he had boxes and boxes piled to the ceiling. Sadly, his accumulated junk eventually collapsed on him, pinning him down and making it impossible for him to escape, and his body was only found when the scent of decomposition made it clear that he had died. At the time of his death in 2006, Shunk had no will and no family, so his estate fell to the Public Administrator of New York County. An initial review of his possessions showed that he had priceless original works of art, including many by Andy Warhol, and the most valuable pieces were removed and sold at an auction for more than $2 million (Bennett 2012; Leland 2012).

After the initial rescue of the valuable art work, building manager Steve Neil hired a company to clear out the remaining debris from Shunk's apartment. Lead by Darryl Kelly, they filled several dumpsters with Shunk's junk. Kelly recalls the apartment was so full that items were piled to within inches of the ceiling, and he had to send his skinniest employee in first to begin creating a pathway for their work (Leland 2012). As Kelly noticed several people retrieving items from the dumpster, he also retrieved items that might be considered "artworks" as well as photographic negatives and slides. Kelly stowed these items in his apartment for many years, apparently until his wife was fed up and demanded that he get rid of the "junk." Kelly sent a cell phone photo of artwork to Matthew Russas of the Westbeth office staff to inquire whether it was significant. Matthew then summoned Jack Dowling, the Westbeth Gallery Director, and showed him a blurry photo that Jack immediately recognized as one of Warhol's Marilyn Monroe prints.

Russas arranged for Darryl Kelly to bring the items back to Westbeth to be examined. Jack recounted the discovery of the importance of Kelly's trove:

Darryl Kelly and a helper brought a heap of mixed material to the Westbeth Community room. I began riffling through what was piled on a large table helter-skelter, pulling out things like dime store framed prints and other cheap articles when my eye was caught by what I knew was a Christo mock-up for on installation in a Western US valley. As I picked through more things it became clear that the major part of this heap of art and artifacts were important. Letters, photos, boxes of slides, prints, paintings, lithographs and other art works, along with another Christo mock-up.

I told Darryl to please just stay and do nothing. I then ran to the Liechtenstein Foundation down the street. It was about 4:45pm. I knocked and Registrar Natasha Sigmund opened the door. She was obviously ready to leave for the day. I persuaded her to come to the Community Room and take a look. She graciously did and after looking over the collection she asked if we could keep everything there overnight so that Jack Cowart, the Executive Director could see it. She expected him in the morning. Darryl immediately became suspicious and concerned about leaving the "goods" in the room. I convinced him that they would be safe, as did Matthew. We assured him that the building had watchmen who toured the premises all night long. He reluctantly agreed and said he would come back in the morning.

The following morning, Jack Cowart came and spent a good deal of time going over everything piece by piece. Darryl, Matthew, Darryl's handyman and I more or less stood back. Cowart made no comment, he just examined everything with care. When he seemed satisfied he asked Darryl if he would agree to bring everything across the street to the foundation's space. He stated that he felt that it should be documented, photographed and examined in more detail. Darryl was leery about this turn of events…the material, the value of which he had no clue…being moved out of his hands. He had no idea who was Roy Lichtenstein was nor what was the foundation. I talked with him to ease him off any mistrust and assured him that he would be dealing with a very respectable and well-known organization. With the help of staff from the Foundation, we carried everything across the street. Sometime later I saw in the New York Times the article with photos of Darryl, his wife and the other handyman at the auction where many of the pieces sold at a very decent price. (Dowling 2019)

Jack Dowling was very frustrated with the whole process of the dissolution of Harry Shunk's estate, most especially with the building management, who had no idea who Shunk was or the potential value of his collective works. As Jack noted, all they would have to have done was a quick Internet search to learn that Shunk was an important figure in the art world through the late 1950s. Neil and Russas claimed to have no idea what happened to the Shunk estate, but evidence to the contrary suggests they were intimately involved in the estate's dissolution. Ultimately, 200,000 of Shunk's slides were placed in five major museums around the world, and Westbeth received nothing from any of these transactions. This was especially galling to Jack, as in a film about the dissolution of the Shunk estate, *Harry's Gift*, there are scenes of dressed up Darryl Kelly and his wife at the auction of the items Kelly had salvaged (Isles 2015). Despite protestations to the contrary, clearly Neil and Russas knew what was to become of the remaining valuable items from Harry Shunk's trove, and they did nothing to ensure that some of the value would accrue to Westbeth. Other residents were less charitable and suspected that Neil and Russas personally profited from the transactions and concealed this from their employer, the Westbeth corporation.

Beyond Eccentric

In any community of several hundred people, there will be a few who suffer from mental illness. In a community of several hundred artists, there is perhaps an even greater likelihood that there will be people who are mentally ill. In the early years of Westbeth's existence, when the neighborhood was rough and dangerous, the residents had to contend with homeless people who would attempt to gain entry into the building and then find a secluded corner in the basement and become squatters. Jack Dowling recalls the residents formed tenant patrol teams to secure the safety of the building and evict squatters, and many women carried whistles to blow if they felt they were in danger (Dowling 2018, 2020). Doris Mare has lived with her artist husband, Emil, in Westbeth since its inception, and she spent many years working in a local psychiatric clinic. This placed her in an awkward situation, as she would recognize clients who were being treated at the clinic as Westbeth neighbors, and because she wished to maintain their anonymity, she intentionally remained disengaged from community events to avoid awkward conversations until long after she retired (Mare 2018).

A few residents' mental illness resulted in behaviors that were not merely erratic, but threatening. Pat Lasch lives in one of the hallways that is only accessible from one direction, and in order to access her apartment, she had to pass the door of a neighbor who was very disturbed. Her neighbor threatened residents along their shared corridor, wielding hammers and kitchen knives and threatening to hurt them. As the management was unable to alter her behavior, she was eventually evicted for the sake of the community, and Pat had to testify at a court hearing about witnessing her threatening behavior. One notoriously unstable long-term resident has intimidated neighbors with his behavior. Barry is thought to be schizophrenic and would terrorize his neighbors by pounding on their shared walls, screaming, and being abusive. His behavior led both Barton Lidice Beneš and Lucille Rhodes to switch units in the building because he frightened them (Rhodes 2019). As the population of the building aged and more elderly residents began to exhibit dementia and other erratic behavior, Westbeth added a social worker to the staff, who is able to help prevent vulnerable elderly people from being taken advantage of or harmed.

Westdeath

The most distressing examples of behavior associated with mental illness are the suicides that have taken place in the community. For many years, Westbeth was the tallest building in the West Village, and it became known to troubled souls around the city as a place for committing suicide by jumping from the roof. In the spring of 1971, two suicides by jumping occurred at Westbeth, one from a stranger who found her way to the rooftop, and the other, resident photographer Shelley Broaday. A few years later, painter Philipp Weichberger jumped as well, and former Westbeth resident Ana Mendieta fell to her death in a nearby apartment high-rise that she occupied with her husband and artist Carl Andre. In several of these cases, alcohol played a role in the mental anguish of the person who died. Weichberger's children recall their father's compulsive drinking. Neighbors recall raucous, alcohol fueled fights between Mendieta and Andre, and they doubt the story of Mendieta's suicide and believe Andre pushed his wife to her death (Bosworth 1984; Bruner 2011; Davidson 2017; Lasch 2017).

During the 1970s, many people in the building saw suicides either by witnessing the act or seeing the body on the pavement outside the building. Jack Davidson recalls having dinner with friends in his apartment when a body flew past the window, and he remains haunted by this image. Davidson's wife worked in the psychiatric unit at Mt. Sinai Hospital, and he occasionally temped there as well. He commented that when a very mentally troubled person was suddenly calm and seemed to be getting better, it was often because they had made a plan for their suicide and saw a way out of their torment (Davidson 2017). Irving Vincent recalled a late-night knock on the door and being greeted by police, inquiring whether everyone in his family was safe and accounted for. The body of a woman had been discovered just below the tenth-floor windows where the family slept, and he was asked to identify the deceased woman, whom he recognized as the mother of his twins' playmate (Vincent 2023).

Some of the people who grew up at Westbeth have macabre memories of witnessing dead bodies and often feared that their parents may follow suit, as their peers' parents died. The images of a mangled body that fell thirteen stories and was lacerated during the fall by the large lanterns on the exterior of the building remain vivid in the memories of children who grew up in Westbeth. The suicides and the reputation of the building as a magnet for those who wished to jump led the younger generation to dub the building Westdeath or Deathbeth (Prete and Sonnenberg 1995; Bottoms-Newby 2020; J.a.E.M. Maile 2019). Some of the adults in the building, including my aunt Shami, formed groups and invited the teenagers to talk about their feelings and fears, in hopes of diminishing the trauma they experienced from witnessing suicides.

The most famous of Westbeth's tragic suicides is that of famed photographer Diane Arbus, although she chose a more private method to end her life. Arbus is famous both for her photographs that challenged and discomforted the viewer and for her unconventional sex life, even for the 1960s. She came from a wealthy family and had been raised among the elites of New York City, but she eschewed the trappings of her wealthy but staid family and intentionally flaunted their expectations. She married young to an established photographer, and they separated in 1960. For the next decade, she supported herself as a freelance photographer, shooting for commercials and the fashion industry. In her spare time, she chose to spend time on the fringes of society and reveled in taking photographs of people she termed "freaks," including those who exhibited themselves in carnivals, people with profound developmental disabilities, nudists, burlesque performers, drag queens, and especially twins and triplets. Her photos were not the traditional say-cheese smiling faces but rather captured looks that were haunted, threatening, and grim. Nadia Dajani recalls when her mother was approached by Arbus to photograph her twin brothers Tarik and Geeby. As Arbus introduced herself, the twins rolled by. Nadia said, "My mother said it was like right on cue. . . my brothers, the little terrorists, are behind her and then go rolling by, like setting each other on fire, like a jackhammer and a Tasmanian devil ball," upon which Arbus thanked them and left. The lively Dajani twins didn't have the somber, stoic, creepy appearance of the faces in her art photos (Bosworth 1984; Dajani 2020).

Arbus gained increasing notoriety during the 1960s for her photographs and for her unbridled sexuality. She had "sex with as many people as possible, partially to test herself, partially *to see what it was like*," and her sexual encounters were more about a nihilistic exploration of others without emotional consequences. Yet these sexual adventures masked a deep and chronic depression that had followed her for years (Bosworth 1984). She moved to Westbeth in January 1970 at the same time as her friend and visual artist Mary Frank. For a time, she was happier and more stable, living in this community of kindred spirits, although she was worried about her financial stability. A few months after her arrival at Westbeth, she learned that her work had been accepted to the Vienna Biennale scheduled for summer 1972. This was a major success, since this show was one of the most prestigious in the world and had never before accepted the work of a photographer. Yet despite the growing acclaim for her work, she remained deeply self-critical and insecure. Her friends recounted in retrospect that there were signs that she was wrapping up her life and contemplating suicide, but they only recognized these omens through the lens of the rearview mirror. A few days after sharing dinner with her famous brother, US Poet Laureate Howard Nemerov, Arbus laid down in her bathtub and took her life by swallowing drugs and slashing her wrists. Ironically, the Westbeth founders' expectations that residence in this vibrant community would result in a fluorescence and fame for the artists in essence came true for Arbus, as her work received positive global attention soon after her tragic death, including at the 1972 Vienna Biennale.

6

Bye Bye, Baby Buddha

Early Days

WHEN WESTBETH FIRST opened in 1970, the restaurant across Washington Street was a little luncheonette that was frequented by the butchers from the nearby meatpacking plants. Emil and Doris Mare recall being able to run a tab at the luncheonette and rubbing shoulders with butchers in white coats covered in blood as they took a break after working since before dawn. Later, the luncheonette was replaced by an inexpensive Chinese restaurant, Baby Buddha, which was very popular. Everyone loved their garlicky green beans, and it was the hub of the neighborhood for many years. There were no traffic lights or streetlights in the area and little traffic. The nearby building that now houses D'Agostino's grocery store was manufacturing iron fencing.

The Westbeth building itself was unfinished as many of the first residents moved in, almost all coming from substandard housing, so they didn't mind the rawness of the industrial building. Each tenant had options to configure their space as it best suited their needs, which, for some, was a simple matter of unpacking their clothes and setting up a writing desk. For visual artists who worked on large three-dimensional pieces or used toxic materials such as oil paints or musicians that played in ensembles, the small Westbeth apartments were never entirely suitable. There had been plans to include within the complex shared studio space for welding equipment and a foundry, but these plans were soon scrapped, as the fire danger they presented was apparent. While most of the first-generation residents were eternally grateful to have a space in Westbeth, a few complained endlessly that their needs were not met. Emil Mare chalked most of this up to ungratefulness. He said, "With some people, you could give them stacks of money, and then they would complain you didn't give them a wheelbarrow to carry it in" (Mare 2018).

The first years were very challenging in this neighborhood that had never been used for residences, especially for children. The residents, especially those who had ground floor apartments experienced crime, including one rape, and several people were mugged in the area, especially returning home late at night. They had not yet installed security grates on windows of the ground floor units, and women, in particular, felt vulnerable. Lucille Rhodes owned a car, which she needed to commute to her job, and it was vandalized many times when parked near the building, with locks broken and windows smashed. After paying for repeated repairs, she surrendered to the thieves by leaving the vehicle unlocked and empty, just to avoid paying for repairs. Sherry Lane often returned from events associated with her work very late at night and would park her car under the elevated highway and walk home. She said there were often unsavory characters on the streets in the wee hours when she was returning, so she consciously walked with a swagger and attitude to appear tough and discourage threats. The residents soon began a tenant patrol, with volunteers taking turns patrolling at night to discourage incursions by shady characters or just those looking for a place to squat. Women were given whistles to wear around their necks and blow to attract attention if they felt unsafe. Those who spent their childhood in Westbeth were all wary of the dangers of the neighborhood, and Julian Maile recalled as a sixth grader, his friend Adam Davidson was mugged, which he guiltily noted was because he ran faster than his friend Adam and evaded the assailants (Caplan 2020; Lane 2019; J.a.E.M. Maile 2019; Rhodes 2019).

On the Bethune Street side of the building, the Superior Ink company manufactured ink for printing the city's newspapers, and on the opposite side of Westbeth, the printing press for the city's newspapers lined Bank Street. A block to the south was a jail used for holding accused criminals, and children who grew up in the building recall being frightened by men being escorted in and out of the jail. Ethan and Julian Maile said the adjacent Meatpacking District served as a moat or buffer, keeping the rest of Manhattan at bay (J.a.E.M. Maile 2019). The Meatpacking District was a mixed-use area of refrigerated warehouses where wholesale butchers broke down carcasses for resale to retail groceries, interspersed with porn shops and gay clubs (Fig. 30, 31).

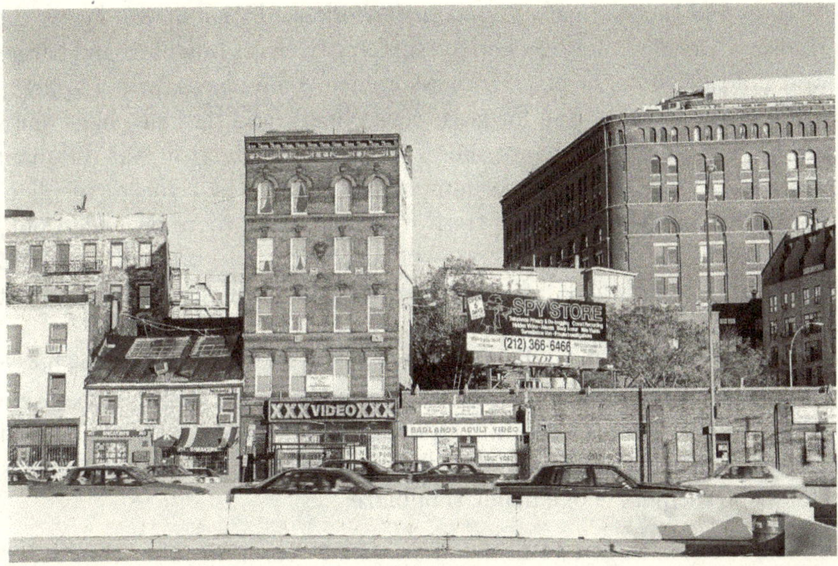

Figure 30. West Street near Westbeth ca. 1990. Krawchuk Collection Image Courtesy of Village Preservation.

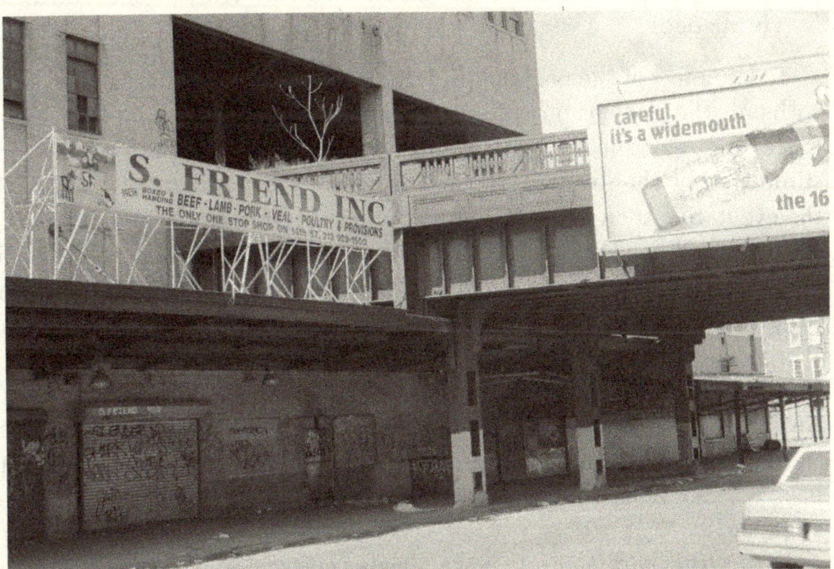

Figure 31. Meatpacking District ca. 1990. Krawchuk Collection Image Courtesy of Village Preservation.

Hans and Linda Haacke's apartment overlooked West Street, facing the Hudson River, and they watched the shipping traffic as freighters and barges were unloaded onto the piers by longshoremen. A few blocks further uptown, a major pier was mooring for large ocean liners, and they saw huge ships sail by regularly. The current site of the Whitney Museum was the plant where the city's garbage trucks dumped their loads. The Haacke's recollections differ as to whether the trash was incinerated there or loaded onto barges to be dumped elsewhere—but suffice it to say, proximity to NYC Garbage Central was hardly a selling point for residential development (Haacke and Haacke 2019).

In 1976, one of the nearby piers burned, and Denise Hurd recalls being terrified of the massive smoke cloud that engulfed the neighborhood. No longer the playground for kids, the pier fire required city fire boats, several coast guard vessels, and hundreds of firemen to extinguish the blaze. Denise's childhood memory is of a malevolent blaze:

> The fire started at 1:30 in the afternoon. I don't remember the fire, but I do remember the smoke. It didn't billow; it didn't blow. It rolled like a living thing across the water. A real-life "Blob" consuming the sun. The smoke chased us. I remember running through Westbeth's inner courtyard to escape it and then watching in horror as the smoke crawled over the walls and oozed through the courtyard. (Hurd 2020)

Today, a few of the original piers have been rebuilt, but most are gone with only their pylons protruding from the river as evidence of their existence (Fig. 32). Shelley Seccombe's interest and future profession were stimulated by the fire on the piers, as she took her camera to document the event. She soon began to photograph the adjacent elevated highway, the piers, and waterfront, capturing buildings as they progressively decayed and collapsed. Her subjects included people sunbathing on the decks in summer, and the passing tugboats and garbage scows. Her book *The Lost Waterfront: The Decline and Rebirth of Manhattan's Western Shore* includes images that are radically different from the contemporary views. An avid nature lover, Shelley often strolled along the river long before sunrise with her camera, but in the early years, she said she would not have felt safe being along the waterfront at 4 in the morning (Seccombe 2008, 2018).

In the gritty early years, teenage Magda Dajani walked her dog along the waterfront and the condemned pier buildings despite the absence of police

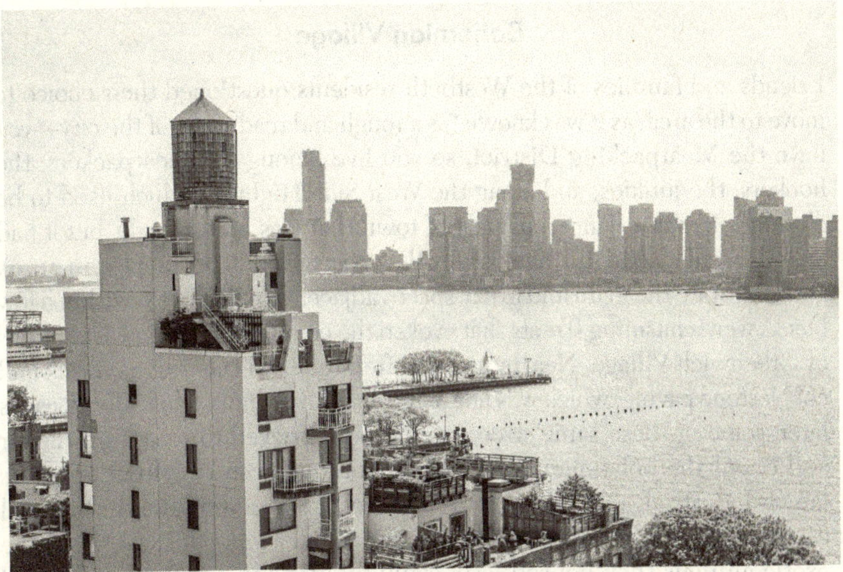

Figure 32. View over Hudson River with Pier Pylons. Image Courtesy of Tom Conelly.

presence. "It was outlaw land; you kind of take your life in your hands when you go there, but we did it on a daily basis. I would walk my dog and take pictures, and it was a whole subversive world along the river" (M. Dajani 2020a).

At night, the waterfront piers and the trucks parked below the elevated highway were transformed by a different form of commerce than shipping, as gay and transgender sex workers used the area for hookups with clients. The residents, even those with children, were never concerned about the sex workers that were doing business but were fearful of their clients, who they associated with rough elements (allegedly all from New Jersey) and gangs. Ron Faber walked his dog late at night and often passed by the parked trucks used for sexual assignations and also feared men who would come to attack the LGBTQ sex workers and clients. Charlie Seplowin and others were concerned about the thugs that came to the riverfront to target the transgender sex workers specifically and said that building residents some-times heard victims screaming for help, and they would open their windows wide and all blow whistles to help summon the police to intervene (Faber 2018; Haacke and Haacke 2019; Seplowin 2019).

Bohemian Village

Friends and families of the Westbeth residents questioned their choice to move to the area, as it was known "as a rough and ready part of the city—you have the Meatpacking District, so you live among the meatpackers, the hookers, the junkies, and along the West Side Highway, which used to be elevated. It was a dangerous part of town that was kind of ugly, but it had an industrial look to it, which is why the artists lived here" (Seplowin 2019).

Yet despite the grim and gritty spaces adjacent to Westbeth, within a few blocks were charming streets that evoked the counterculture and artsy ethos of Greenwich Village. Nearby streets often retained the original brick and cobblestone paving, which was not yet covered by asphalt. Ironically, decades later, some of these same streets would be rebricked to recapture the air and era of the bohemian West Village. Although the riverfront area was largely industrial, a few blocks away on Bleeker Street were funky shops and cafés. Pat Lasch frequently brought her daughter to a pet store to see the exotic animals they housed, especially the parrots. Sandra Caplan and Christina Maile took their children to the nearby horse paddock where New York City police stabled their police horses, and kids would admire the ponies, and Ralph Lee collected manure to use as fertilizer for his house plants (Caplan 2020; C. Maile 2017; Mare 2018). Another improbable neighborhood site was a farm a few blocks heading downtown on Washington Street. The eccentric owner of this lot stabled ponies, goats, and other farm animals in a small paddock. This was a popular destination for Westbeth kids to visit and pet the animals (Stock 1969).

Bleeker Street was home to hardware stores, furniture stores, coffeehouses, and a famous antique store that became a de facto salon for famous Broadway performers and notorious characters, including Andy Warhol. Samantha Gillison's childhood included lengthy visits to Ruth Berk's antique store, where Ruth kindly looked after her while her parents did their errands. Samantha recalls learning soft shoe routines from dancers from Broadway, being serenaded by an angelic singer, and conversations with noted gay rights advocate Bayard Rustin (Gillison 2006).

Julian and Ethan Maile remembered Westbeth as being sort of a small town surrounded by an industrial area. Many of their fellow children were latchkey kids who largely took care of themselves, but it was not unusual for one of them to return home with twenty kids in tow and announce they had brought their friends over to play. In reflection, they noted that their community was highly diverse in a city characterized by strong ethnic enclaves, diverse in every respect. Their friends included the children of one of the original architects of the building who lived in the apartment after their parents' separation, together with their mother and her transgender boyfriend, at a time when this was rare. They counted ethnically diverse playmates among their peers and were of mixed ethnicity. The Westbeth kids shared a solidarity and looked out for each other, especially as they reached middle school age and attended a school that included tough boys who had been held back several grades and were thus bigger and older than the average sixth grader. Mark Vincent, later known as Vin Diesel, was respected for his toughness even as a boy, and they said friendship with him afforded them some "protection," as the tough boys didn't wish to incur his wrath if they picked on the more vulnerable children from the building (J.a.E.M. Maile 2019).

Despite the gritty and somewhat dangerous nature of the neighborhood surrounding Westbeth, everyone is nostalgic for those days when the neighborhood was more authentic and less gentrified. In the wild early years of Westbeth, there was a sense of magic about the place and community, and it is in this context that the famous Halloween Parade originated. The parade was started in 1974 by Ralph Lee, an actor and puppeteer who conceived the event. Ralph created a scavenger hunt for participants who walked the parade route to see scary tableaus and haunting images. The first parade started at the Theater for the New City on nearby Jane Street and later moved to the Westbeth courtyard. Ralph made gigantic Tim Burton-esque papier-mâché puppets, including massive spiders that launched the parade in the Westbeth courtyard by rappelling down the walls eleven stories from the roof. All of the participants, adults and children alike, wore costumes as they walked out of the Bank Street courtyard and around the corner, eventually turning onto Bethune and ending the parade four blocks away at Abingdon Square. Along the route were many performances, jugglers, musicians, and actors. Perched on fire escapes, or the stairs of nearby brownstone buildings, the route was lined with events. Nancy Gabor and other actors dressed as witches and other scary imagery and positioned themselves along the parade route, acting out Halloween appropriate tableaus, to scare the children. One year, Ralph's son flew a moth-like kite puppet over the assembled crowd in the courtyard, and another year, son Josh rappelled down the side of the building dressed in a smoke-emitting costume. A puppet made of many segments each held aloft on a long pole by a person made up an undulating snake that slithered along the parade. Many of Ralph's puppets, like his most famous "Land Shark" from vintage Saturday Night Live, were not small puppets to be worn on a hand but were larger than the human who stepped inside the costume. Many had additional limbs attached by dowels and operated by the wearer, so the costume might stand ten or twelve feet high in total (Gillison 2006; Columbia 2021; Lee 2018)

Gwynne Duncan and Hans Haacke recall all the fantastic costumes—as all the adults in the building were artists, they poured their creativity into the costumes they prepared, and everyone indulged in the high-energy, spirited event. Soon, the event expanded beyond the Westbeth population. The cross-dressing sex workers and drag queen performers joined the parade, and eventually, gays began making floats to be part of the parade festivities. Hans and Linda Haacke recall this annual event as the crown jewel of Westbeth and a magical experience that grew organically each year (Duncan 2020; Haacke and Haacke 2019; Lee 2018).

Nadia Dajani recalls one parade where she heard a loud thwack as she walked along the route on the Washington Street side of the building. Realizing that she had narrowly missed being beaned with an egg dropped from above that instead cracked on the sidewalk, she looked up to the level where the High Line train formerly ran and saw a group of boys. Soon realizing the pranksters included her twin brothers, Geeby and Tarik, "and their idiot friends were hurling eggs at everyone down below at the Halloween parade. My brothers and friends were frickin terrorists." (N. Dajani 2020b; Lee 2018). Eventually, the parade became so large that the route was shifted from commencing in the Westbeth courtyard to the center of Greenwich Village, about the same time that Ralph Lee passed the torch to let others manage. Today, the parade is thought of by most New Yorkers as the gay Halloween Parade of Greenwich Village, but for the first decade of its existence, the parade was integrally tied to the building and residents of Westbeth.

The Ugly 1980s

The second decade of Westbeth's existence coincided with a period of general decline for much of New York City and the slow-moving emergence of the HIV/AIDS pandemic. People recall this era as a time of great sadness because many lost friends and colleagues to the disease or to drugs, many relationships ended, families broke apart, and the vibrancy of the civil rights activism of the 1970s gave way to cynicism. Times Square wasn't a glitzy plaza with giant electronic billboards but was dirty and famous for porn shops and sex shows. Rampant intravenous drug use left used syringes as part of the litter, and the parks for which the city is rightfully famous were unkempt and unused. Muggings and robbery were common, and housing across the city was both expensive and derelict. Buildings, subway stations and trains, and other infrastructure were filthy, falling apart, and covered with graffiti. People with means began fleeing to the outer boroughs, even if working in Manhattan, leaving behind those at the bottom of the socioeconomic spectrum. While there was nostalgia among Westbeth people for their early days in the building and their youthful optimism, they recalled the 1980s with sadness.

Emil and Doris Mare lost many friends to the AIDS epidemic and noted that, at the same time, many residents lost faith in the building management. There were equipment thefts from studios and workspaces, and the management sold off part of the building that was refurbished as a tony event space for wealthy clients in a deal that everyone viewed as suspect. Rumors that the managers were paid kickbacks to facilitate this deal persist today. Ed Field said that some residents began hosting "drug parties" to earn money to pay rent, and the hallways would have visitors who were high, loitering, and sometimes engaging in unruly behavior. Others recall intruders and squatters taking over vacant spaces, especially in the basement. One of the oddest intrusions happened to playwright Susan Yankowitz, who was asleep in a loft bed in her apartment. When she woke up in the morning, a strange man was sound asleep with a bag of potato chips on his chest beneath her bed. Susan and her partner woke him up and demanded an explanation. He claimed to have mistakenly come into their apartment, but before he left, he finished eating his chips and washed off in their bathroom (Field and Derrick 2017; Mare 2018; Yankowitz 2019).

Businesses opened up in the Westbeth neighborhood, including iconic restaurants such as the bistro Florent, which catered to residents and meatpackers by day and club-goers and sex workers by night. Florent's owner, Florent Morellet, credits himself with beginning the trend of gentrification and diversification of the neighborhood, and said that his restaurant welcomed "political drag queens, suicidal libertines, secular surgeons, transvestal virgins, lunatic ravers, steroidal saviors, twelve-stepping two-steppers, infidel lepers, sadistic humanists, lunatic sensualists, wondering Jews, multicultural views, leftist rituals, and delectable victuals" (Moss 2017). Several restaurants within a block's radius opened, including Tortilla Flats, bringing Mexican food and cheap drinks, but none were more iconic than Baby Buddha. Directly across from Westbeth's main entrance, this small Chinese restaurant became the mainstay for everyone in the building, and their delivery guys shuttled food across the street at all hours. The building hallways were often perfumed with the smell of garlic and ginger at dinner time from the Chinese takeout deliveries.

With the greater activism in the gay rights movement, more visible gay presence was seen throughout the West Village. Clubs opened in the area that catered to the gay partying clientele and ranged from standard gay bars to those with more kinky orientations such as Spike, Hellfire, and the Mineshaft, and the pants-optional Rawhide Bar (Moss 2017).

One of the most significant symbols of this period of decay was the abandoned elevated West Side Highway, which aligned with Westbeth parallel to the river at a level between the second and third floors. The highway, built over several decades beginning in the 1920s, had long been deteriorating, carrying more traffic and heavier vehicles than it had ever been designed to carry. The area beneath the highway was used to park vehicles and empty tractor trailers for commerce brought in by ships at the adjacent piers, but at night, they were commandeered for sexual transactions by sex workers and gay men. Also the site for many drug transactions and drug use, the narrow strip between Westbeth and the river could be dangerous territory. After decades of deferred maintenance and corrosion from salting the highway deck in winter, in the mid-1970s, a heavy truck crashed through the upper deck of the elevated highway a few blocks from Westbeth at 14th Street, causing the whole thoroughfare to be closed to traffic below 18th Street. While it was a boon to bicycle riding and children skating as a road deck devoid of cars, the mangled metal pylons remained and were slowly rusting away. The abandoned roadway remained for almost a decade as city officials debated about what to do and how to pay for demolition and replacement (Strausbaugh 2013; Field and Derrick 2017).

For Westbeth residents whose apartments faced the river and were on the lower floors, the highway impeded air and light from filtering into their apartments and, once abandoned, became even more of an eyesore. As a photographer, Bob Gruen was especially attuned to the light in his apartment, and he cheered the news that after a decade, the city would begin demolishing the highway. The deconstruction took years, as first the highway decking was removed, then later, the support pylons. Jackhammers worked day in and day out, chipping the concrete and steel into pieces small enough to be trucked away bit by bit. For years, Bob watched the progress of the demolition until it finally came south from 14th Street and approached Westbeth.

Finally the work got in front of the building. I'd been waiting ten years to see the river. Then they got to my windows, it was like six beams, the main support beams on the end and in the middle. They were removing the four big beams, and they had gotten three of them, and one beam was left, right in front of my window. I could see the superintendent and the contractors and they are all looking at their watches and pointing to the beam. I screamed out the window—take it down, take it down! It's like twenty to four and they had to quit at four. But they looked and saw me and I shouted again take it down. And they did! I had two six-packs of beer here, and I went out and gave it to them. I had big stereo speakers and I put them in the window and played The Who song *I Can See for Miles*, and then I looked out the window, and I'm looking at Hoboken. It's like, where's the purple mountain majesty? It's just New Jersey. (Gruen 2018)

The impetus for the demolition of the West Side Highway was partly due to a plan to rebuild the highway as a subterranean road on reclaimed land, extending the riverbank and impinging the flow of the Hudson. Part of this grand plan, which remained on the books for years and multiple mayoral administrations, was to build Westway, a mixed-use commercial and residential strip of buildings on top of the subterranean highway. This proposal included acres and acres of reclaimed land and would have resulted in a wide swath of buildings and development between Westbeth and the riverfront. This controversial plan remained under discussion for a decade and was hotly contested by both Westbeth residents and their neighbors. The idea of losing waterfront views and commercial developments enriching additional billionaires was anathema to locals. Many locals participated in protests against the Westway plan, led by activist musician Pete Seeger, who wanted to see the polluted and foul river cleaned up but without the massive construction project proposed as Westway (Faber 2018). The project remained under discussion, and multiple sets of engineering plans were developed over a decade until 1985 when the Westway plan was finally scrapped. The demolition of the elevated highway was not completed until 1989.

Preparing for the New Millennium

Many of the changes in the neighborhood during the 1990s ended up being the first drafts of sweeping changes that came with the turn of the millennium. During the Rudy Giuliani mayoral administration, the reimagining of the West Side Highway was finally approved as a scaled-down street-level road between the riverfront and a newly envisioned green space and the sidewalk adjacent to Westbeth. The park was under construction for a decade and now includes bike and walking paths, playgrounds, venues, and recreational facilities, and was completed in 2014. The new riverside park was New York City's largest park construction since the establishment of Central Park and is used by thousands of residents and tourists daily. Bob Gruen notes with irony that the vegetation planted for the park has thrived so much that now his view of the river is partially blocked by trees, but he would trade the trees and light over the industrial blight any day (Gruen 2018).

The neighborhood retained vestiges of its bohemian history as small businesses occupied storefronts on nearby Bleeker and Hudson Streets and were largely locally owned rather than corporate outlets. The restaurants were mostly either diners, like the Bus Stop Café at the terminus of the number 11 bus that ran uptown, or ethnic eateries offering Chinese, Thai, or Mediterranean food. Westbeth residents frequented the hardware or used furniture store, the bookstore, the pet store, and got takeout from the inexpensive restaurants nearby.

The late 1990s was also when the High Line Park was envisioned, and Joshua David and Robert Hammond started Friends of the High Line to raise enough funds to begin construction of the park on the remains of the elevated railbed. Beginning near Gansevoort Street, the park was built on the rail deck and opened in 2009 after donations from many, including New York celebrity Barry Diller and fashion designer Diane von Furstenburg. When it first opened, it was a neighborhood gem, regularly frequented by locals who strolled and enjoyed the plants and the views. Today, it is one of the top tourist destinations in the city, and on busy summer days, the stroll becomes more like a slow-moving mosh pit inching along in unison heading uptown. Like all tourist destinations, there is money to be made at the High Line, whether by the gelato vendors or enterprising musicians like Westbeth painter Ken Wade, who is an occasional busker playing and singing on the High Line for tips (Wade 2019).

Twenty-First Century *Sex and the City* Tourism

The twenty-first century has ushered in wholesale changes in the West Village, especially around the waterfront and Westbeth. The popularity of the television show *Sex and the City* contributed to what some have called the Disneyfication of Greenwich Village, aided by Mayor Bloomberg, who wanted to raze gritty buildings and eliminate what he deemed low-class influences, such as street buskers, hot dog vendor carts, and drumming groups. While the changes at this time did sanitize the Village, it also resulted in exponential increases in property values and the loss of affordable housing and storefronts. Iconic, historic Village landmarks like the Minetta Tavern (established 1937), the Waverly Inn (1920), and the White Horse Tavern (open since 1880, where poet Dylan Thomas drank himself to death) were purchased by soulless businesses and gussied up to evoke bygone eras in what has been termed *fauxstalgia* (Moss 2017). Businesses cultivated the bohemian image, yet the Village's original bohemians would not stand in line for two hours for a table at a popular restaurant and spend more on a single cocktail than a full meal would have cost at Florent. Several successive mayoral administrations had pushed tourism as a means to revitalize the city and infuse cash, which were launched campaigns such as the use of Milton Glaser's now famous graphic of "I Heart NY." Leaders pleaded with New Yorkers to be nicer to wandering tourists and help them with directions and subway routes—to counter the archetype of the rude and pushy New Yorker.

The Magnolia Bakery where the *Sex and the City* ladies bought cupcakes was originally a single storefront on Bleeker Street serving as a neighborhood bakery, but the popularity of the show resulted in swarms of tourists standing in long lines to purchase the cupcake du jour. Magnolia capitalized on this massive free advertising and is now a multinational corporation with stores across the US and as far away as India and Qatar. Rents for businesses on Bleeker that were $75 per square foot escalated to $300 and then $550 per square foot, driving many businesses out (Moss 2017). There is a an irony that, in a year 2000 episode, the character Samantha moves into the Meatpacking District and has conversations with transgender sex workers in sky high stilettos, and now it is tourists in equally impractical footwear that frequent the neighborhood (Moss 2017).

Businesses have closed left and right, with the COVID-19 pandemic dealing the final blow to some holdouts. As late as the late 1990s, there were as many as seven Chinese restaurants within a couple blocks of the building, and the best was right across the street at Baby Buddha. When Baby Buddha was forced to close because they could no longer afford the rent, they held one final meal to thank the loyal Westbeth customers and invited hundreds of people to join them as their guests for one last meal. Residents still wax nostalgic about how much they miss cheap restaurants, and Baby Buddha is at the top of that list (Cominskie, Maile, and Lee 2020; C. Maile 2017).

The businesses that had catered to the gay scene also closed one by one, some in the late 1980s as the ravages of HIV/AIDS decimated their clientele. The city had forced the closure of many bathhouses, bars, and other local venues that were perceived as being places where gay men hooked up or used drugs. Rawhide was the last bar to close in 2013, having withstood the pressures of neighborhood anti-gay protests and rent hikes. At the same time, the gay community turned its energies into fighting for cures and prevention for AIDS, with groups like Act Up and the Gay Men's Health Crisis, and to caring for their friends and loved ones ravaged by the disease. Skyrocketing rents put other LGBTQ-friendly businesses in jeopardy. The Rainbows and Triangles boutique closed, as their monthly rent was raised from $7K monthly to $24K. Writer Kate Walter also decried the end of the neighborhood gay enclave with the closure of the Oscar Wilde bookshop (Moss 2017; Strausbaugh 2013). Many of those once coveted Bleeker Street and Hudson Street commercial spaces shuttered, and with the combined impact of recessions, natural disasters, and the COVID pandemic, some remain empty.

In addition to the riverfront and High Line parks, the other major innovation in the neighborhood was the 2015 opening of the new Whitney Museum of American Art. Founded in 1930 by heiress and artist Gertrude Vanderbilt Whitney, the museum's mandate from the beginning was to showcase innovations in American art. Many Westbeth artists have had work shown at the Whitney, including the first major exhibition by a video artist, with the works of early Westbeth resident Nam June Paik. The original museum was located uptown but moved to the West Village location, and the connections to the Westbeth community persist. In addition to Veronica Ryan and Debra Jenks showing works in the 2022 Whitney Biennial, Nat Oppenheimer, who grew up in the building, was one of the lead engineers on architect Renzo Piano's industrial and edgy design of the museum. The proximity to Westbeth has fostered new collaborations, as now the Gallery hosts an annual exhibit of works by artists who are also staff at the Whitney (Oppenheimer 2020; Whitney).

While a couple of meat processing facilities remain, most storefronts in the Meatpacking District now cater to a wealthy crowd. A Tesla showroom joins stores selling luxury brands like Hermès and Christian Louboutin. On nearby Bleeker and Hudson Streets, once the epicenter of the bohemian Village, Magnolia Bakery is joined by pricey boutiques that sell garments that equate in price to the monthly rent of Westbeth residents.

The exponential gentrification continues with the newest destination of Little Island, a manmade "island" park that projects into the Hudson. Opening in 2021, this wholly artificial island is composed of precast concrete tulip-shaped segments, with the stem of each tulip sunk into the river bed, joining other segments to form an undulating platform. Now completed, Little Island includes playgrounds, an amphitheater, and lushly landscaped walking paths accessible to all—if you have a timed entry during peak hours (Island 2023).

Where Is My Village?

Juanita Neely has been wheelchair-bound for many years and seldom left her Westbeth apartment where she painted and lived unless she had a medical appointment. She said that every time she went out, she looked around and asked herself, "Where is my Village?," because the area is so unrecognizable from when she first occupied her space facing the river and the old highway. In reflecting on her history at Westbeth, she said that despite the elevated highway blocking her windows for years, having a jail just outside her door, and seeing shackled prisoners transported across the street, her life was very rich in the early days. On weekends, everyone would take their coffee and newspaper and sit out on the piers, and the performing artists would practice their plays or dances, making the piers into impromptu open-air rehearsal spaces. Like most long-term residents, she sees both good and bad in the gentrification (McNeely 2019).

Bob Gruen and his wife, Elizabeth Gregory, are among the many residents who commented on the buildings that have gone up in place of the ink factory and other local landmarks. On the Bethune side of the building, there were originally plans for a tall, shiny, mirrored skyscraper that would take up a square block, but later the developer redesigned the plans in response to pressure from both Westbeth Artists Resident's Council and the heritage preservation group Village Preservation (Cominskie, Maile, and Lee 2020). Today, most of Bethune is lined with faux brownstones, the front of which look like historic structures but which actually house apartments connected to a high-rise on the corner of Bethune and West. The seven brownstone facades are just that, facing on an apartment building that is connected to the high-rise on the corner where residents enter and park in a subterranean garage. Bob and Elizabeth say the high-rise building blocks views for many units that formerly had unobstructed views toward the river, and the galling part is that most of the building appears unoccupied years after its completion. At night, few windows are illuminated. No one comes and goes, except for occasional parties where men clad in business suits drinking cognac mingle with bikini-clad women in hot tubs on the open balconies. Many residents speculate that these apartments were purchased by corporations and not intended for permanent residents, or by foreign tycoons, or are purchased as part of money laundering schemes, and so they remain empty, and symbols of greed and the one percent (Cominskie, Maile, and Lee 2020; Ciarrocchi 2020; Gruen 2018; Gregory-Gruen 2018).

On the other side of Westbeth, artist Julian Schnabel bucked the building trends of glass skyscrapers and faux brownstones and built his bright pink Palazzo Chupi as a towering addition on top of a conventional brick building. Schnabel's Palazzo, built in the style of an Italian palace, has endeared some neighbors who see it as an extension of the edgy arts traditions of the Village and enraged others who see it as a monument to his ego. Like other new constructions in the neighborhood, the apartments he has sold within the building go for millions of dollars, keeping the neighborhood one of the highest-priced real estate markets in the US.

Favorite restaurants and shops are mostly long gone, and a huge blow to the neighborhood was the closing of St. Vincent's Hospital in 2010 after serving the area for 161 years. The hospital had been ground zero for the HIV/AIDS epidemic, and the first patients treated in the nation were cared for by St. Vincent's. At the height of the epidemic, half of the hospital's beds were devoted to critically ill AIDS patients, and the hospital was one of the pioneering centers to turn the tide with the use of protease inhibitors to treat HIV (Project). Westbeth residents turned out for protests at the plans to close the hospital, which would create a huge void in health care access for the area. My aunt Shami was one of the leading voices at these protests, wheeled there in her wheelchair because she knew she was alive because of St. Vincent's care. A year before, she had been in a massive accident and crushed by a truck in the bike lane at Abingdon Square as she rode her mobility scooter toward the YMCA that she had frequented for decades. She spent several months in the intensive care unit at St. Vincent's after breaking many bones and suffering internal damage, and she (and we) attributed her survival to the care she received at St. Vincent's. The proximity to Westbeth allowed many of her friends to visit and monitor her status and support her through her recovery. On one memorable day, when she had yet to regain consciousness, a group of Hasidic men came to pray over a patient in a nearby curtained area and were approached by Shami's sister Miriam, and asked if they would also pray for Shami. After asking what her Hebrew name was, the men prayed and bobbed up and down in the traditional davening manner, and my aunt Miriam turned to me and whispered, "There are Buddhists in New Jersey praying for her too." When she was finally released months later, the nuns and medical staff who ran the hospital dedicated to the poor and needy lined the corridor as she was wheeled past. Wishing her well and crossing themselves as she said farewell, they all felt they had witnessed a miracle.

Where St. Vincent's once stood is only the façade of the building, now attached to new construction medium-rise apartment structures. The century of needed maintenance for the old hospital made it impossible for operations to continue, and after more than a century of serving the needs of New York's poor, the hospital declared bankruptcy. Sold to developers, the building was demolished save for part of the historic brick façade, and made into apartments. Now, apartments at the site sell for $6 million for a small one-bedroom unit, and well over $20 million for the larger apartments. The value of the property is emblematic of the changes in the area surrounding Westbeth and reflects the indelible changes that have occurred in Greenwich Village.

Some of the wealthiest people in New York are now neighbors to the quirky artists of Westbeth. Maya said the neighbors are a wholly different class, the people who also own mansions in the Hamptons. Magda noted that the presence of very wealthy people frequenting local bars and restaurants has increased muggings as the inebriated, well-dressed tourists teetering in high heels make an easy mark as they leave late at night. Susannah Kelly said the Westbeth folks retain their ragtag archetype. Yet when they walk the local streets, they are confronted by a different caste of rich spandex-wearing women talking on iPhones while power walking along the river. The contrast between the artist bohemians and the other residents of the area could not be stronger, and like castes elsewhere, they don't interact (Kelly 2020).

Steve Lomprey was struck by the fact that the Hudson River is now so clean that you can see schools of fish from the piers, which was never true in the industrial days. The Maile brothers shared the sentiment that the nostalgia for the gritty old days expressed by many Westbeth residents is a reflection of the fact that artists love decay and industrial chic, as they see the potential for creative improvement—and Charlie Seplowin's current studio made of an abandoned freight elevator shaft full of pigeon poop was the epitome of that ethos. Expensive restaurants and stores have replaced neighborhood dives, and the area's reputation as the cool place to hang out has made it the mecca for tourists. Josh Hamilton said the streets aren't as quiet at night as they were, and the area is definitely "not as interesting, but you know, that's true for all of New York" (Ciarrocchi 2020; M. Dajani 2020a; Hamilton 2020; Lomprey 2020; J.a.E.M. Maile 2019).

But the neighborhood gentrification has also had some benefits for Westbeth. Everyone can access the building's rooftops and enjoy the million-dollar views of the Empire State Building toward the east (Fig. 33) and see across the Hudson River and park on the west with views of the Statue of Liberty

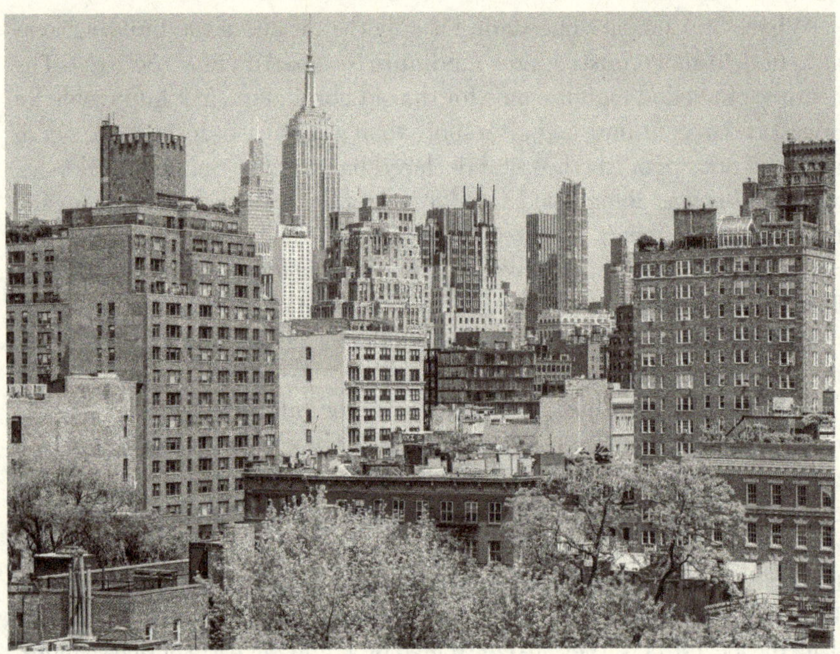

Figure 33. City View Toward Empire State Building from Westbeth Roof. Image Courtesy of Tom Conelly.

and New Jersey (Fig. 34). Hans and Linda Haacke note that everyone enjoys walking along the Hudson River Park, using the bike lanes, and sitting and having a coffee while relaxing along the river. Everyone notes that it is now easy to hail a cab right at the Westbeth entrance, whereas, in the old days, taxis never ventured into the grimy neighborhood. A grocery, although expensive, is now accessible and open long hours a block from Westbeth instead of having to schlep over to groceries ten blocks away. Shelley Seccombe often took her camera to the riverfront before sunrise and always found joggers and yoga enthusiasts already there, whereas, in the old days, she would never have felt safe being out at that hour (Seccombe 2018).

The gentrification in the neighborhood has brought in wealthy neighbors, and the opening of the Whitney Museum has brought more art lovers to the area. Both of these have stimulated Westbeth residents to be more outward looking, and events at the building now draw neighbors. The biannual flea market is an important fundraiser for the building beautification committee, and people from around the Village now come in search of bargains, including works of art from residents. Open studio weekends bring

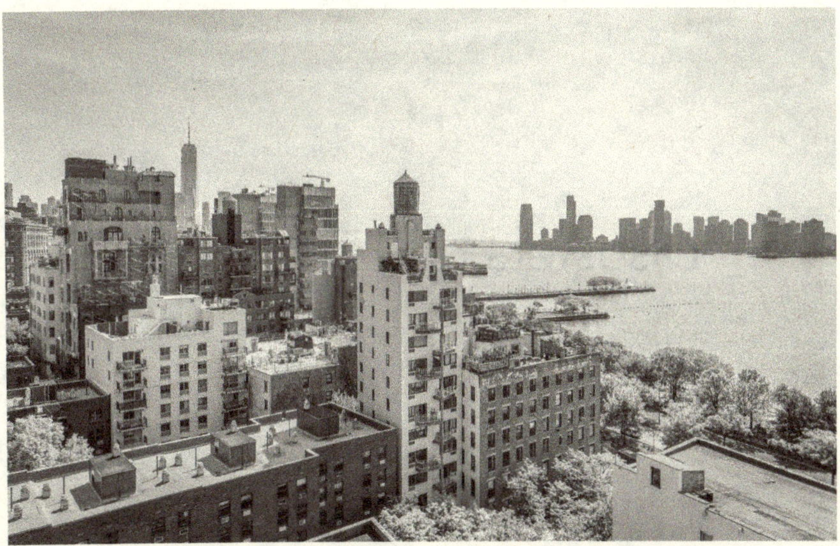

Figure 34. View over Hudson River from Westbeth Roof. Image Courtesy of Tom Conelly.

hundreds of potential art patrons to see works in the visual artists' homes and studios, and the Westfest event schedules dance performances around the building including in hallways and stairwells. A few residents suggested that the presence of Westbeth is a draw for the neighborhood and has attracted wealthy neighbors, but this is a stretch, as the impact of the High Line, the Hudson River Park, and the new Whitney Museum are surely more significant. Yet Sherry Lane says that these changes in the neighborhood have brought many Westbeth artists together and joined in welcoming the broader community, which makes them less of an isolated enclave. The older generation at Westbeth see themselves as pioneers who endured amid many challenges, and they made the area an attractive place to live and served as a draw for others to move in and settle (Lane 2019).

7

Disasters and Traumas

THE PEOPLE OF Westbeth have experienced more than their share of challenges and disasters over the past fifty years. Some of these events, like the 2020 COVID-19 pandemic, affected the world as a whole, but other events have had an impact unique to Westbeth. A decade after Westbeth's inception, the HIV/AIDS epidemic began. About the same time, in the early 1980s, many of the artists experienced mid-life crisis, as their aspirations for artistic success hadn't panned out as planned. Residents recall the 1980s as a grim time, and everyone lost friends to the AIDS epidemic. The most notable resident whose life was linked to HIV was Barton Lidice Beneš, who lived for decades with the virus due to being one of the first generation of out gay men to participate in the drug trials for the earliest anti-retroviral drugs, which prolonged his life long after his partner, Howard, had succumbed to Kaposi's sarcoma and AIDS. Barton's work as an artist was profoundly influenced by his HIV status, which was woven as a theme in his work. Most notable was the *Lethal* Weapons project, an ensemble of vessels including vials, hypodermic needles, and tubes filled with his own and his friends' HIV+ blood.

Barton was a legend, and many of his neighbors on the ninth floor said Barton was their best friend. They, in turn, were Barton's best friend. Most perceived their relationship with Barton as totally unique, seeming not to notice that others also claimed him as their best friend. Joan Hall said that no matter what time of night or day she would return from traveling, she would knock on Barton's door and he'd prepare martinis so she could recount her adventures, and her relationship with him was a marriage minus sex. Roger Braimon moved into the building only in Barton's last few years but counts his friendship with Barton as one of the most meaningful of his life. Other residents took friends, almost as tourists, to visit Barton's one-of-a-kind apartment/art installation crammed full of his collections of African masks, taxidermy, paintings, antiques, oddities, and ephemera. My aunt Shami was one who considered Barton her best friend, and they had daily phone dates while sitting in their respective apartments on opposite ends of the ninth floor to simultaneously watch and chat about Judge Judy on TV. Many evenings, Barton would make them dinner to share, and Shami would wash the dishes. On one memorable day in January 2009, Barton called Shami and while breathlessly telling her about a plane that he had seen on TV that had just ditched in the Hudson River. He dragged his oxygen tank on a wheeled cart the full block length of the Westbeth hallway and burst into Shami's door, still talking on the phone, to tell her to look out her window. Her apartment faced the river, and beneath them in midstream was the "Miracle on the Hudson" plane that had floated downstream some blocks from where it first touched down. Together, they watched the passengers being rescued by water taxis and Coast Guard vessels, and miraculously everyone survived this wreck (Braimon 2020; Chaikin 2017–2020; Hall 2018).

The grim decade beginning in the early 1980s coincided with many premature deaths from HIV, and everyone recalls with sadness watching vibrant friends grow frail and pass away. For the performing artists in particular, being cast in roles or offered gigs to play their music often meant hiding their HIV+ status, and often the fact they were gay. While the cause of many of the deaths in those early years was disguised or left unspoken, for those within the gay community, the epidemic of HIV was simultaneously profoundly sad and a call to action. Jack Dowling said he stopped counting the number of funerals he attended after the number reached one hundred (Fig. 35). Others channeled their anger into activist groups demanding research and treatment about the disease or became deeply committed to caring for those who were failing and sick. George Cominskie, who long served as the president of the Westbeth Artists Resident's Council and was later key in establishing protocols to protect building residents in the early days of the COVID-19 pandemic was one of those who began a life of service to the care of others. For decades he has been a Wednesday volunteer at God's Love We Deliver, a nonprofit organization that delivers prepared meals to people with chronic illnesses. First established to help people living with HIV/AIDS, this organization has grown exponentially as the needs of

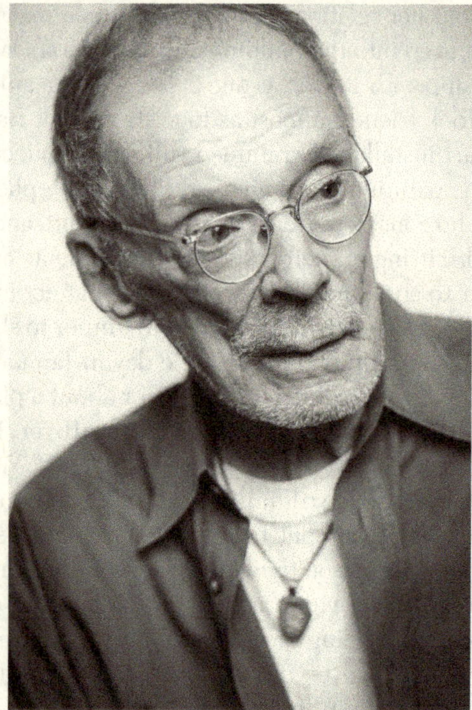

Figure 35. Jack Dowling. tribesnyc Project. Image Courtesy of David Plakke.

many vulnerable populations were addressed, and now serves more than 4.4 million meals annually (God's Love 2022).

Congregation Beit Simchat Torah, now the largest LGBTQ synagogue congregation in the world, was housed at Westbeth for forty years beginning in the early 1970s. As the HIV/AIDS crisis emerged the congregation was hard hit, as about a third of the male members perished before the anti-retroviral drugs became available. Two members of the congregation, microbiologist Regina Linder and infectious disease expert Mark Beiber, were instrumental in encouraging fellow congregants and Westbeth neighbors to enroll in the early trials of the AIDS drugs, no doubt saving the lives of many men, including Barton Lidice Benès (Linder 2023). As awful as were the ravages of the HIV epidemic, it brought many people together to fight a common enemy and care for each other, foreshadowing the later disasters and traumas that were experienced by the Westbeth community.

September 11

The terrorist attacks of September 11, 2001, felled the Twin Towers in New York, but this tragedy was felt worldwide. That moment became frozen in time for nearly all who lived through it as one of those "I remember where I was" snapshots in the same way that the assassinations of JFK and MLK or the explosion of the space shuttle *Challenger* had done in earlier generations. For the people of Westbeth, these attacks were not just an existential threat but a real one, as the World Trade Center towers were only blocks away.

September 11 coincided with the day for primary voting in New York City, and Maya Ciarrocchi recalls walking home after casting her vote and saw a crowd gathered staring at something in the distance. As she stopped to watch, she saw the first tower had been hit and was burning. She arrived at Westbeth, and instead of going to her own apartment, she went to her parents' unit to tell them what she had seen and recalls they turned on the television and watched with horror as the events unfolded (Ciarrocchi 2020).

Allison Armstrong was also walking home after having met a friend for breakfast and heard the crash of the first plane. When she reached Seventh Avenue, she saw everyone looking up and saw the first tower with fire blazing out of the top floors with smoke billowing out and papers floating out of windows. Later, she realized, with horror, that she thinks she witnessed people jumping from the building as she reconstructed the events in her mind. As she continued home, she tried to call her friend from a pay phone on Christopher Street when she heard the second crash. As she continued walking, she heard from the radio of a parked truck President Bush announcing that the crashes were not chance accidents, but a deliberate attack. She recalls feeling desperate to get home, to feel safe amidst the trauma and turmoil of the crowds. As she stood outside Westbeth with her dog and several neighbors, the second tower imploded and they saw a slow fountain of gray dust engulf them and crowds of terrified people running uptown on West Street away from the towers (Armstrong 2019).

David Greenspan was in nearby Washington Square when he noticed a plane flying extremely low to the ground and then heard the loud impact of the first plane hitting the tower. His partner, Bill Kennon, was at home and joined other residents on the roof of Westbeth and saw the collapse of the first tower soon after impact. After watching the collapse Bill went to the riverfront and saw a wall of smoke, dust, and debris barrel out toward the river and along the streets north of the WTC site. Bill thought he was seeing the end of the world, as the fire and smoke cloud appeared ready to engulf all the buildings in its path.

Many residents moved to the roof of Westbeth, which gave them a vantage point toward the Twin Towers, and Maya began filming the events, using the video camera she used for her art pieces but quickly realized she didn't have the stomach to film such a horrific scene. She knew she could never be a documentary filmmaker. Geeby Dajani went to the roof after running back from Eleventh Street and burst into tears at the sights (Ciarrocchi 2020; N. Dajani 2020b). Painter Jayne Holsinger photographed her husband, poet Hugh Seidman, gazing across Manhattan at the burning tower in the distance, and Jayne's quick snapshot became the basis for her painting of Hugh's back as he focused binoculars on the burning towers a few blocks away. Jayne's painting freezes that moment in time and gives a visual to the collective memory of the attacks, and the painting has been exhibited widely including internationally, including in a show *Meditations on the American Spirit* that included works by Sally Mann and Roy Lichtenstein (Fig. 36) (Holsinger 2018; Stoller 2017).

Maya's parents, Ray Ciarrocchi and Sandra Caplan, remembered watching the Twin Towers being built after they had settled in Westbeth and recalled the contentious reaction to the plans for the tallest buildings in the city. Like everyone else, they watched numbly as the landmark vaporized.

Gayle Kirschenbaum had been working in her apartment when her mother phoned to tell her of the attack, and she immediately walked out to the river and joined a group beginning to gather. One man had a radio, and she heard from the broadcast that people were jumping from the towers and that the president had ordered all the airports to close. One of the people clustered together said his father had helped build the Twin Towers and said the buildings would stand—tragically he was wrong. Gayle remembers hearing fighter jets fly over the river and felt a moment of hope that the military were coming to help and protect New York. A decade earlier, Gayle had lived through the turmoil in Los Angeles following riots provoked by the acquittal of the police officers accused of beating Rodney King, and she recalled most Angelenos' reaction was to avoid the topic and build barriers. With the 9/11 attacks, her first instinct—and that of many New Yorkers—was to volunteer to help in any way they could. She joined others at nearby Chelsea Market to volunteer, but volunteers soon realized they were not going to be helping survivors. However, they could still mobilize support. Equipped with a clipboard, Gayle began to record contact information, languages spoken, and experience with running heavy equipment for the

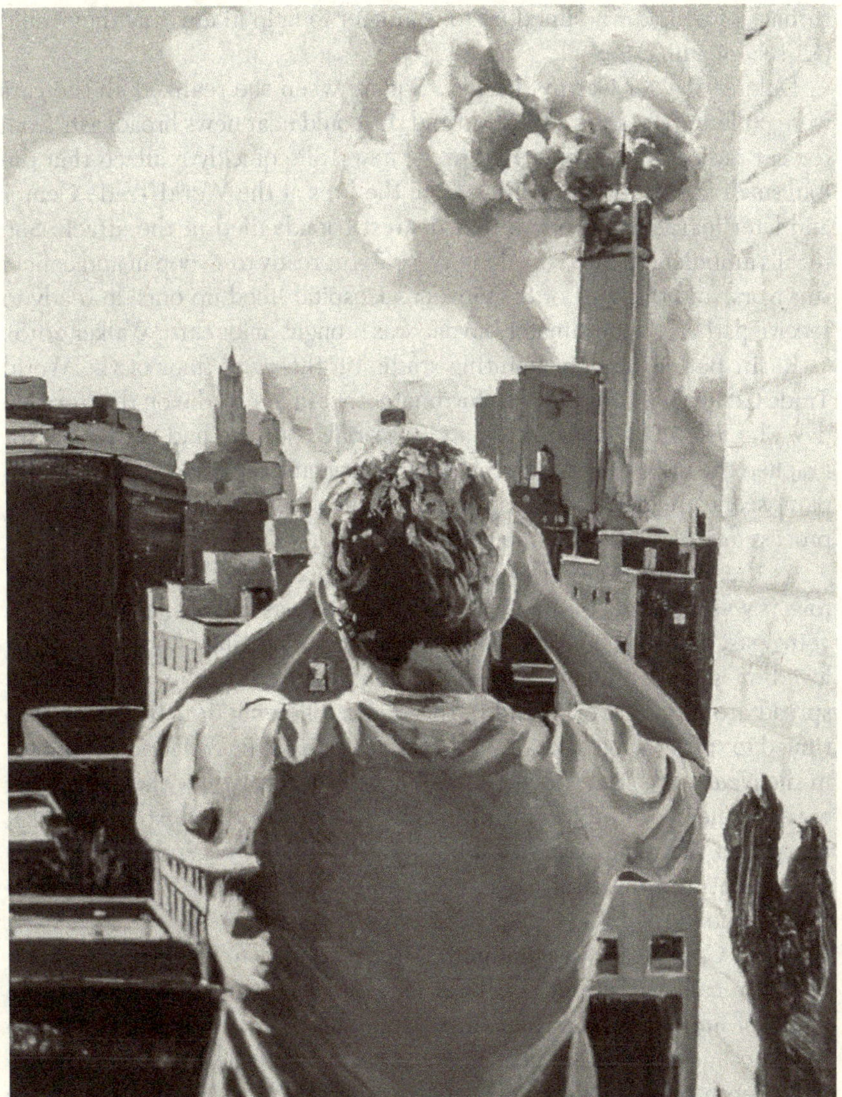

Figure 36. Painting of Hugh Seidman on Westbeth Roof during collapse of World Trade Center, September 11, 2021. Painting by Jayne Holsinger. Image Courtesy of Jayne Holsinger.

throngs of people who lined up to volunteer to help in any way they could (Kirschenbaum 2020).

Dolores Walker was in Sheridan Square when she realized all the cars were pulled to the side of the road and she could hear news broadcasts from the car radios as everyone tried to get news. She quickly realized that the foul smell in the air was coming from the fires at the World Trade Center and later learned that one of her dearest friends died in the attack. She recalls ambulances lined up along West Street ready to swoop in and collect survivors, and the staff of St. Vincent's Hospital lined up outside ready to receive patients, but ultimately no one was brought in for care (Walker 2018).

Karin Batten had her painting studio on the 92nd floor of the World Trade Center building and was fortunately not in her studio on that terrible day. She lost all of her artwork and materials, but she had earlier photographed the view from her perch in the tower, and later used that image to paint scenes related to the tower, which she said was part of her healing process and helped overcome her grief and fear (Batten 2018).

As the city responded to the attacks, the area in the vicinity of the towers was off limits for many weeks. The area was full of sounds of sirens going past day and night, and soon people began posting photos of missing loved ones at St. Vincent's Hospital. The images of the mangled towers spread around the world, and in the weeks following 9/11 the press continued to splash photos of New York City in crisis. One collection of photos in the *New York Times* included an image of a tiny lady with a face mask covering her nose and mouth to protect her from the dust and smoke, carrying a shopping bag with a bottle of OJ as she returned home. This photo captured my aunt Miriam as she walked back to Westbeth from D'Agostino's grocery.

David Greenspan was commuting to New Jersey to teach at Princeton, and he recalls each train ride back into the city gave new witness to the plume of smoke for many weeks after the attack. Like everyone living in the area, he had to show identification to get into the neighborhood below Fourteenth Street. The whole area remained covered in white dust for months following the towers' collapse, and many bought vacuums or air filters with HEPA filters to avoid breathing in the highly toxic dust (Greenspan 2019).

Within moments of the attacks, local and national authorities closed the skies to all commercial air traffic, forcing thousands of planes to land at the closest airport regardless of their destination. The city closed the major bridges and tunnels that connected the island of Manhattan with the rest of New York and New Jersey, and remained closed for days to commuter traffic. Subways and trains were temporarily halted, and thousands of people working in Lower Manhattan walked miles home across various bridges, including the Brooklyn Bridge, and the George Washington Bridge connecting to New Jersey. Slowly, over the succeeding days, transportation routes began to partially reopen, but some of NYC transit buses and subway trains had altered or curtailed service, often lasting a year or more.

A few weeks after the terrorist attacks, another plane crashed after takeoff from JFK airport, and Maya recalls having almost a worse reaction to this disaster—even though it was an aviation accident and not an attack. It was a trigger for many, bringing on mass PTSD and forcing them to recall the fear and sadness that engulfed the region in response to 9/11 (Ciarrocchi 2020).

Allison and Jayne recall the weeks following 9/11 as a time when New Yorkers were kinder and gentler to each other, as they dealt with the collective shock. Gayle recalls everyone trying to help each other in any way they could, and the tens of thousands of volunteers who wanted to serve. She noted in contrast when there were riots or earthquakes when she lived in Los Angeles, there was no collective response; instead it was everyone for themselves (Armstrong 2019; Holsinger 2018; Kirschenbaum 2020).

Nancy Gabor and her husband, Paul Binnerts, had been living in his native Holland, and Nancy's daughter had been staying in their Westbeth apartment, but the events of 9/11 were a catalyst for Nancy to return home to New York City. She realized that after a decade of living largely in Europe, she had no roots there comparable to her New York roots, and soon after the terrorist attacks, they moved back to Westbeth permanently. Fortunately, their success as a theater director and playwright respectively helped them gain jobs teaching at Princeton, so they could make the move and begin to reestablish their stateside networks (Gabor 2018).

Like millions of New Yorkers, the trauma of the 9/11 terrorist attacks haunted people of the Westbeth community for a long time. Several sought therapy in the aftermath to deal with their grief and fear. Others increasingly saw their building as a safe zone in a dangerous city, and retreated more into the comfort of the familiar. While this attack was truly heinous and cost thousands of lives, it also made New Yorkers kinder toward each other, and it became commonplace to ask acquaintances how they are, but with deeper significance. The whole world stood in sympathy with the people affected by the 9/11 attacks, and Milton Glaser's famous "I Heart NY" logo and the emblems for the hero fire fighters and police adorned garments across the globe as a symbol of their solidarity with New Yorkers. While no one would argue there was any positive outcome from this tragic day, the support for the people of the city was undeniable and brought many Westbeth residents closer with their neighbors—ultimately a preview of the response to the devastation of Hurricane Sandy years later.

Hurricane Sandy

The Atlantic hurricane season in 2012 was extremely active, and in October, a storm began to form that would ultimately sweep through the Caribbean and march up the eastern seaboard of the US, causing devastation in its path. Outer bands of Superstorm Sandy approached New York City on October 29, and the full impact of the storm arrived the following day. Torrential rain and high-velocity winds combined with tidal cycles resulted in massive disruption—from power outages and business closures to the flooding of tunnels connecting Manhattan to New Jersey and those used by the subway train system. The storm produced the highest storm surge ever recorded in the area, raising the level of the Hudson River to well above its banks.

The mayor and other city leaders tried to prepare for the storm's impact, by measures such as closing schools, opening evacuation shelters, and freezing many mass transit routes in an effort to encourage people to remain home and shelter. In areas close to the waterfront, these measures were grossly inadequate.

Magda Dajani tried to prepare for the storm and followed recommendations to move her car from the streets outside Westbeth to a location a few blocks further from the river. After several hours she reconsidered and moved her car home, reasoning she was a plucky New Yorker and had weathered other problems, but as she watched the water level rise, she decided it was best to heed the warnings and again moved her car away from the building. Soon, she realized how fortunate she was, as cars began floating down flooded Bethune Street. Jack Davidson was not so fortunate, as he had a brand-new car that he'd parked near Westbeth. Having not heard the warnings about possible flood risks, Jack's car was indeed submerged and never started again (M. Dajani 2020a; Davidson 2017).

Everyone was instructed to stock up on groceries and fill pots and pans with water in expectation of the power outages. My aunt Faye was visiting her older sisters who lived at Westbeth, and she walked to D'Agostino's market a block away to buy groceries. The manager of the store was barring entrance from anyone who wasn't one of the "regulars." But as she was Shami and Miriam's sister, the manager let Faye in to forage. She found the shelves completely bare and said people were standing in line to buy food that was actually rotten—everyone was in a panic and ill-prepared for a crisis (Pearl 2022).

Karen Santry was at work at the Fashion Institute of Technology in Midtown Manhattan when the storm began in earnest, and her students showed her live videos of the storm and urged her to go home. As she arrived at the Bethune Street entrance to the building, she stood with several of the building staff as they watched the swell of water rise over the highway at the end of the block. They saw an orange Volkswagen Beetle lifted by the water and disappear, and they feared the car had been swept out into the river, not knowing whether there was anyone inside. As the water surged toward them, they retreated into the building and Karen joined members of the staff as they ran through the ground floor hallways screaming at everyone to run upstairs. She recalls this as a terrifying moment, and that the subsequent stress caused from losing her life's work in the aftermath of the hurricane, combined with weeks of trudging up- and downstairs, she soon experienced heart problems necessitating a pacemaker, all of which she attributes to the hurricane (Santry 2019).

The impact of the storm on the Westbeth building was nothing short of catastrophic. The Hudson River rose from its usual level, many feet below West Street, and continued to rise until the riverside park, six lanes of the Westside Highway, and adjacent sidewalks were all submerged. Water streamed inland along the streets perpendicular to West Street, so Bank and Bethune Streets became raging streams as the river water flowed inland along them, submerging everything in its wake. The water flowed into the first level of Westbeth and filled the block-long and block-wide basement of the building—both by streaming to the lowest point through elevator shafts and stairwells and by actual breaches in the basement walls allowing water to flow in below grade. The building is built on century-old landfill and the water seeped through cracks in the basement walls (Fig. 37). Karen Santry described the water acting like a malevolent being, moving from space to space causing the most damage possible, as it coursed through the basement studios. The watermarks in the basement showed that the water level reached the ceiling of the laundry room, and on the Westside Highway there was a high watermark on the building's walls at the height of 14 feet (Santry 2019; Armstrong 2019).

The building had a long history of deferred maintenance, and much of the building's mechanical works were a far cry from modern building technology or in compliance with building codes. Heating came from a basement boiler which heated water that passed through radiators in each apartment, effectively being either on or off without the benefit of modern temperature

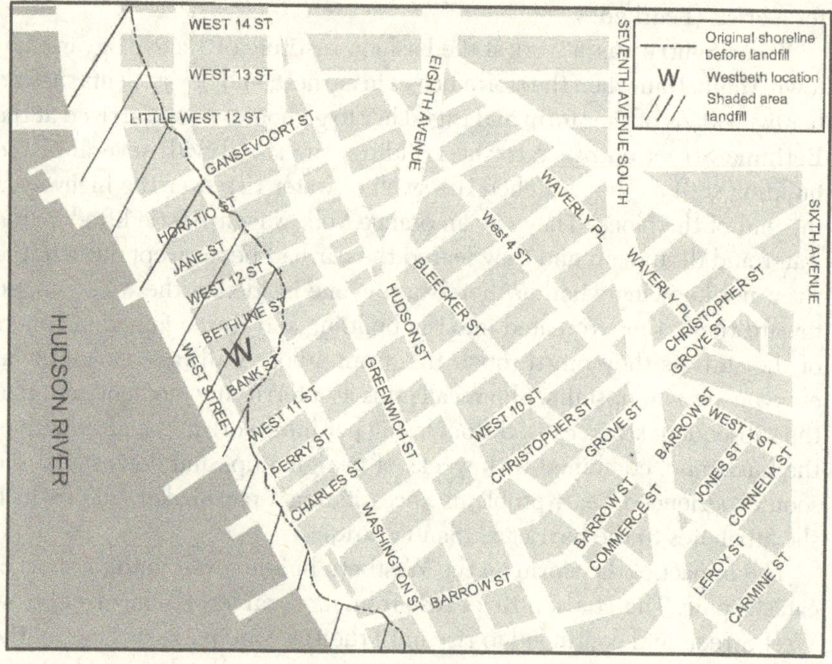

Figure 37. Map of Historic Hudson River coastline and landfill. Prepared by Mehran Pourakbar after image in *Maritime Mile*. Courtesy of Stuart Waldman.

regulating thermostats. The mechanical works that pumped water throughout the building, the apparatuses that worked the elevators, and the electrical transformer were all housed in the basement, and all were rendered inoperable when the basement flooded. Because the water was a mix of river water and salt water from the storm surge, copper telephone wiring was also corroded, after having remained submerged for weeks. Residents were left with no light, no power, no water, and no heat—just as the days grew colder and darker.

The only justice from the storm was that it affected rich and poor equally. Alison Armstrong recalls that the pricey faux brownstone apartments across Bethune Street had recently been completed, replacing the old ink factory. These newly-occupied apartments flooded, and giant dumpsters soon appeared where the furnishings from their fancy apartments were dumped. Bob Gruen and Elizabeth Gregory-Gruen had connections in the fashion industry, and knew designer Marc Jacobs who had moved into one of the new apartments across Bethune Street. They commented that all of the furniture from Jacobs's apartment also ended up in the trash and noted it was some of the largest furniture they had seen. Bob had another friend who lived nearby who prided himself on his extensive wine cellar, and when his basement also flooded, the labels on the bottles all came unglued and he was left with thousands of bottles of drinkable wine of unknown vintages (Armstrong 2019; Gregory-Gruen 2018; Gruen 2018).

As the storm buffeted the brick building, residents on the side facing the river could feel the impact of the high winds, especially as many apartments retained the original century-old wooden frame windows. Beverly Brodsky lived alone and feared her windows would shatter or blow out because of the intensity of the storm. She was very relieved when her friend Alison Armstrong, who lived on the opposite side of the building, invited her to ride out the storm in her apartment where the impact of the winds was much less (Brodsky 2019).

In the aftermath of the storm, everyone tried to figure out how to survive without light, power, or heat. The basement contained the boilers for the building-wide heating system, and without electricity no one had a functioning fridge or stove. Water pumps ceased working and soon there was no longer running water in the building, making it impossible to get a glass to drink or flush a toilet, much less have a shower. The hallways of the building are almost all devoid of any windows as they are in the interior of the building with apartments on both sides. The halls became pitch black caverns, and many had to walk a full block's length to get to a stairwell to exit. None of the elevators functioned, so everyone had the choice to remain marooned in their apartment or climb the many flights of stairs to enter or exit. The whole neighborhood was devoid of streetlights or traffic lights, and Bill Kennon describes walking through the neighborhood after the storm as the "scariest Halloween I ever experienced." Everyone was unnerved by the spooky air in the neighborhood. Bob Gruen said the only saving grace was that as the transit systems were not running, no one could get into the neighborhood to bother residents in the early days following the storm (Gruen 2018; Kennon 2019).

Soon after the storm passed, Westbeth began convening tenants' meetings in the Community Room, both for residents to check up on each other and identify the residents who were most vulnerable and in need of help. Susannah Kelly recalls telling others that she was fine, but she was concerned about her elderly mother who would never be able to navigate the nine flights of stairs to exit the building, and she expressed concern for the other frail and elderly tenants who remained isolated in their apartments without food or someone to look after them. The tenants formed teams of hall monitors to check on their elderly neighbors, and the building staff were heroic in their efforts to protect the vulnerable. Many of the staff temporarily moved into the building, camping out to be available almost 24/7 to help. The presence of the maintenance and security staff was critical, as unlike most residents who knew their immediate neighbors, but might not know people several floors away, the staff knew all of the community. Given the number of quite elderly residents, the staff is credited with ensuring there were no fatalities or critical injuries during the weeks of darkness and cold. No matter how capable the building staff or the city utilities were, replacing a 2,000-pound transformer in a waterlogged basement was no easy task, as Bob Gruen noted, you can't just go and buy a replacement at Home Depot (Kennon 2019; Greenspan 2019; Gruen 2018; Kelly 2020).

The restaurant across the street from the Bethune and Washington entrance rigged up a garden hose from their kitchen and ran it out the window so residents could use this to fill water containers to ensure they had water for their daily needs. Bob recalls the owner becoming very annoyed that people were using more water than he thought was fair, including to flush their toilets, and he said he would not provide water any longer. Bob sheepishly admits he became livid and said that of course everyone's hygiene depended upon being able to flush toilets, as well as having potable water, and he shouted at the man and threw money at him saying "take the money for the water." He noted that it was ironic that if the owner had not rescinded his generosity until a few hours later, he would have been heralded as a neighborhood savior—as soon after their shouting match, the city installed faucets on fire hydrants that allowed people to collect as much water as they needed (Gruen 2018).

Magda Dajani was able to drive into Brooklyn to a big box store and purchase a barbecue grill, and she set it up in the Westbeth courtyard. Soon neighbors joined her, taking food at risk of spoiling without refrigeration down to the courtyard to cook it before it went bad. She viewed the inconveniences philosophically and ultimately saw the post-Sandy days as a good life's lesson for her children, who were recruited to walk a block away to fetch water and to help carry containers of water up the stairs to assist older neighbors. Taking on the role of caregivers for nine elderly neighbors was in some ways a gratifying experience. In reflecting on that time, Magda said, "It wasn't terrible, not like people hanging on for their lives. It was an inconvenience, but it wasn't a tragedy" in large measure due to the collective ethos the storm engendered (M. Dajani 2020a).

Susannah Kelly shared Magda's view that the impact of the storm was not all bad, although she noted that the effect on her frail, elderly mother was much more negative. She had moved back to a split-level duplex apartment where she had grown up to help her brother care for their aging parents. Her mother was still living when the storm arrived, but she was not ambulatory and was stranded on one level of the apartment because their stairlift no longer functioned. Her mother was unable to get up the stairs to the level with the bathroom, so the Kelly siblings found a portable commode to help their mother. Facing this isolation and sense of imprisonment, her mother began having panic attacks, and Susannah feared leaving her for even a short while. She recalls the support her family received from one of the men new to the Westbeth staff, who supplied strong trash bags for disposing of the toilet waste, and who cleared the bags away, carrying them down pitch black hallways and nine flights of stairs without complaint (Kelly 2020).

Susannah said her brother and a friend who had a car ran around the city trying to find supplies to keep their own family and their neighbors safe. She recalls the generosity of friends and other New Yorkers as she used her iPad to send messages to people who offered to help. She recalls, "We had the most amazing experience, with the most extraordinarily generous people coming in and out of our home with food, blankets, cooking supplies—we saw the best of human behavior. For me, it was a wonderful experience." For about a year before the storm arrived, Susannah had been helping her mother Sonia Gechtoff—who had been a noted painter—work with NYU students to catalog and inventory Sonia's life's work. After the storm hit, the young women from NYU rode their bicycles to check on their elderly mentor and found Sonia and Susannah stranded. Soon they returned, one with a whole roasted chicken and flowers, the other with a dozen boiled eggs and gallon containers of water, and they climbed the nine flights of stairs to help take care of Sonia (Kelly 2020).

The outpouring of help for the refugees from the storm was almost overwhelming. Susannah recalls at one point there was almost too much being delivered and remembers that Vin Diesel arranged for meals to be prepared nearby at the Bus Stop Café and delivered door to door for those who remained in Westbeth. Jack Davidson's friend and fellow actor Cherry Jones also brought food to those marooned in their apartments. Jack Dowling remembers a knock on the door of his tenth-floor apartment and being greeted by a woman from the nearby Tea and Sympathy restaurant, who brought him a hot meat pie after days with no warm meals (Kelly 2020; Davidson 2017; Dowling 2018, 2020).

Many of the frailest eventually evacuated the building and went to stay with friends or family until at least the power and elevators were restored. Beverly Brodsky fortunately had family in New Jersey and Pennsylvania and went to stay with nephews for weeks following the storm, but she too suffered trauma at this time. Her 100-year-old mother died during the storm, and because of the flooding, she was unable to bury her mother in a timely fashion, which was extremely distressing. Jack Davidson left his apartment and stayed with his ex-wife and several friends in the weeks after the storm, ultimately ending up at a friend's place close to the Broadway theater where he was performing daily at the time. As New York City returned to normal, Jack needed housing within walking distance of the theater where he was performing, which was essential as there was no transportation functioning to get him to his work. Others such as Bob Gruen looked into moving to a hotel, reasoning that the cancellation of the New York City Marathon would mean there were lots of empty hotel rooms. Instead of finding deeply discounted rates in nearby hotels, perhaps in part as a gesture of goodwill toward displaced neighbors, nearby hotels doubled their rates and quoted him $600 to $700 per night (Brodsky 2019; Davidson 2017; Gruen 2018).

My two aunts were both fortunate that their younger sister Faye had been visiting from California, and she had friends who lived near Central Park and were unaffected by the storm. Soon after, the friends came to Westbeth and their children walked door to door all twelve floors of the building, handing out sandwiches to people stranded in their apartments. Faye was concerned about the welfare of her two older sisters whose health was not as robust as hers, and she recalls the terror of feeling her way along pitch-black stairwells as she moved from Shami's apartment on the ninth floor to Miriam's on the third floor to check on each sister. She said she thought they were all going to die. After a few days, her friend realized that it was untenable for the sisters to remain in the building, and she and her husband came and helped Shami navigate down nine floors, and Miriam three, and took them to her apartment uptown where they were safe and warm (Pearl 2022).

Susannah was able to enlist help from one of her mother's former students who lived in Westchester to move Sonia to a safer and more comfortable place. After reaching out to ask for help, Sonia's student arrived within twenty minutes with her car, and Susannah's brother and his friend stood on either side of Sonia and guided her down the dark stairwell for nine floors. Sonia couldn't wait to escape the building where she had been having panic attacks in the cold and dark, and she happily spent the next couple weeks in a guest room all to herself, where she was able to enjoy a wood-burning fireplace and listen to classical music while warm and safe, watching as it snowed outside (Kelly 2020).

Once Sonia was safely relocated, Susannah returned to her Buddhist community center where she found solace with chanting. At the event one person asked if anyone was still without electricity and she raised her hand, and a friend immediately invited her to her home and prepared lunch for her while Susannah was able to enjoy a long, hot shower. The weeks following the storm engendered a great deal of kindness.

Others might not share Magda and Susannah's view that the impact of the storm fell short of a tragedy, especially the visual artists who had studios in the basement with their life's work. Jayne Holsinger, Karen Santry, David Seccombe, and Charlie Seplowin were among those who lost decades worth of their paintings and sculptures. Acquiring basement studio space required patience and strategy, despite the terrible lighting and ventilation, most visual artists did not want the studios in the I building that required taking stairs. Karen had multiple spaces in the basement including some niches that were like catacombs or bunkers, and she noted that some studios were almost like secret vaults with obscure entrances. Her first space had previously been used by a sculptor, and she was left with mountains of chunks of marble that took her a long time to clear out. She needed multiple small spaces in the basement as she had a large body of work, and her artwork pieces were very large. Just before the storm she had acquired additional studio space on the top floor of the I building, which required walking up three flights of stairs with her pieces, and it was not climate controlled, so most other artists rejected this space as unlivable. Fortunately, she had just moved several huge pieces—paintings on plywood cutouts of figures dressed in Kabuki theater costumes, each of which stood eight or nine feet tall—to this new upstairs space (Fig. 38) (Santry 2019).

The artists were initially barred from entering the basement to try to retrieve their work as it was hazardous even when the water was gone, but several of them ventured into the space despite the prohibition. As pieces were recovered, many were laid out on the ground in the Bank Street courtyard to dry, along with other items like bicycles, and the artists stretched police tape around the items to signal they were off limits. This didn't dissuade thieves, who stole items from the courtyard, including Karen's models of horses which were prepared for the Lord of the Rings films. Both the damage to their work and the theft of pieces were a very low moment for all of those affected, and several recall this resulting in depression and anxiety (Santry 2019).

Jayne recalls that some curators from city museums visited them at Westbeth to give them advice about how to dry out and clean their work,

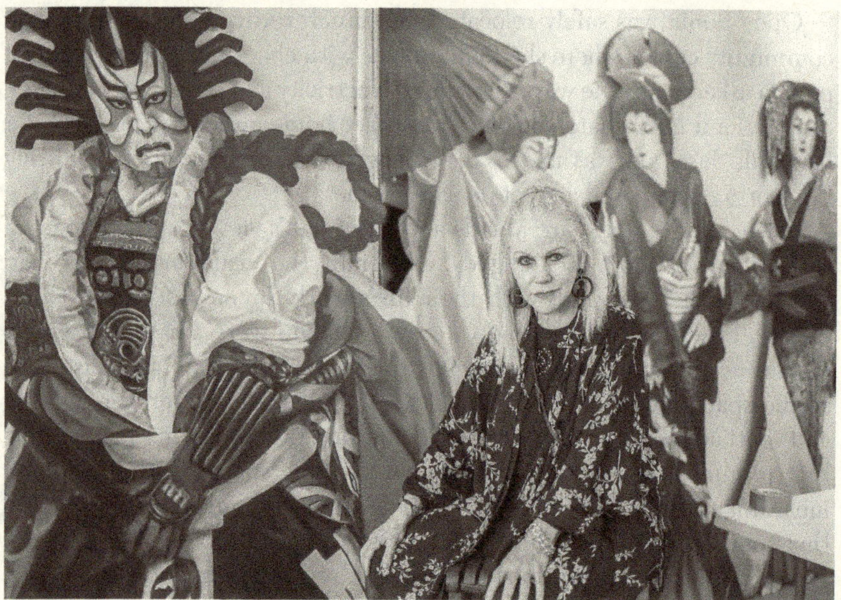

Figure 38. Karen Santry in her Studio with Kabuki Pieces. Image Courtesy of Tom Conelly.

which had been submerged for days in filthy brackish water. Her studio had been on the river side of the basement and everything was very damaged. As she slowly recovered pieces she removed the canvases from their frames, and with funding from a grant, later tried to restretch the paintings onto new frames. She took photographs of the mess, which helped her secure grants to restore what could be restored, but she acknowledges that so much was lost that it would be impossible for her to ever stage a retrospective of her work. She describes living through this experience as feeling like a war zone, but paused and said as a pacifist former Mennonite, she is grateful she never had to live through a real war (Santry 2019; Holsinger 2018; Seplowin 2019).

Charlie Seplowin also lost his life's work from his basement studio, and he said the loss of this work was both one of the worst and one of the best experiences of his life. He was devastated when his art was destroyed, and felt for a long time that he simply couldn't go on as an artist as every piece he'd retained was lost in the flood. But after some time, he felt unburdened and liberated, as he began to rethink how he did art and what he would produce. He has since given up his metal cast pieces and now uses 3D printers to carve his three dimensional pieces with intricate, interlocking

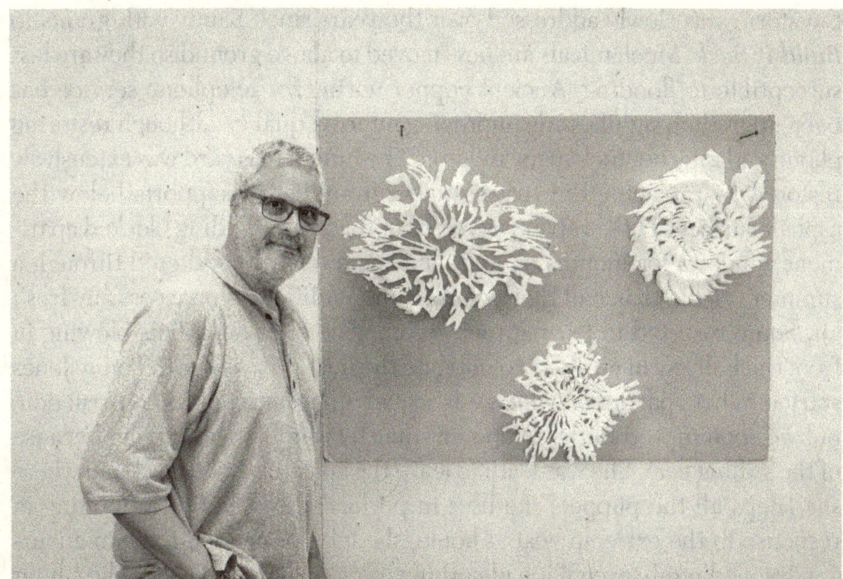

Figure 39. Charlie Seplowin and his sculpture. Image courtesy of Tom Conelly.

geometrical pieces, and he notes this would not have happened had he not lost his entire studio (Fig. 39) (Seplowin 2019).

Sherry Lane remained in her apartment for the first couple of days after the storm but soon realized the conditions were bad and left to stay with a friend. She returned on November 9, her birthday, because she had already made plans to host a small celebration with friends at a nearby restaurant on Hudson Street. She had called the restaurant to be reassured they were open and functioning, and came home to her apartment to change her clothes before the party and found the space ice cold. When she returned later that evening, she could feel the pipes leading to the radiator were exuding a little warmth, which meant the boiler was back on line and would slowly bring heat throughout the building. But given the size of the building and the way the mass of concrete, steel, and brick retained the cold, it was a long time before space felt warm (Lane 2019).

Ultimately, the aftermath of the storm forced the building to deal with some of the consequences of the years of deferred maintenance. The financial footing of the building has long been precarious, as the rent stabilized apartments never generated the revenue stream realistically needed to maintain—much less upgrade—a century-old building. The damage from the storm was slowly addressed over the years since Sandy with grants to *Build It Back*. Mechanicals are now moved to above ground so they are less susceptible to flooding. Ancient copper wiring for telephone service has been upgraded, significantly improving internet quality, although restoring phone and internet took many months. The inner courtyard was extensively restored by replacing the rusting underground steel supports below the asphalt surface. These repairs were disruptive as scaffolding blocked apartment windows for months on end, and some tenants sweltered through a summer unable to install their window air conditioners or access any fresh air. Some resorted to leaving their doors wide open with fans blowing in from the hallway in an effort to mitigate the heat. My visit with Penny Jones started in her apartment, which was sealed up because of the construction, but we soon moved to the temporary quarters she was occupying because of the stifling heat. She was loath to leave the apartment she loves and where she keeps all the puppets she uses in performances, but after fainting in response to the extreme heat at home, she felt she needed to be in an air-conditioned room, even if it had nothing more than a simple cot. The center core of the building was sealed off for several years, and depending upon what space one wished to access, getting from point A to point B sometimes necessitated exiting the building and walking around the block to enter on the opposite side. The repairs were disruptive, but essential to protect the building from future damage and to make the space safe for habitation (Armstrong 2019; Jones 2019).

Playwright Paul Binnerts wrote a play about Hurricane Sandy's visit and impact called *Lost and Found*. Actor Jack Davidson served as narrator and the cast included Paul, and fellow actors Nancy Gabor, and Sandy Kingsbury. Binnerts's play asks the question about how one regains a sense of self after losing everything. The eight performances in Westbeth brought the cast and audience together, as they traveled throughout the building. Beginning in the Westbeth Gallery at street level, the roving theater piece traveled around the building including parts of the performance in apartments, in the basement, and the community room, before returning to the Gallery for the conclusion. For the performers and participants, this immersive piece was part theater, part therapy (Davidson 2017; Binnerts 2018).

Pandemic

The spring of 2020 upended lives across the world with the emergence of the COVID-19 virus, and New York City was one of the places hardest hit. The daily news was full of terrifying accounts of this mysterious new virus that felled strong young people and left others entirely asymptomatic but capable of transmitting the disease. Commerce and industry slammed on the brakes, and within days, people ceased commuting to work, and work and schooling gave new meaning to the word "zoom." New York went into lockdown, and suddenly trains and buses that were usually packed to the gills were empty. Restaurants, schools, and churches closed their doors. The governor gave daily updates about the spread of the virus and efforts being taken to mitigate the impact and support the besieged medical systems. People lined up outside and at their windows to give noisy tributes to the first responders and medical professionals who were helping those felled by the disease. At the outset of the pandemic, few understood how transformative the disease would be on so-called normal life, and few comprehended how enduring the pandemic.

Ellen Salpeter had recently accepted the position as executive director at Westbeth when the pandemic hit. While she was prepared to deal with fundraising for the arts and challenges of managing the building, staff, governing structure, and residents, no one could have been prepared for how best to manage a pandemic. Partnering with the Westbeth Artist Resident's Council (WARC) and its longtime president George Cominskie, Westbeth quickly formulated protocols intended to minimize risk and protect the most vulnerable. The first step was to go into lockdown mode, well before the rest of the city or other parts of the nation, and to restrict access to the building and interactions in person. Westbeth implemented a mask mandate, and restricted elevators to one person or household at a time. All deliveries had to be left at the front reception area. Volunteer floor captains checked on vulnerable elderly and brought them deliveries of food and mail so they did not have to venture out. Spaces were disinfected, and any urgently needed repairs were done by maintenance staff wearing full hazmat suits. As with the aftermath of the hurricane, some staff moved into the building so they would not have to engage in risky behavior like riding mass transit to commute to and from work. Residents who returned home after being away from the building were required to quarantine in their apartments. Ellen recalls the biggest challenge was getting everyone to trust the process and decision making about rules to keep everyone safe, and most residents were happy to comply as the strict protocols gave comfort that measures were in place (Salpeter 2020).

Westbeth had been working on plans for a series of celebrations to commemorate the 50th anniversary since the founding of the community, but the plans for in-person events were soon scrapped. While the big celebrations had to be cancelled, virtual events were established, and the photo exhibit that had been planned was modified. Photographer Frankie Alduino had captured some magical images of the most senior members of the community, and instead of small prints shown on a gallery wall, selections of Frankie's photos were blown up to be one story high and adorned exterior spaces around the building so they were visible to passersby. WARC Literary Chair Terry Stoller had the idea to commission writing by current and past residents of the building, and the Westbeth Chronicles published short essays and recollections to capture memories and the collective history of the community.

The pandemic limited options for some residents but created new ones for others. Photographer David Plakke's commercial commissions temporarily evaporated, but he was moved by the eerily empty streets of the city (Fig. 40). His documentation of the streets devoid of vehicles or people look like a post-apocalyptic horror movie, but his images of people giving tribute to the hospital staffers is heartwarming. He enlisted a dancer friend to pose for stunning photos, en pointe, leaping across empty New York City streets (Plakke 2018).

Susannah Kelly recalled going for a walk in the empty streets, which were normally swarming with tourists. The fancy stores in the Meatpacking District nearby, the Whitney Museum, and all along Gansevoort Street the building fronts were boarded up with plywood sheets, which were soon embellished with murals and tagged with graffiti. She commented that New Yorkers are always mindful of personal space, even trying to avert gazes in crowded subways where people are packed in, and in the pandemic, the equivalent of this was to continue to wear masks outdoors, even when riding a bike along the river, or sitting alone at the park. Places that failed to enforce the mask mandates, or permitted crowded gatherings soon found the city's response, such as restaurants that failed to comply having a temporary suspension of their liquor license (Kelly 2020).

Gayle Kirschenbaum developed a habit of trying to get fresh air by taking a snack and a bike ride early in the morning, and filming Facebook live posts. One morning she saw the US Naval hospital ship *Comfort* sail up the Hudson to moor a few blocks away. Although the impact of the help the hospital ships were able to render was ultimately controversial, the sight of the ship was buoying for Gayle and many New Yorkers (Kirschenbaum 2020).

Miraculously, none of the deaths that occurred in the first months of the pandemic were attributable to COVID-19, including the death of my last surviving aunt. Shami died at the end of March 2020 after a long illness, and her care during the final weeks of her life was greatly complicated by the virus, as moving her to a hospital was an impossible prospect. Two

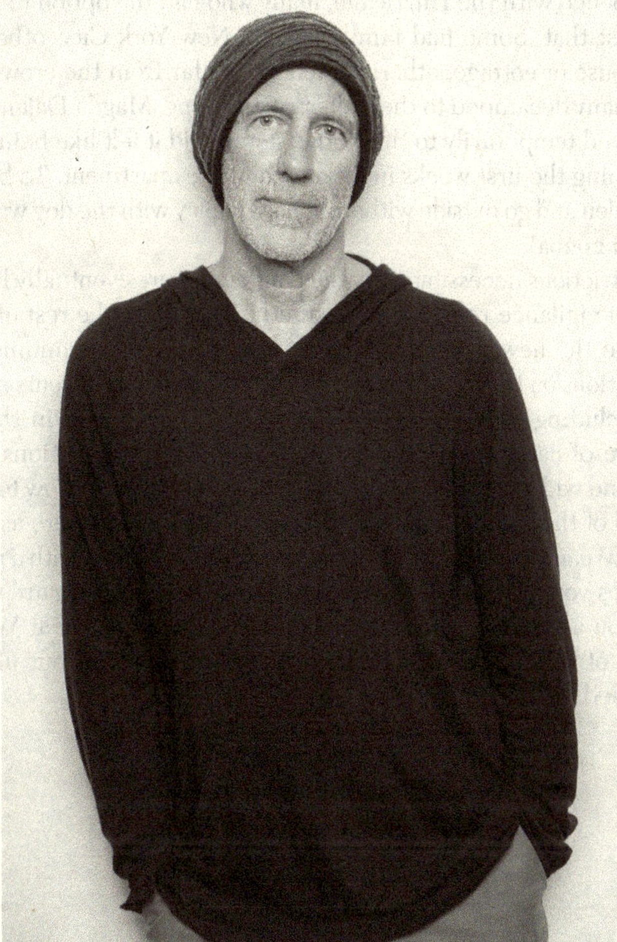

Figure 40. David Plakke. Self-Portrait Courtesy of David Plakke.

residents who had been earlier moved to rehab centers died of COVID, but the others who succumbed in the early months of the pandemic died of natural causes.

The residents remained very fearful of the spread of the virus but comforted knowing that all measures that might help prevent the spread of the disease were rigorously implemented. Maya said, "I feel safe, there are very clear protocols established, there is no ambiguity," which was a sentiment echoed by many (Ciarrocchi 2020).

As happened with the Hurricane, many who had the option to leave the city did just that. Some had family outside New York City, others had a country house or cottage, others rented spaces far from the crowds of the city, and many decamped to their alternate housing. Magda Dajani and her family moved temporarily to the Midwest and said it felt like being reborn after spending the first weeks in lockdown in the apartment. To be able to grow a garden and go outside without a mask to play with the dog was freeing (M. Dajani 2020a).

The restrictions necessitated by the pandemic were eventually lifted one by one, but vigilance remains at Westbeth. Long after the rest of the city returned to the new normal, in-person events in the Community Room had restrictions on the numbers that can attend, and many events remained virtual, including exercise classes that were formerly held in the space. Each surge of cases, including in 2022, long after vaccinations became available and widespread, is met with new reminders about how to staunch the spread of the virus. Posters in the elevators and elsewhere ask people to "Kindly Wear a Mask" in all public spaces in the building, with a reminder "Sometimes you have to be kind to others, not because they are nice, but because you are." With each successive disaster or tragedy at Westbeth, the bonds of community and collective action are tested but ultimately strengthened.

8

The Village

For most of my life, the Westbeth building was a place I would visit to see my aunts and uncle, who were long-term residents. In the course of these visits, I met a few other residents, sharing lunch with Christina Maile at Aunt Molly's favorite local greasy spoon diner, or having Shami take me on the "tour" of Barton Lidice Beneš's exotic apartment after he mixed up a batch of apple martinis. I commiserated with Molly when her dear friend Sally Gross's cancer returned, and I was so grateful to Halina Warren who helped clear out Molly's apartment after her death. I enjoyed sitting in Shami's Wednesday morning Around the Table writing circle and hearing Karen, Joyce, Dawn, Diane, and Christina read their compositions. When Shami had her terrible accident and spent many months in St. Vincent's hospital, I became close to her dearest friends Karen Ludwig and Suzanne Little, who hovered over her like guardian angels during her long hospitalization. When Shami died, her ashes were buried at the base of a tree, joining those of her beloved brother Joe, at Karen's upstate lake house. I came to love George Cominskie (known in our family as Georgeous) and his husband, John Turner, who have hearts of gold and look after many of the frail and elderly residents, making daily visits to see how they are faring. These people comprise a small part of the village of Westbeth.

My career has been spent in villages, and as a cultural anthropologist, I have lived for long periods in small communities in the Philippines and Kenya and worked in other villages throughout Africa. In many ways, Westbeth is a vertical version of the village life that is familiar to me. The correspondence between Westbeth and the archetypical village isn't an observation unique to me. My photographer friend Frankie Alduino, who captured gorgeous portraits of some of Westbeth's elders, published his work in *Vertical Village*, a title suggested to him by Westbeth resident Alison Armstrong. When I talked with actor Josh Hamilton, who grew up at Westbeth, he said his mother Sandra Kingsbury often comments that she is taking meals to a neighbor or helping another in some way as she lovingly did for my aunt Molly in her final days. Noting that everyone he knew as a child is now elderly, he said the pool of residents effectively all become a hospice care team, encircling the frail to allow them to remain at home, surrounded by caring friends, preserving their dignity. "They are part of a community that takes care of each other. This is unheard of in a big city. It's something, from an anthropological view. It happens in all villages, where people get old and you have a support system. It feels like Westbeth is this anomaly in that it is an incredibly caring community that really takes care of its own. In most of New York, people grow old alone, and it's lonely" (Hamilton 2020). Penny Jones said living at Westbeth is like permanently being in a college dormitory; within this enormous city is a small place where "you can find friends and camaraderie and a network, and it keeps you young. You can get away from the great big city out there if you want to, Westbeth is a lifeboat" (Jones 2019).

Late Bloomers

When Westbeth was first conceived, the planners assumed that most of the first-generation of artists would stay at Westbeth for five years until they made it big and then move on, making room for the next generation to replicate the cycle. But this didn't come to pass, and many of the first generation remained in their apartments for the rest of their lives. Yet without the financial stability that Westbeth afforded, many of the now-celebrated artists would not have had the freedom to produce work that has gained praise and recognition in their advanced years. Perhaps with the exception of some performing artists, very few artists are celebrated in their youth. Rather, it is their body of work that establishes their reputations.

Juanita McNeely's paintings and prints have graphic and visceral depictions of women's bodies and functions, and for decades galleries would not exhibit her works because of the often disturbing imagery. Art critic Deborah Solomon noted that museums are replete with angelic images of mothers holding dimpled babies, but she added "For ninety years of its existence, the Whitney Museum of American Art did not own a single painting that explicitly deals with abortion. But that has changed. The museum recently purchased Juanita McNeeley's "Is It Real? Yes It Is!" (1969), a mural-sized painting that recounts, in a fragmented narrative spanning nine separate panels, her harrowing experience of having an abortion in the early '6os, when the procedure was illegal. Her "Is It Real? Yes It Is!" adopts an angled, expressionist style to chronicle a medical emergency that left her bleeding profusely and in critical condition before she found a doctor willing to disregard the law and perform an abortion that she believes saved her life." Although this important piece was produced about the time that McNeeley moved into Westbeth as a young woman, it was not purchased until 2022 when she was 86, shortly before her death, after the Supreme Court struck down abortion rights. This significant museum sale came at a time when Juanita was enjoying growing recognition, with shows in major museums and galleries (Solomon 2022).

In the 2022 Whitney Museum Biennale, one of the most prestigious contemporary art juried shows in the world, Veronica Ryan was one of the sixty-three artists from around the world included in the show—achieving global recognition at the age when most people retire. She has had numerous solo shows in museums and galleries over the past few years in Europe and the US, and as a British citizen she was awarded the OBE by Queen Elizabeth in 2021. Soon after, she won the Turner Prize for contemporary art, the oldest person to receive this prestigious international award.

Lorraine O'Grady is an essayist, novelist, and conceptual performance artist who first gained recognition by arriving at art openings dressed as *Mademoiselle Bourgeois Noir*, wearing a "gown" made of layers of long, elbow length white gloves that might have been worn by debutantes. Her work continued to challenge conventions in art and the racism common in the world of contemporary art and galleries, and she continues to be a working artist as she approaches age 90. Her body of work was highlighted in a 2021 exhibit at the Brooklyn Museum and, in 2022, featured in a lengthy article in the *New Yorker* magazine, as another example of a Westbeth artist achieving well-deserved recognition late in life (St. Felix 2022).

Jazz and blues singer Bobby Harden was a journeyman musician since his arrival in New York City decades ago. Now advancing in years, he recently released a new album of original music in 2023 with his band the Bountiful Saints (Fig. 41). The new work has rave reviews and is likely to eclipse his earlier recordings (Plakke).

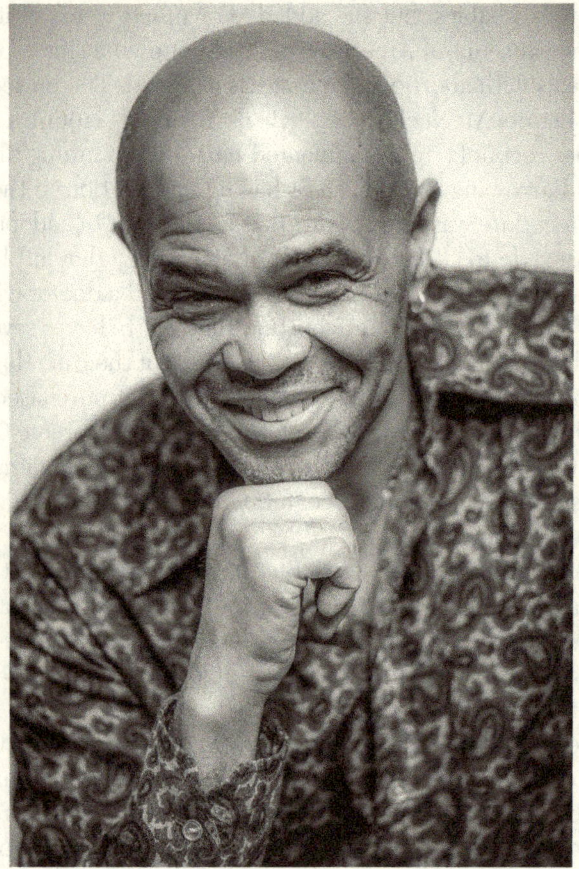

Figure 41. Singer Bobby Harden. tribesnyc Project. Image Courtesy of David Plakke.

Similarly, dancer Vija Vetra, now 101 years old, remains vibrant. To celebrate her 90th birthday and her seventieth year on the stage, she danced her Jubilee performance in her native Latvia (Fig. 42). Like a number of the early residents, she was a penniless refugee after World War II and spent several years in a displaced persons camp before relocating to Australia. After years of touring on five continents, she settled in New York City and had a full career as a dancer and choreographer (Plakke).

Like these noted artists, many of Westbeth's residents waited years to gain recognition. Photographer Bob Gruen's memoire about his lifetime embedded in rock and roll was published when he was in his mid-70s, and poet Ed Field was in his 90s when his early poem was made into a

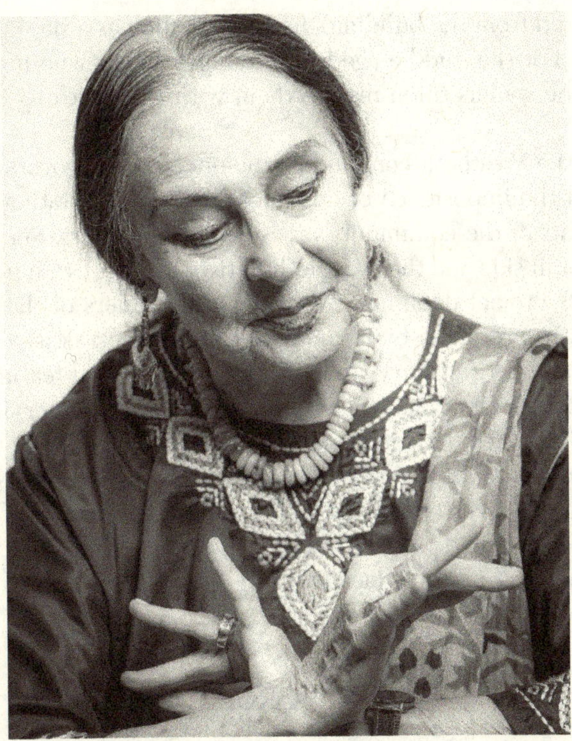

Figure 42. Dancer Vija Vetra. tribesnyc Project. Image Courtesy of David Plakke.

prize-winning animated documentary, and he published his most recent 2021 book at age 97. Classical music composer and pianist David Del Tredici won a Pulitzer Prize in 1980 for his compositions but regained visibility as a composer whose works were shaped by and reference his gay identity with the 50th anniversary of the Gay Pride movement when he was 83. Dancer and choreographer Edith Stephan took up filmmaking in her 80s when unable to dance any longer and continued to work on short films about her perception of the world well into her 90s.

Performer/puppeteers Ralph Lee and Penny Jones were prominently featured in a major exhibit at the Museum of the City of New York in 2022 when they were both well beyond 80 years of age. All of these artists labored in near obscurity in the first decades of Westbeth's existence at the time when the founders expected them to launch. Yet these people and many of their peers were driven to continue to produce their art by a passion for their work, and perhaps in part by decades of breathing the creative ozone that stemmed from the building's first incarnation as a site for innovations in science. For the middle-aged and younger artists who now live in the building, the seniors often inspire them with their lifelong dedication to their craft.

Within the Westbeth community, members of the governance council recognized the importance of documenting and celebrating the lifetime achievements of the community's most senior members. Spearheaded by George Cominskie and the Westbeth Artists Resident's Council (WARC), the ICONS Project documents the illustrious elders of the community. The films are produced by filmmaker Ted Timreck assisted by Frankie Alduino, Sandra Kingsbury, and Christina Maile, and feature the Chair of the Literary Arts Committee, Dr. Terry Stoller, interviewing these artists, interspersed with still images from throughout their careers. The team has now produced more than a dozen documentary films available to view through the Westbeth website. These moving portraits of these artists capture their spirit and passion, and all are timely as both 102-year-old Edith Stephan and 90-something Jack Dowling have passed away since the films were made.

NORC

Actor Jack Davidson first introduced me to the term *NORC*—a naturally occurring retirement community. Jack said when Westbeth was first envisioned and occupied, no one imagined staying for the rest of their lives in the community—they all expected to get rich and famous, or at least famous, and move on and up—but the financial and logistical realities, combined with the strong sense of community, made staying at Westbeth irresistible and inevitable. I am amused every time I see Jack, who has an illustrious resume acting on stage, film, and television, and now appears in a laundry product commercial as the rumpled grandpa alongside his rumpled spouse, raising his grandson's eyebrows as he suspects they were up to hanky-panky in the linen closet. Jack is a perfect example of the Westbeth NORC experience—older, with knees that might not work so well and in need of support—but still vital, active, creating his art, and independent at 86 (J. Davidson 2017).

Jack Dowling said that Westbeth is more of a family than it was twenty years ago, in part because many have served in roles that benefit the whole community, such as Gallery Director, or a position on WARC. The shared governance and responsibilities led to collaborations and an ethos for everyone to take care of each other. Jack noted there have been factions and friction, one faction of visual artists wanted to break off from the gallery and establish their own exhibit space—much like the *Salon des Refusé*, but that eventually blew over. Jack recalled with amusement a painter whose work he included in one of the gallery shows, and she became enraged with him and demanded that her work be moved because he had hung it next to work by another woman she accused of "trying to seduce my husband"— such are the dramas in villages. Yet when this woman was frail and dying, neighbors visited and cared for her daily in her Westbeth home (Dowling 2018, 2020).

David Greenspan and Bill Kennon are regularly summoned to neighbors' apartments when someone has fallen and can't get up without assistance, and they recalled the young people in the building carrying containers of water to their stranded neighbors for weeks following Hurricane Sandy. Jayne Holsinger and others commented that the presence of so many people with needs related to their aging resulted in the building hiring a social worker whose office is on the ground floor, and she assists many people with building a safety net around them, and helps find options for people who need increased levels of care due to dementia or severe physical limitations. A visiting nurse checks on elderly residents and can perform assessments about their physical and medical needs. This ensured that actress Pawnee Sills, conceptual artist Helène Aylon, and dancer Edith Stephan were moved to senior care facilities when needed, such as the nursing home run by the actors' guild. The social worker ensured that more than a dozen elders with dementia and without family became wards of adult protective services and had aides to ensure they were safe and not exploited while vulnerable. Christina Maile welled up with tears as she talked about a neighbor who had to be involuntarily committed due to dementia after a lifetime of mental illness yet was an astoundingly productive painter. She wondered how and if his work can still be exhibited when he lost touch with reality and noted that "many people in Westbeth have had—maybe mental problems is too strong of a word—but they have always been eccentric characters, and having this unusual character is the source of some of their creativity." The WARC board secured grants and funding for these services, activities such as seated yoga classes to keep seniors flexible, and weekly singing groups. Ellen Salpeter, who briefly served as Westbeth's executive director, commented that the younger residents recognize the challenges of the indignities of aging and loss of autonomy for their elders, and many feel compelled to pay it forward and be part of the social safety net for the elderly (Greenspan 2019; Holsinger 2018; Maile 2017; Salpeter 2020).

The most visceral symbol of Westbeth as a NORC is something that several dubbed the Death Board (Fig. 43). In the space where everyone comes to retrieve their mail is a notice board where staff posts the names of the recently deceased, and the Westbeth website includes full obituaries for residents. These obituaries are sometimes the only way that younger residents learn that the wizened lady who shuffled to the elevator with her walker was once a famous dancer, or a nonverbal old man was once an *avant garde* painter who challenged conventions. Gayle Kirschenbaum commented that witnessing so many people who have died has affected her deeply. She notes, "When I got to know them, they were already little old people. Like my mother says about living in Florida, it is God's waiting room. And then when they die, there is a huge spread in the *New York Times*, and I had no idea of their stature. I found out that one deceased neighbor was a famous feminist painter. Sometimes I fear going to get my mail because I'll learn about another who has passed." Others joked that they steered clear of the board for fear they would see their own name. Octogenarian filmmaker and writer Lily Rivlin admitted that she sometimes avoided looking at the infamous board, as nearly every week someone has died. Lily tries to avoid confronting her own mortality and refuses to write a will—but she did acknowledge with pride that her papers and work will eventually end up in an archive at Brandeis University. Lucille Rhodes said that the best thing about her life at Westbeth was the diversity of people who live there—diverse in ethnicity, religion, and imbued with a strong ethos of tolerance. She said the mix of people includes difficult people and those with mental illness who might not be tolerated in other places, but in Westbeth, they can be part of the community, in part because of "people like George Cominiskie; you couldn't pay for someone who has that much generosity and has respect from people across the building," as he coordinates neighbors taking care of each other (Kirschenbaum 2020; Rhodes 2019; Rivlin 2018).

The passing of Westbeth's elders has generated an important legacy for those who remain. When people die and their families claim what they want to keep from their elders' apartments, volunteers at Westbeth clear out everything else and many of the bits and pieces, old artworks, clothing, and ephemera end up in the building's basement where a twice annual flea market is held. Items are organized and marketed by volunteers, and it has now become a famous neighborhood event visited by thousands. The flea market generates substantial revenue that is allocated to building beautification, such as landscaping the exterior, and permits the village of Westbeth to help others in need with large donations to causes they collectively champion, such as fighting hunger.

Figure 43. Infamous Memorial Board in Westbeth mailroom. Image Courtesy of Tom Conelly.

Old People, Old Building

Just as the half-century of life at Westbeth has aged the people, so too, has the building weathered. Some of the challenges of maintaining a building over 100 years old are expected, others due to catastrophes such as Hurricane Sandy, and yet others attributable to the checkered history of building management. The building has had both a management team and the Westbeth Corporation has had a Board of Directors—and over the past decades there have been examples of both capable and inept players in the management staff and the Board. Adam Davidson is a renowned writer on the world of finance, and he is one of the people who grew up at Westbeth. Adam now serves on the Executive Board and recalls times when the board was wildly out of touch with the mission of Westbeth. When he first joined the board, there had been a coup of sorts that pushed three building residents off the governance board—Adam's father Jack, Christina Maile, and George Cominskie. He was proposed by residents concerned about the lack of representation of their voices as a candidate for the board, and because of his expertise in finance, he was seen as a viable candidate by the then-current Board members who were in the real estate and finance industries. He was soon alarmed at the ways the board members talked about the residents and the contempt they showed for their welfare:

> The board became a real estate board, not an arts board, and it's a self-perpetuating entity so the board voted in others with similar views. Most of the members were these real estate guys who all knew each other, and many of them had served on the governing board that nearly destroyed Cooper Union. There are huge articles about it, their decisions were tone deaf, stupid, self-destructive, idiotic, and much of that board became the board of Westbeth. This destructive board was locked in amber for twenty years. These guys had open contempt for the tenants, they would say things like "the tenants are not stakeholders and we don't need to care about them," they were really nasty. They had a whole plan to try to convert some of Westbeth into luxury housing, to make money to fix the rest of the building, to sell off a quarter of Westbeth to a developer to build a separate high-rise tower with a separate entrance.

> At first, I tried to be respectful, but eventually I would go to these meetings and just scream my head off; it got ugly. When they kept pushing the idea of selling off part of Westbeth, I said the building is going to be circled by old activists in wheelchairs—they're just dying

for something like this. And there was no way the city council was going to allow this. At one meeting, they discussed an incident when the building manager pushed a tenant and the police were called. The board was calmly discussing how they would tell him not to push tenants instead of firing him immediately. I never heard a good thing about him, and the whole time he was manager there were no records of what was going on in the building. As a business reporter who has covered corruption, I know that when someone has autonomy and no one is checking, there is going to be corruption.

I made a decision; I'm here to protect the people who live here now. I'd love also for Westbeth to have a deeper purpose in the world, but I'm not going to be part of kicking everyone out or buying them off to generate two billion dollars for a real estate development. (A. Davidson 2020)

Eventually the real estate–oriented board members were removed or cycled off, and today the board is much more representative of the tenants' interests and the greater arts world of New York City. Yet the challenges of addressing the real needs of the building remained, as the original industrial building was never intended to be residential space. There have long been discussions among both residents and the governing bodies about expanding the commercial spaces to generate revenue, such as having a restaurant, a café, performance venues, and possibly even a boutique hotel, but it is unclear if any of these could generate the $50 million needed to shore up the building without even tackling any improvements or modernization that would likely cost an additional $50 million. The annual budget for the building operations is about $8 million, which in the tony real estate world of Manhattan is paltry, less than the cost of a single apartment in an adjacent building. With most apartments rent stabilized, the opportunity to greatly increase revenue from rent is unfeasible.

Complicating matters, the turnover of apartments is very slow. According to former director Ellen Salpeter, the financial prospects for the building are complex. The laws that protect tenants' rights results in apartments being retained for decades in perpetuity, as residents' children often remain and take over their parent's apartment when the elders die, and rent stabilization prevents raising rents substantially to the current market value. She questioned the viability of what essentially amounted to a lifetime guaranteed subsidy for residents who are allocated an apartment, especially as she noted that gaining entrance to Westbeth does not guarantee a lifetime of artistic innovation and productivity. She commented with frustration, "There are some who have spent the past fifty years painting the same painting" (Salpeter 2020). Yet for every artist whose productivity stagnated, there are many examples of residents who remain productive until the end of their lives.

Over the previous five years, approximately 50 of the 383 apartments turned over, but nearly half of these turnovers were due to in-house moves of existing residents, freeing up only a handful of apartments in any given year. The legendary waiting list that had been established decades ago was closed, as people on the list were by now geriatric and not likely to be the vibrant, productive, yet financially needy artists that Westbeth wished to attract. In 2018, the management opened an application process for about a month to create a new pool of potential residents, and they received more than a thousand applicants, and three quarters of those appeared to be eligible on the basis of the criteria used for admission (a combination of financial need and stature in one's art genre). To ensure fairness and impartiality, an independent nonprofit organization is responsible for determining final eligibility and matching eligible prospective tenants with appropriately sized vacant units, with input on the merits of their artistic quality reviewed by committees for each genre (literary, performing, or visual arts). As an apartment is vacated, the building oversees a renovation to replace half-century-old kitchen cabinets, plumbing fixtures, and appliances as well as a cosmetic refresh, and each unit costs $60,000 to update. Some residents have complained that the pace of placing a new tenant when a unit is empty is slow, and the building has empty, unrenovated apartments in its inventory. However, part of the challenge is having the funding to finance these much-needed renovations. Some residents are also a little jealous that their homes aren't eligible for the same level of renovation unless they pay for the renovations themselves (which many have done), and they have voiced their beliefs that the renovations are intended to make a unit qualify for substantially higher rents according to the fair-market regulations that govern housing. In some ways, the residents' concerns are valid, but they also have enjoyed the benefits of both the community of artists and the affordable housing that Westbeth has provided—harkening back to Emil Mare's comments about his neighbors: "With some people you could give them a million dollars in cash and they'd complain you didn't give them a wheelbarrow to carry it in" (Mare 2018).

Celebrating a Half-Century and Planning for the Next

In the fall of 2019, the residents and staff at Westbeth began planning a series of events for spring 2020 to celebrate the fifty years of the Westbeth community. Events planned included exhibits at the gallery, a new informational exhibit about the history of Westbeth, and an effort to develop a new master plan (Mare 2018). A few months later, the world stopped cold as the emergence of the COVID-19 pandemic swept through New York City with a vengeance beginning in February 2020. Instead of throwing an epic party, the residents retreated into quarantine, and all in-person events were canceled for well more than a year. It was important not to let Westbeth's landmark anniversary pass without any recognition, so an innovative art show was staged outside, using the building itself as the canvas on which the images appeared. Graphic artists worked with photographer Frankie Alduino, who had moving images of some of Westbeth's most illustrious octogenarians, and these portraits were enlarged to be one story high and were put on the outside of the building so anyone walking down Bethune or Bank Street courtyard would be able to enjoy them. WARC created a list of fifty important moments or individuals associated with Westbeth and used these to create informational timeline panels to celebrate significant achievements.

As the grip of the pandemic eased and people and organizations began designing new ways to work, play, and live, WARC has creatively found ways to innovate and expand the visibility of Westbeth and its residents. Literary Committee Chair Terry Stoller invited current and former residents to write short essays about their experiences in the community, and the more than eighty essays in the online *Westbeth Chronicles* include both poignant and funny remembrances.

The long-standing ethos of social justice and equity that has prevailed since Westbeth's inception has engendered a new program. The Artist Safe Haven Residency Program is designed to house and nurture international artists who are persecuted on the basis of political affiliations, ethnic, locational, religious, and/or gender-based persecution; forcibly displaced; artists who need a respite from dangerous situations; or artists from countries experiencing active, violent conflict. In collaboration with other New York City organizations, Westbeth has provided artists of all disciplines a residency for six months to two years from countries around the world, including Uganda, Haiti, Iran, Tunisia, and Congo. Visual artist Faten Gaddes is one who benefitted from this program (Fig. 44). She was optimistic in 2011 when her native Tunisia was part of the Arab Spring that cast off long-standing despots. She had exhibited her thought-provoking works throughout north Africa and in Paris. One of her notable installations entitled "Punching Bag" featured several heavy, suspended punching bags like the type used in gyms for training boxers. Each bag was adorned with images of women, and the

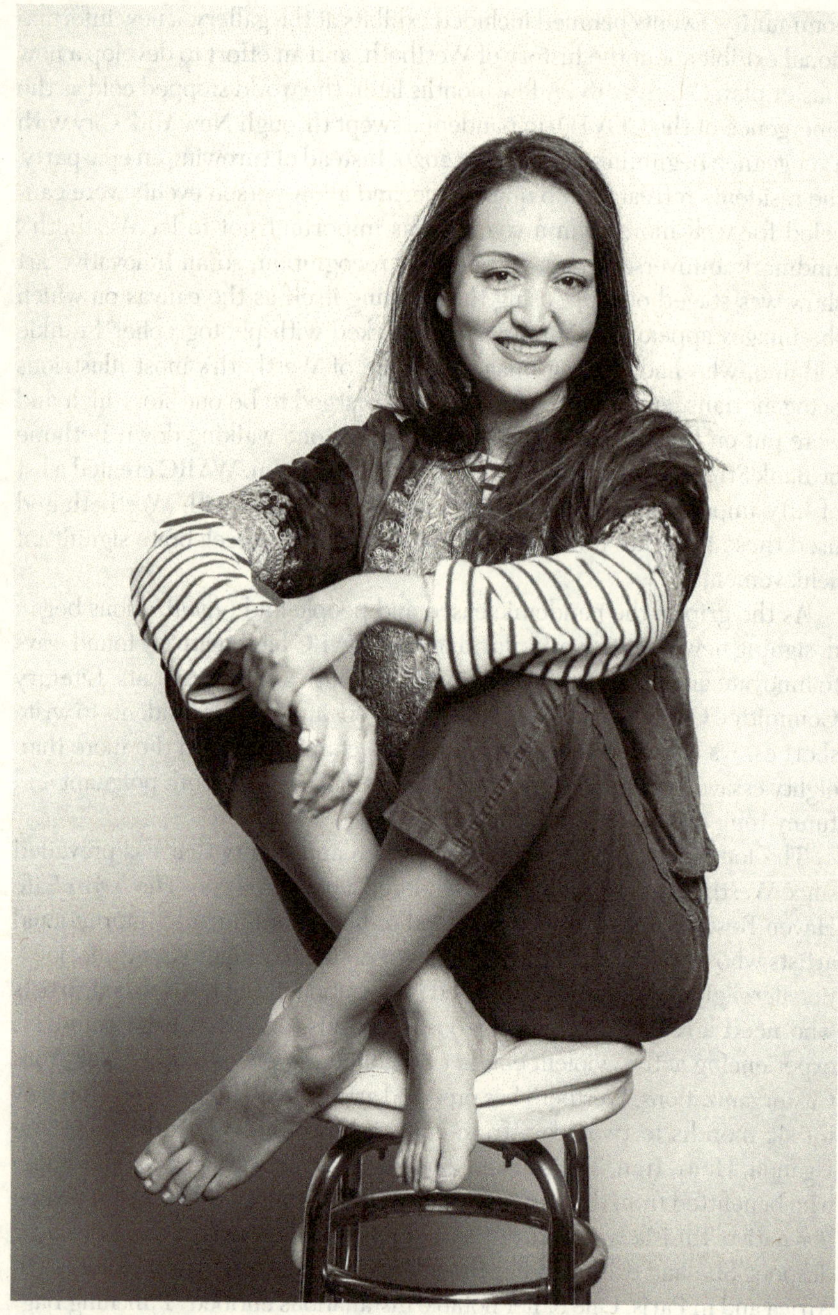

Figure 44. Faten Gaddes. Participant Westbeth Endangered Artist Program. tribesnyc Project. Image Courtesy of David Plakke.

piece was meant to symbolize the problem of violence against women. Her work was destroyed by an extremist who deemed her work blasphemous—in part because it included representation of humans, which is forbidden in strict Islam (Plakke). She is typical of the artists who have benefitted from the Safe Haven Program and is a continuation of the long-standing political activism that has been in the DNA of Westbeth. Issues large and small, from left of center public rallies to successfully protesting the planned elimination of a much-used bus route nearby, Westbeth artists remain lifelong, left-leaning activists.

Building collaborations for programming and funding have been critical for renewed vitality of the community and brought greater visibility. Collaborations with the Whitney Museum include an annual exhibition in the Westbeth Gallery of works by Whitney staff. The organization Village Preservation (formerly the Greenwich Village Society for Historic Preservation) has many links with Westbeth, from recording and preserving oral histories from Westbeth residents and founders to including the building in thematic public information opportunities such as their Civil Rights and Social Justice map. The Village Voices project in 2022 features photographs, artistic creations, artifacts, and soundscape recordings that tell the story of some of the history-making people and events connected to sites throughout the area. The newly created park and event space at Little Island a few blocks from Westbeth has created new opportunities for collaboration, and the art space The Kitchen has moved from its previous location into Westbeth.

Annual events such as the Westfest Dance event, the open studios weekends, the readings from prominent writers through collaboration with the Pen Literary Awards, performances in the Community Room or courtyard all bring thousands of visitors to the Westbeth community annually. The efforts of WARC and individual residents have created networks of outreach to greater New York City and, at the same time, brought New Yorkers to Westbeth.

As the visibility of Westbeth has grown, so too has the justification for ensuring its survival. Building on successful grants that rebuilt and updated infrastructure that was damaged in Hurricane Sandy, recent Directors have secured millions of dollars in funding to fix Westbeth. The first phase of removing mechanicals from the vulnerable basement and removing lead paint and asbestos are complete, and recently secured funds will improve livability for residents. The 100-year-old wooden windows will be replaced with custom energy efficient, well-fitting windows that will open and close easily. The equally antiquated and extremely heavy radiators that heat the building will be replaced with modern fixtures that have thermostats, so residents don't juggle a wasteful calculus of having heat on and windows cracked open in the dead of winter to moderate temperatures. The notoriously finicky antique elevators will be replaced, toxic substances like lead and asbestos will continue to be abated, and the building will improve energy conservation. The roofs will become green with new rooftop gardens inspired by the nearby High Line Park. At last, the critically needed infrastructure repairs and modernization will be tackled while preserving the historic status of Westbeth.

The governance of Westbeth is being passed from the vulnerable elders to the younger generation, just as the building also gets a refresh. The recently forged alliances with local cultural institutions like the Whitney Museum and City Island and with advocacy organizations such as Village Preservation will continue to enhance the visibility and stature of Westbeth in both the city and the art world.

Years ago when I was in a taxi en route to Westbeth, I would have to provide detailed directions for the driver to follow and where to turn because of the narrow one-way streets in the West Village. On a more recent trip, as I chatted with my Ethiopian cab driver about my work in his country, after hearing I wanted to be dropped at the corner of Washington and Bethune, the driver said, "Oh, you must be going to Westbeth." The building has stood on the same corner for more than a century but was not always visible to the surrounding city. The half-century of creativity of the villagers of Westbeth and their efforts in activism, the arts, advocacy, and inclusion have put this community on the map. Life's challenges in a very old building remain, but as new artists join the community and the elders pass on, the next half-century for Westbeth is built on a solid foundation.

ACKNOWLEDGMENTS

I AM GRATEFUL to Margot Lee Shetterly, author of the bestselling book *Hidden Figures*, about the inspiring African American women mathematicians who made the early years of NASA a success. A chance meeting with Margot and reading her wonderful book inspired me to look at the people of the Westbeth community in a new light. I remain responsible for errors or omissions.

My father's family of talented artists who lived at Westbeth gave me entrée into the Westbeth sphere and made this book possible. My aunt Shami was my champion as I began working on the research, and it saddens me deeply that none of my relatives lived to see this project to fruition. I take some solace as several in the Westbeth community have become close friends and sounding boards, including Karen Ludwig, Christina Maile, Joan Hall, Jack Dowling, and Ze'eva Cohen. This book would never have happened without the support, insights, and connections shared by the amazing Mayor of Westbeth, George Cominskie. George, forever grateful.

As an anthropologist, my role is to take the words shared with me by others and weave their stories into a coherent whole. For the more than one hundred people who sat with me for interviews, answered my follow-up questions, and spent hours with me on Zoom during the pandemic, all of you from the Westbeth community are the source for everything in this book. For the elders, some of whom are now gone, and for those of you who grew up at Westbeth and shared your memorable stories of your youth, thank you. I hope you enjoy this book and hope it brings back positive memories.

Many friends and colleagues shared information, feedback, and suggestions for avenues to explore in writing this work. Friends Marjorie Arnett, Lynn Botelho, and Vaughn Clay from my Pennsylvania days, and New Mexico colleagues Julia Barello, Becky Corran, Liz Gamboa, Meg Goehring, Amy Lanasa, Andrea Orzoff, Enrico Pontelli, Mary Prentice, Marisa Sage, Monica Torres, and Connie Voisine all provided generous advice. Rus Bradburd and his grad students in his nonfiction writing class gave me helpful guidance as I retooled my writing style to tackle this book. Manuscript reviewers for Fordham University Press, Jan English-Lueck and Gabrielle Selz, made very helpful suggestions for revision that made the final product stronger.

The pictures in this book are worth thousands of words, and I am indebted to Tom Conelly, Frankie Alduino, David Plakke, and Nate Smith for their generosity in sharing their photographs. Brigitte Freed kindly shared the image of the pony corral on Washington Street from her late husband Leonard Freed, and Westbeth friends Samantha and Stephen Hall, Jayne Holsinger, and Christina Maile shared photos. For important historic photos, I thank Cara Gilenbach of the Kent State University Archives and Special Collections and historian Sheldon Hochheiser at the AT&T Archives and History Center. Mehran Pourakbar prepared the maps by with helpful guidance from Professor Chao Fan.

Staff at Village Preservation, including Andrew Berman, Leeanne G-Bowley, and Sam Moskowitz, have all expressed enthusiasm for this project from the very beginning of my inquiry. At Fordham University Press, I have benefited from wonderful support and guidance from Fredric Nachbaur, Will Cerbone, Kem Crimmins, and the very professional staff.

My deepest debt is to my family, who encouraged me throughout the research and writing of this book. My father, Israel ben Zion Chaiken, provided my connection to Westbeth through his sisters and brother who lived there, and he was so very proud of all of them. My sisters Sara and Rebecca Chaiken have my love and gratitude; I could not ask for better siblings. My husband, Tom Conelly, was my unflagging supporter, encouraging me as I conducted interviews, taking photos that were essential to this book, and assuring me this was important work when I doubted myself. Thank you, my loved ones.

APPENDIX: CAST OF CHARACTERS

MANY PEOPLE, BOTH living and gone, are included in the story of the community of Westbeth. Borrowing an old convention from works of fiction, the cast of characters will help you place people mentioned in the text in context. A code of NR next to a name indicates they were never a resident of Westbeth. Code CHILD indicates a person spent childhood at Westbeth, and RET indicates they returned to live at Westbeth as an adult.

Joyce Aaron—Obie award–winning actress, member of Open Theater

Frankie Alduino (NR)—photographer and author of *Vertical Village* about Westbeth

Bill Anthony (1934–2022)—visual artist, died in fire in Westbeth apartment

Diane Arbus (1923–1971)—iconoclastic photographer, first suicide at Westbeth

Alison Armstrong—writer and literary scholar, painter, and musician

Helène Aylon (1931–2020)—ecofeminist visual and conceptual artist

Karin Batten—painter, formerly had studio in World Trade Center

Pele Bauch (CHILD, RET)—dancer and choreographer

Barton Lidice Beneš (1942–2012)—visual artist and HIV+ activist

Paul Binnerts—theater director, playwright, theater scholar

Louise Bourgeois (NR) (1911–2010)—conceptual feminist visual artist, collaborator

Beverly Brodsky—painter

Sandra Caplan—painter

Joseph Chaikin (1935–2003)—Obie award–winning actor, director, playwright, founder of Open Theater

Miriam Chaikin (1924–2015)—editor, author of children's literature and Judaica

Shami Chaikin (1931–2020)—actress, singer, dancer, member of Open Theater

Maya Ciarrocchi (CHILD, RET)—dancer and visual artist, grew up at Westbeth

Ze'eva Cohen—dancer, choreographer, director of dance company, dance scholar

Paul Collins—musician and composer

George Cominskie—photographic agent, leader in Westbeth governance and tenants' rights

Geeby Dajani (1961–2019) (CHILD) —rock band roadie, DJ

Magda Dajani (1959–2023) (CHILD, RET)—screenwriter, editor

Nadia Dajani (CHILD)—actress

Adam Davidson (CHILD)—financial journalist, member of Westbeth Executive Board

Jack Davidson—actor, Westbeth governance leader

David Del Tredici (1937–2023)—Pulitzer Prize–winning composer, gay rights activist

Neil Derrick (1931–2018)—writer

Vin Diesel (aka Mark Sinclair, aka Mark Vincent)(CHILD)—actor, film producer

Michel Dobbs (CHILD)—Buddhist leader, baker

Jack Dowling (1931–2021)—painter and later writer, antique dealer, and art restoration

Gwynne Duncan (CHILD, RET)—painter, workshop leader

Ron Faber (1933–2023)—Obie award–winning actor, member of Open Theater

Edward Field—writer, principally poetry

Nancy Gabor—actor, director, theater scholar, member of Open Theater

Faten Gaddes—visual artist from Tunisia, Endangered Artist Residency participant

Sonia Gechtoff (1926–2018)—painter

David Gillison—ethnographic photographer, educator

David Greenspan—Obie award–winning actor, playwright

Elizabeth Gregory-Gruen—visual artist

Bob Gruen—rock and roll photographer

Moses Gunn (1929–1993)—film, stage, and TV actor, civil rights and tenants' rights activist

Hans Haacke—conceptual visual artist, founding member of Art Workers Coalition

Joan Hall—multimedia visual artist, writer, former dancer, and mime

Stephen Hall—painter

Josh Hamilton (CHILD)—actor

Barbara Hammer (1939–2019)—feminist filmmaker and photographer, gay rights activist

Bobby Harden—jazz and blues singer, composer

Carol Hebald (1934–2022)—writer

Jayne Holsinger—painter

Denise Hurd (CHILD, RET)—actor, fight coach, theater educator

Hugh Hurd (1925–1995)—actor, civil rights activist

Michelle Hurd (CHILD)—TV and film actor

Chuck Israels—jazz musician

Jacob Kaplan (NR) (1892–1987)—philanthropist and visionary founder of Westbeth

Joan Kaplan Davidson (NR) (1927–2023)—philanthropist and early Westbeth organizer

Penny Jones—puppeteer and children's theater director

Marc Jacoby—musician and children's music educator

Susannah Kelly (CHILD, RET)—visual artist

William Kennon—painter

Sandra Kingsbury—actor, collaborator on Icons Project

Gayle Kirschenbaum—filmmaker and writer

Bettye Lane (1930–2012)—photographer and documentarian of Stonewall Uprising

Sherry Lane—visual artist and cartoonist

Patricia Lasch—multimedia visual artist

Ralph Lee (1935–2023)—actor, puppet maker (Land Shark), theater director

Jenny Lombard (CHILD, RET)—writer, educator

Kirk Lombard (CHILD)—owner of Sea Forager Seafood, fisherman, writer, musician

Steve Lomprey (CHILD)—multimedia artist, painter

Karen Ludwig—actor, playwright, director, theater educator

Christina Maile—printmaker, writer, landscape architect, leader in Westbeth governance, cofounder of Westbeth Feminist Playwright Collective

Ethan Maile (1972–2024) (CHILD)—painter, writer, actor

Julian Maile—(CHILD)—musician

Doris Mare—health care administrator, Westbeth Artists Resident's Council governance

Emil Mare—painter, art educator

Juanita McNeely (1936–2023)—feminist painter

Gloria Miguel—actor, singer, dancer, cofounder of Spiderwoman Theater Company

Gilbert Moses (1942–1995)—actor, cofounder of Free Southern Theater, civil rights activist

Eric Moskowitz (CHILD)—multimedia artist and video producer

Alice Neel (NR) (1900–1984)—painter and portraitist, collaborator with Westbeth painters

Madeleine Yayodele Nelson (1948–2018)—musician, founder of Women of the Calabash

Caitlin Newby-Bottoms (CHILD)—visual artist

Lorraine O'Grady—multimedia conceptual and performance artist, cultural critic, writer

Joel Oppenheimer (1930–1988)—poet and sports journalist

Nat Oppenheimer (CHILD)—engineer on bespoke arts projects

David Plakke—photographer, musician

Cordell Reagon (1943–1996)—singer and civil rights activist

Lily Rivlin—feminist filmmaker and documentarian

Lucille Rhodes—visual artist

Muriel Rukeyser (1931–1980)—writer, feminist, and social critic

Suzanne Ruta—widow and archivist of painter Peter Ruta, human rights activist

Ellen Salpeter (NR)—Executive Director of Westbeth 2019–2021

Karen Santry—painter, fashion illustrator, art educator

David Seccombe (1929–2022)—sculptor and mixed-media artist

Shelley Seccombe (1938–2023)—photographer

Hugh Seidman (1940–2023)—poet

Talia Selz (1925–2010)—fiction writer, early work in Westbeth admissions

Charles Seplowin—mixed-media artist, sculptor, art educator

Pawnee Sills—actor, theater educator, civil rights activist

Harry Shunk (1924–2006)—photographer, notorious hoarder

Gil Sorrentino (1929–2006)—writer

Anita Steckel (1930–2012)—feminist mixed-media artist

Edith Stephan (1919–2021)—dancer, choreographer, filmmaker

Terry Stoller—actor, writer, theater educator, collaborator on ICONS Project, Chair of WARC Literary
Ted Timreck—documentary filmmaker, collaborator on ICONS Project
John Turner—photographer, photographic agent
Rachel Urkowitz (CHILD, RET)—sculptor, mixed-media visual artist
Irving Vincent—theater and TV producer, director
Samantha Vincent (CHILD)—film producer, management
Ken Wade—painter, musician
Dolores Walker—writer, original member of Westbeth Feminists Playwright Collective
Hannah Wilkie (1940–1993)—feminist visual artist
Susan Yankowitz—playwright, dramaturg, member of Open Theater
Eve Zanni—jazz singer and music educator
Jamie Zaretsky (CHILD) (d. 2021)—graphic artist

WORKS CITED

Aaron, Joyce. 2017. Interview. Edited by M. S. Chaiken. Unpublished.

Alduino, Frankie. *Vertical Village: A Book of Photographs from Westbeth Artist Housing*. Self published. 2020.

Allison, Raphael C. "Muriel Rukeyser Goes to War: Pragmatism, Pluralism, and the Politics of Ekphrasis." *College Literature* 33, no. 2 (2006): 5.

Armstrong, Alison. 2019. Interview. Edited by M. S. Chaiken. Unpublished.

Art, North Dakota Museum of. "Barton Lidice Beneš Apartment, Permanent Collection." Accessed 27 September 2021.

Ashrawi, Sama'an. *"The Life and Times of a Palestinian Punk-Rocker-Turned-Hip-Hopper in New York City."* *Palestine in America*, 2020.

Aylon, Helene. *Whatever Is Contained Must Be Released: My Jewish Orthodox Girlhood, My Life as a Feminist Artist*. New York: Feminist Press, 2012.

Bain, Dixon. Oral History. Edited by Jeanne Houck. New York: Greenwich Village Society for Historic Preservation, 2007.

Batten, Karin. 2018. Interview. Edited by M. S. Chaiken. Unpublished.

Bauch, Pele. 2020. Interview. Edited by M. S. Chaiken. Unpublished.

Beneš, Barton Lidice. *Curiosa: Celebrity Relics, Historical Fossils, and other Metaphoric Rubbish*. New York: Harry N. Abrams, 2002.

Bennett, Sarah. "Dead Artist Horded Socks, Warhols." *New York Magazine*, 2012.

Berger, Susan. "Westbeth Chronicles." 8 December 2020.

Binnerts, Paul. 2018. Interview. Edited by M. S. Chaiken. Unpublished.

Bosworth, Patricia. *Diane Arbus: A Biography*. New York: Alfred A. Knopf Press, 1984.

Bottoms-Newby, Caitlin. 2020. Interview. Edited by M. S. Chaiken. Unpublished.

Braimon, Roger. "My Friendship with Barton Beneš." *Westbeth Chronicles* (blog), 29 June 2020. https://westbeth.org/westbeth-chronicles/roger-braimon-multimedia-artist-3/.

Brodsky, Beverly. 2019. Interview. Edited by M. S. Chaiken. Unpublished.

Bruner, Betsy. "Their Father's Art." *Arizona Daily Sun*, 2011.

Caplan, Sandra. 2020. Interview. Edited by M. S. Chaiken. Unpublished.

Chaikin, Shami. 2017–2020. Personal communication.

Ciarrocchi, Maya. 2020. Interview. Unpublished.

Cohen, Jem. 2020. Interview. Edited by M. S. Chaiken. Unpublished.

Cohen, Ze'eva. 2017. Interview. Edited by M. S. Chaiken. Unpublished.

Collins, Paul. 2019. Interview. Edited by M. S. Chaiken. Unpublished.

———. "What Westbeth Means to Me." *Westbeth Chronicles* (blog), *Westbeth Artists' Residence*, 8 September 2021.

Columbia, David Patrick. "Memorializing America's Holiday of Wit and Artistry." *New York Social Diary*, 2021.

Cominskie, George, Christina Maile, and Ralph Lee. The Art of Community: A #Westbeth50 Oral History Conversation, 2020.

Cotter, Holland. "Bliss and Anger in Balance: The Art of Lorraine O'Grady." *New York Times*, 2021, 9, C.

Dace, Tish. "Making Their Own Opportunities: Women's Theater in New York." *Backstage Magazine*, 2001.

Dahl, Per-Johan. "The Story of Westbeth: Discovering the Abstract Lines of an Artists' Colony." *The Journal of Architecture* 19, no. 3 (2014): 305–328.

Dajani, Magda. 2020a. Interview. Edited by M. S. Chaiken. Unpublished.

Dajani, Nadia. 2020. Interview. Edited by M. S. Chaiken. unpublished.

Dajani, Nadia. 2020b. Interview. Edited by M. S. Chaiken. unpublished.

Davidson, Adam. 2020. Interview. Edited by M. S. Chaiken. Unpublished.

Davidson, Jack. 2017. Interview. Edited by M. S. Chaiken. Unpublished.

Del Tredici, David. 2017. Interview. Edited by M. S. Chaiken. Unpublished.

Dobbs, Michel. 2020. Interview. Edited by M. S. Chaiken. Unpublished.

Dobbs, Michel. 2020a. Interview. Edited by M. S. Chaiken. Unpublished.

———. 2020b. "Westbeth Chronicles." March 7, 2020.

Dolkart, Andrew S., and Greenwich Village Society for Historic Preservation. National Register for Historic Places Nomination for Westbeth. Edited by National Parks Service. National Register Database: US Government, 2009.

Dowling, Jack. 2018, 2020. Interview. Edited by M. S. Chaiken. Unpublished.

———. 2019. Interview and email correspondence. Edited by M. S. Chaiken.

Duncan, Gwynne. 2020. Interview. Edited by M. S. Chaiken. Unpublished.

Faber, Ron. 2018. Interview. Edited by M. S. Chaiken. Unpublished.

Field, Edward, and Neil Derrick. 2017. Interview. Edited by M. S. Chaiken. Unpublished.

Finnegan, Sharon. "Juanita McNeely: Art and Life Entwined." *Women's Art Journal* 9 (2011).

Foley, Dylan. "Jack Dowling." The Last Bohemians. Accessed 19 March 2020. http://lastbohemians.blogspot.com/2020/04/jack-dowling-in-his-loft-in-1967-jack.html.

Gabor, Nancy. 2018. Interview. Unpublished.

Gass, Alison. "The Art and Spirituality of Helene Aylon." *Bridges* 8, no. 1/2 (2000): 6.

Gillison, David. 2019. Interview. Edited by M. S. Chaiken. Unpublished.

Gillison, Samantha. "Growing up in Westbeth." *The Literary Review (Teaneck)* 49, no. 4 (2006): 150–155.

Gilmore, Lyman. *Don't Touch the Poet: The Life and Times of Joel Oppenheimer.* Jersey City, NJ: Talisman House Publishers, 1998.

God's Love, We Deliver. "God's Love We Deliver." Accessed 28 June 2022. glwd.org.

Goertzen, Chris. "Freedom Songs: Helping Black Activists, Black Residents, and White Volunteers Work Together in Hattiesburg, Mississippi, during the Summer of 1964." *Black Music Research Journal* 36, no. 1 (2016): 29.

Gopnik, Blake. "Hans Haacke, Firebrand, Gets His First U.S. Survey in 33 Years." *New York Times*, 2019. https://www.nytimes.com/2019/10/11/arts/design/hans-haacke-new -museum.html?rref=collection%2Fsectioncollection%2Farts&action=click&content Collection=arts®ion=rank&module=package&version=highlights&content Placement=9&pgtype=sectionfront.

Greenberger, Alex. "Helene Aylon, Eco-Feminist Artist Who Pondered Change, Is Dead at 89 of Coronavirus-Related Causes." *Art News,* 2020.

Greenspan, David. 2019. Interview. Edited by M. S. Chaiken. Unpublished.

Gregory-Gruen, Elizabeth. 2018. Interview. Edited by M. S. Chaiken. Unpublished.

Gruen, Bob. 2018. Interview. Edited by M. S. Chaiken. Unpublished.

———. *Right Place, Right Time: The Life of a Rock & Roll Photographer*. New York: Abrams Press, 2020.

Haacke, Hans, and Linda Haacke. 2019. Interview. Edited by M. S. Chaiken. Unpublished.

Hall, Joan. 2018. Interview. Edited by M. S. Chaiken. Unpublished.

Hall, Stephen. 2019. Interview. Edited by M. S. Chaiken. Unpublished.

Hamilton, Josh. 2020. Interview. Edited by M. S. Chaiken. Unpublished.

Hauser, Christine. "Down a Tall Chimney, and Out of It Alive." *New York Times*, 2008.

"The High Line." Accessed 3 December 2020. https://www.thehighline.org/.

Holsinger, Jayne. 2018. Interview. Unpublished.

Holst, Sebastian. 2020. "Fences Make Good Neighbors" Westbeth Artists' Residence 50th Anniversary.

Holst, Sebastian. 2020. "Westbeth Chronicles." *Westbeth Chronicles (blog),* 15 July 2024. https://westbeth.org/westbeth-chronicles/.

Hoover, Clara. "An Interview with Hugh Hurd." *Film Comment* 1, no. 4 (1963): 3.

Hurd, Denise. 2020. Interview. Edited by M. S. Chaiken. Unpublished.

Island, Little. Accessed 13 October 2023. littleisland.org.

Isles, Alexandra. Harry's Gift. Chalice Well Productions, 2015.

Israels, Chuck. 2023. Interview. Edited by M. S. Chaiken. Unpublished.

Jacoby, Marc. 2019. Interview. Edited by M. S. Chaiken. Unpublished.

Jones, Penny. 2019. Interview. Edited by M. S. Chaiken. Unpublished.

Kaplan Davidson, Joan. 2019. Interview. Edited by M. S. Chaiken. Unpublished.

Kelly, Susannah. 2020. Interview. Edited by M. S. Chaiken. Unpublished.

Kennon, Bill. 2019. Interview. Edited by M. S. Chaiken. Unpublished.

Kiger, Patrick. "Bettye Lane: A Feminist Photojournalist's Arresting Images." Accessed 22 March 2012. https://blog.aarp.org/legacy/bettye-lane-a-feminist-photojournalists -arresting-images.

Kingsbury, Sandra. 2018. Interview. Edited by M. S. Chaiken. Unpublished.

Kirschenbaum, Gayle. 2020. Interview. Edited by M. S. Chaiken. Unpublished.

Kosch, Rachael. "Westbeth Chronicles." 8 March 2022. https://westbeth.org/westbeth -chronicles/.

"LAByrinth Theater." LAByrinth Theater Web Site. labtheater.org. Accessed 6 December 2020.

Lane, Sherry. 2019. Interview. Edited by M. S. Chaiken. Unpublished.

Lasch, Patricia. 2017. Interview. Edited by M. S. Chaiken. Unpublished.

Lee, Ralph. 2018. Interview. Edited by M. S. Chaiken. Unpublished.

Leland, John. "Surprise Bounty for a Cleanup Artist." *New York Times*, 2012, 1.

Linder, Regina. 2023. Interview. Edited by M. S. Chaiken. Unpublished.

Lombard, Jenny. 2020a. Interview. Edited by M. S. Chaiken. Unpublished.

Lombard, Kirk. 2020b. Interview. Edited by M. S. Chaiken. Unpublished.

Lomprey, Steve. 2020. Interview. Edited by M. S. Chaiken. Unpublished.

Ludwig, Karen. 2018. Interview. Edited by M. S. Chaiken. Unpublished.

Maile, Christina. 2017. Interview. Edited by M. S. Chaiken. Unpublished.

Maile, Julian, and Ethan Maile. 2019. Interview. Edited by M. S. Chaiken. Unpublished.

Mare, Emil, and Doris Mare. 2018. Interview. Edited by M. S. Chaiken. Unpublished.

McNeely, Juanita. 2019. Interview. Edited by M. S. Chaiken. Unpublished.

Merjian, Ara. "Hans Haake." *Frieze* 150 (2012).

Miguel, Gloria. 2017. Interview. Edited by M. S. Chaiken. Unpublished.

Mitter, Siddhartha. "Lorraine O'Grady: Still Cutting into the Culture." *New York Times*, 2021.

Moskowitz, Erik. 2020. Interview. Edited by M. S. Chaiken. Unpublished.

Moss, Jeremiah. *Vanishing New York: How a Great City Lost its Soul.* 1st ed. New York: HarperCollins, 2017.

Museum, Guggenheim. "Hannah Wilke." Guggenheim Museum Collections. Accessed 1 July.

"The New School Drama." Accessed 7 December 2020.

O'Neill-Butler, Lauren. "Helene Aylon." *ArtForum* 1 (2019).

Oppenheimer, Nat. 2020. Interview. Edited by M. S. Chaiken. Unpublished.

Pearl, Faye. 2022. Interview. Edited by M. S. Chaiken. Unpublished.

Plakke, David. "David Plakke Artist's Website." Accessed 1 August 2022. https://www.davidplakke.com/work-category/photo-journalism.

———. 2018. Interview. Edited by M. S. Chaiken. Unpublished.

Prete, Allison, and Ben Sonnenberg. 1995. Growing Up in Westbeth. Undistributed.

Prete, Allison, and Ben Sonnenburg. n.d., unpublished video.

Project, NYC LGBT Historic Sites. "St. Vincent's Hospital Manhattan." Accessed 21 June 2020. https://www.nyclgbtsites.org/site/st-vincents-hospital-manhattan/.

Project, SNCC Legacy. "Cordell Reagon." Student Nonviolence Coordinating Committee Digital Archives. Accessed 16 February 2020. https://snccdigital.org/people/cordell-reagon/.

Ramscale. "Ramscale." Accessed 13 September 2021. ramscale.com.

Rhodes, Lucille, and Margaret Murphy. 1978. They Are Their Own Gifts. Women Make Movies.

Rhodes, Lucille. 2019. Interview. Edited by M. S. Chaiken. Unpublished.

Rivlin, Lily. 2018. Interview. Edited by M. S. Chaiken. Unpublished.

Ruta, Suzanne. 2023. Interview. Unpublished.

Salpeter, Ellen. 2020. Interview. Edited by M. S. Chaiken. Unpublished.

Santry, Karen. 2019. Interview. Edited by M. S. Chaiken. Unpublished.

Saxon, Wolfgang. "Hugh Hurd Obituary." *New York Times*, 1995, Obituaries.

Seccombe, Shelley. *Lost Waterfront: The Decline and Rebirth of Manhattan's Western Shore.* New York: Fordham University Press, 2008.

———. 2018. Interview. Edited by M. S. Chaiken. Unpublished.

Seidman, Hugh. 2017. Interview. Edited by M. S. Chaiken. Unpublished.

Seplowin, Charlie. 2019. Interview. Edited by M. S. Chaiken. Unpublished.

Sheire, James. National Register of Historic Places Nomination for the Bell Telephone Laboratories. Edited by National Park Service. National Register Database: US Government, 1975.

Sills, Pawnee. 2017. Interview. Edited by M. S. Chaiken. Unpublished.

Small, Zachary. 2020. "Biden Video Uses Artists' Image to Project a Unified Country." *New York Times*, 2020.

Solocheck, Beverly. "It's an Uncertain Eden for the Artists of Westbeth." *New York Times*, 1976, 1.

Solomon, Deborah. "After Decades of Silence, Art About Abortion (Cautiously) Enters the Establishment." *New York Times*, 2022.

St. Felix, Doreen. "Lorraine O'Grady Has Always Been a Rebel." *New Yorker*, 2022.

Stock, Ellen. "The Man from P.O.N.Y." *New York Magazine*, 1969, 49.

Stoller, Terry, and Ted Timreck. Westbeth Icon Series.

Stoller, Terry. "Jayne Holsinger: Painter." *Profiles in Art* (blog), 2017. https://westbeth.org/profiles-in-art/jayne-holsinger-painter/.

Strausbaugh, John. *The Village: 400 Years of Beats and Bohemians, Radicals and Rogues*. New York: HarperCollins, 2013.

Terris, Virginia. "Muriel Rukeyser: A Retrospective." *American Poetry Review* 3, no. 3 (1974.): 5.

Timreck, Ted, and Terry Stoller. Edward Field: Icon. In *Westbeth Icons*, edited by Terry Stoller and Ted Timreck. Westbeth Artists Residence Council, 2018.

Urkowitz, Rachel. 2020. Interview. Edited by M. S. Chaiken. Unpublished.

Urkowitz, Rachel. 2020a. Interview. Edited by M. S. Chaiken. Unpublished.

———. 2020b. "Superhero in Training." *Westbeth Chronicles* (blog). https://westbeth.org/westbeth-chronicles/.

van Gelder, Lawrence. "Cordell Reagon Obituary." *New York Times*, 1996.

Vincent, Irving. 2023. Interview. Unpublished.

Vitello, Paul. "Anita Steckel: Artist Who Created Erotic Works, Dies at 82." *New York Times*, 2012.

Wade, Ken. 2019. Interview. Edited by M. S. Chaiken. Unpublished.

Waldman, Stuart. *Maritime Mile: The Story of the Greenwich Village Waterfront*. New York: Mikaya Press, 2002.

Walker, Dolores. 2018. Interview. Edited by M. S. Chaiken.

Weiss, Diane. A Minor Accident of War. 2019. ww2shortfilm.com.

Westbeth. *40 Degrees 44 Minutes North by 72 Degrees 59 Minutes West: An Evening of New York Scenes (Program)*. Westbeth, 1970.

Whitney, Museum. "Whitney Museum Website." Accessed 16 July 2023. whitney.org.

Wilke, Hannah. "Hannah Wilke." Accessed 1 July 2021. http://www.hannahwilke.com/id10.html.

Williams, Tod. Oral History. Edited by Jeanne Houck. New York: Greenwich Village Society for Historic Preservation, 2007.

Word, Troy. The Presence of Joseph Chaikin. United States: Independent Filmmaker Project, 2011.

Yankowitz, Susan. 2019. Interview. Edited by M. S. Chaiken. Unpublished.

Zanni, Eve. 2019. Interview. Edited by M. S. Chaiken. Unpublished.

Zaretsky, Jamie. 2020. Interview. Edited by M. S. Chaiken. Unpublished.

INDEX

Miriam Chaiken is a cultural anthropologist who has done field research on four continents and then turned her anthropological gaze to the most exotic site yet—Greenwich Village in New York City. Three members of her family were longtime residents of the Westbeth Artists Housing, and this connection opened doors and permitted her to capture the stories of members of this community. After her work in villages in sub-Saharan Africa, she realized that Westbeth is a vertical village, with all the drama and intrigue. *Creative Ozone: The Artists of Westbeth* tells of the artists who left their mark on the city of New York and every artistic innovation and social justice movement of the last half-century. Miriam's earlier writing draws on her anthropological field research in Africa and Asia, focusing on poverty and hunger alleviation, gender equity, and the welfare of children. She has published many articles and co-edited two books on international development and community resilience.

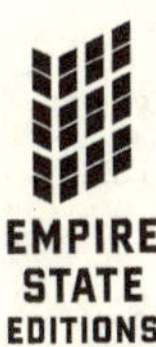

Colin Davey with Thomas A. Lesser, *The American Museum of Natural History and How It Got That Way*. Forewords by Neil deGrasse Tyson and Kermit Roosevelt III

Wendy Jean Katz, *Humbug: The Politics of Art Criticism in New York City's Penny Press*

Jim Mackin, *Notable New Yorkers of Manhattan's Upper West Side: Bloomingdale–Morningside Heights*

Matthew Spady, *The Neighborhood Manhattan Forgot: Audubon Park and the Families Who Shaped It*

Robert O. Binnewies, *Palisades: 100,000 Acres in 100 Years*

Marilyn S. Greenwald and Yun Li, *Eunice Hunton Carter: A Lifelong Fight for Social Justice*

Jeffrey A. Kroessler, *Sunnyside Gardens: Planning and Preservation in a Historic Garden Suburb*

Elizabeth Macaulay-Lewis, *Antiquity in Gotham: The Ancient Architecture of New York City*

Ron Howell, *King Al: How Sharpton Took the Throne*

Jean Arrington with Cynthia S. LaValle, *From Factories to Palaces: Architect Charles B. J. Snyder and the New York City Public Schools*. Foreword by Peg Breen

Boukary Sawadogo, *Africans in Harlem: An Untold New York Story*

Alvin Eng, *Our Laundry, Our Town: My Chinese American Life from Flushing to the Downtown Stage and Beyond*

Stephanie Azzarone, *Heaven on the Hudson: Mansions, Monuments, and Marvels of Riverside Park*

Ron Goldberg, *Boy with the Bullhorn: A Memoir and History of ACT UP New York*. Foreword by Dan Barry

Peter Quinn, *Cross Bronx: A Writing Life*

Mark Bulik, *Ambush at Central Park: When the IRA Came to New York*

Matt Dallos, *In the Adirondacks: Dispatches from the Largest Park in the Lower 48*

Brandon Dean Lamson, *Caged: A Teacher's Journey Through Rikers, or How I Beheaded the Minotaur*

Raj Tawney, *Colorful Palate: Savored Stories from a Mixed Life*

Edward Cahill, *Disorderly Men*

Joseph Heathcott, *Global Queens: An Urban Mosaic*

Francis R. Kowsky with Lucille Gordon, *Hell on Color, Sweet on Song: Jacob Wrey Mould and the Artful Beauty of Central Park*

Jill Jonnes, *South Bronx Rising: The Rise, Fall, and Resurrection of an American City, Third Edition*

Barbara G. Mensch, *A Falling-Off Place: The Transformation of Lower Manhattan*

David J. Goodwin, *Midnight Rambles: H. P. Lovecraft in Gotham*

Felipe Luciano, *Flesh and Spirit: Confessions of a Young Lord*

Maximo G. Martinez, *Sojourners in the Capital of the World: Garifuna Immigrants*

Jennifer Baum, *Just City: Growing Up on the Upper West Side When Housing Was a Human Right*

Davida Siwisa James, *Hamilton Heights and Sugar Hill: Alexander Hamilton's Old Harlem Neighborhood Through the Centuries*

Annik LaFarge, *On the High Line: The Definitive Guide, Third Edition.* Foreword by Rick Dark

Marie Carter, *Mortimer and the Witches: A History of Nineteenth-Century Fortune Tellers*

Alice Sparberg Alexiou, *Devil's Mile: The Rich, Gritty History of the Bowery.* Foreword by Peter Quinn

Carey Kasten and Brenna Moore, *Mutuality in El Barrio: Stories of the Little Sisters of the Assumption Family Health Service.* Foreword by Norma Benítez Sánchez

Kimberly A. Orcutt, *The American Art-Union: Utopia and Skepticism in the Antebellum Era*

Jonathan Butler, *Join the Conspiracy: How a Brooklyn Eccentric Got Lost on the Right, Infiltrated the Left, and Brought Down the Biggest Bombing Network in New York*

Nicole Gelinas, *Movement: New York's Long War to Take Back Its Streets from the Car*

Jack Hodgson, *Young Reds in the Big Apple: The New York Young Pioneers of America, 1923–1934*

Lynn Ellsworth, *Wonder City: How to Reclaim Human-Scale Urban Life*

Walter Zev Feldman, *From the Bronx to the Bosphorus: Klezmer and Other Displaced Musics of New York*

Larry Racioppo, *Here Down on Dark Earth: Loss and Remembrance in New York City*

Bonnie Yochelson, *Too Good to Get Married: The Life and Photographs of Miss Alice Austen*

David Brown Morris, *Ten Thousand Central Parks: A Climate-Change Parable*

Eve M. Kahn, *Queen of Bohemia Predicts Own Death: The Forgotten Journalist Zoe Anderson Norris, 1860-1914*

Stefanie Mercado Altman, Claire Altman, and Stan Altman, *Twice Blessed: A Story of Unconditional Love*. Foreword by Stephen G. Post

Stephanie Azzarone, *Fabulous Fountains of New York*

For a complete list, visit www.fordhampress.com/empire-state-editions.